THE ACADEMY OF GOLF AT PGA NATIONAL

TOTAL GOLF

This edition first published in 1999
Reprinted 2001

Text and photographs © Mike Adams and T.J. Tomasi 1996, 1999
Design and diagrams © Carlton Books Limited 1996, 1999

A CIP catalogue reference for this book is available from the British Library.

ISBN 0-681-32016-8

Printed in Dubai

Acknowledgements

The authors would like to thank Kathryn Maloney who served
as Project Manager. Kathryn is an LPGA Teaching Professional
at Ironhorse Country Club in West Palm Beach, FL, and a
freelance writer.

Photographs
All photographs by Marc Feldman with the exception of the following
photographs on pages 139 (top), 153, 154 and 157, which were taken
by Kathryn Maloney.

Note: for convenience of presentation, we have presented the material in
this book for right-handed golfers. Obviously, the mechanics of the golf
swing will apply to all golfers.

THE ACADEMY OF GOLF AT
PGA NATIONAL

TOTAL
GOLF

MIKE ADAMS & T.J. TOMASI
with KATHRYN MALONEY

SEVENOAKS

Contents

Golf is listed in the dictionary as a game played by striking a small, resilient ball with clubs into a series of holes with natural and artificial obstacles irregularly interposed. It involves striking a ball the fewest number of times possible, over a vast expanse of territory, varying terrain and in changing weather conditions. In no other sport is the disparity between the size of the playing field and the goal (the cup) so large.

Golf is a game that is different from other sports in that it does not require an exceptional physique: you need not be seven feet tall, weigh 200 pounds, or be able to run 100 yards in less than ten seconds. You can excel at golf even if you aren't blessed with the natural attributes that are essential in many other sports. A golfer with a good short game is a match for anyone even if he doesn't drive the ball a mile. It is part of the fascination and frustration of the game that a three-foot putt and a three-hundred yard drive are of equal value on your score card.

In all sports where you have an opponent, your actions are a response to someone else's performance. What they do dramatically affects what you do. A baseball pitcher's choice of a curve ball versus a fast pitch determines the batter's behavior; the server in tennis dictates the response of the competitor on the other side of the net.

However, in golf, everything is self initiated because, by the rules of the game, the ball does not move unless you act on it. What you do to that ball depends solely on your own capabilities laced with a little luck. You have no coach and no team-mates to offer assistance or to blame when things go wrong. All the decisions and actions are your sole responsibility and it is this matrix of self-reliance that gives the game its wonderful character. During a round of golf the golf swing itself gets the most focus, but there is plenty of time for doing other things. In a four-and-a-half hour round where you took 90 swings (the average swing takes about 1.5 seconds), you would spend approximately two minutes and twenty-five seconds actually swinging the club. That leaves about four hours and twenty-seven minutes to relax and enjoy the company of your companions and the beauty of your playing field.

It won't ever be perfect

In golf, we should strive for perfection but never expect it. After all, golf is a target game, and the nature of targets is they can be, and often are, missed. In a game requiring such precision and accuracy, even a slight alteration of your swing can have significant effects on your ball flight. If you contact the ball just a quarter of an inch off of the sweet spot it can result in a loss of 30 yards. Thus it is wise to remember that expecting flawless performance in a game with such a small margin for error is asking for frustration.

Even though you can't attain perfection, it is true that the more sound your swing mechanics are, the more you will be rewarded with golf shots that go where you want them to. Thus it makes sense for you to develop a blueprint for your golf swing that is technically correct. This will allow you to play better golf with more consistency.

Develop a blueprint

The problem is that most golfers don't take the time to construct and follow a blueprint for building their golf swing because they are too busy looking for quick remedies. They want to do it the "easy way" with a tip that instantly makes the ball fly long and straight and they end up putting a band aid on their swing that works one day, and is gone the next.

We believe that you will play better golf if you follow our step-wise learning procedure which is designed to allow you to build a blueprint of your golf swing based on the time-tested fundamentals of what constitutes good golf.

The learning procedure

How can you learn to play better golf? Science shows us that an effective way to learn a skill like the golf swing is to divide it into manageable pieces and then to learn them one at a time. The procedure goes like this:

■ First, you pick a perfect example of what you want to be able to do. It could be Pete Sampras's serve in tennis, or Ronaldo's shooting in soccer or Jack Nicklaus's grip in golf.

■ Then once you have studied that model, you attempt to match it using a trial and correction procedure where your attempts bring you closer and closer to the prototype.

■ Once you can match the prototype perfectly, the next step is to repeat the procedure again and again until it becomes a habit, i.e. you can do it automatically. In our example of learning the grip, you can place your hands on the club perfectly without even thinking about it. Chuck Hogan, an advisor to many tour players and an expert on how golfers learn the game, estimates that it takes at least 60 repetitions for 21 days in a row to produce a motor habit.

Whatever the exact number, there have been many professional golfers, including Greg Norman and Larry Nelson, who built their swing piece by piece using an instructional book as their model guide.

What's in the book

In the following chapters you will learn how to play better golf using this step-wise, piece-by-piece approach.

■ **Chapters One and Two** present the building blocks of the swing, the pre-shot routine and the pre-swing mechanics, including the grip, stance, posture, aim and alignment. These set the stage for the sequential motion of your swing before the club is even set in motion.

Sometimes you have to look at the arrows rather than the archer, so to aid you in the selection of your clubs, we review some essentials of golf equipment so that you can make an informed decision about what is right for you.

■ **Chapters Three to Five** describe the golf swing sequence, focusing in detail on the four key parts: the backswing, downswing, the position at impact and the follow through.

In support of the full swing instruction, special sections are provided that focus in depth on how to hit the driver, the long irons and fairway woods, the mid and short irons as well as the technique of drawing and fading the ball.

And in keeping with our belief that you can learn your own golf swing by copying the swings of others, some frame-by-frame annotated swing sequences of expert players are provided to serve as prototypes from which you can model your own golf swing.

■ **Chapters Six and Seven** cover the specialty shots you need to know out on the golf course. These are the shots that call for some imagination as well as specific technical adjustments to your stance and swing. The special shots section includes advice on how to keep the ball under a tree limb, how and when to run the ball to the flag, how to handle bad lies and what to do when the ball is above your feet or perched on the side of a hill well below your feet.

■ **Chapters Eight to Eleven** focus on the short game. Since 65 percent of the strokes you take are from 100 yards and in, pitching, putting, chipping and sand play make up an important segment of your blueprint for golf.

■ **Chapters Twelve to Eighteen** deal with the actual playing of the game: how you think your way around a golf course, where to position your ball, what kind of shot to play based on your evaluations of the conditions (weather, pin position, lie etc.) and the circumstances of play (match or medal). Of equal importance to good course management is good self-management, so a section dealing with the inner game of golf has been included.

It's been said that practice makes perfect but in reality only perfect practice makes perfect so we've outlined for you some perfectly designed practice routines that will speed you on your way to playing better golf.

Summary

As you can see from this brief overview, the purpose of this book is quite simply to help you play better golf. In the final analysis, your development depends on your ability to take control of your own learning process. Improvement in golf is an evolution—a gradual, continuous process. Our job is to get you started in the right direction.

The authors

T.J. Tomasi is the Director of the Players School at the Academy of Golf at PGA National. With over 20 years of teaching experience, he is also one of the most widely published golf instructors in the world and has served as the instructional editor of *Golf Illustrated* and *Golfing* magazines. Dr. Tomasi has a Ph.D. in Education.

The Academy of Golf at PGA National at Palm Beach Gardens, Florida, is one of America's most comprehensive golf schools. The Academy of Golf affords the student access to the top golf instructors, superb teaching facilities and the latest technology.

Mike Adams, a former PGA touring professional, is Director of the PGA's National Academy of Golf at Palm Beach Gardens, Florida. Known throughout the world as the "Swing Doctor," Adams has a keen eye for detecting swing flaws, and an impressive track record for correcting them. He is one of America's most sought-after golf teachers, teaching more than 3,000 individual lessons each year. Hollywood celebrities who have Adams to thank for their golf skills include Jack Nicholson, Michael Douglas, Willie Nelson and Tom Landry. President Bill Clinton worked with the "Swing Doctor" when he visited the PGA National in March 1995, and former President Gerald Ford was another pupil of Mike Adams. Recently voted one of America's 100 Best Golf Teachers by *Golf Magazine*, Adams writes instruction articles for *Golf Magazine*, *Golf Digest* and *Golfing*.

Equipment

In the past decade, through sophisticated computers linked with video cameras and other measuring devices, the effects of club specifications on the flight of the golf ball, (for example, loft and lie), have been well documented. The results are clear: learning to swing the golf club correctly is directly dependent on having the correct golf club to swing.

To maximize your performance in golf you should fit your golf clubs and your golf ball to your own personal characteristics, such as swing speed, strength, and body type. For example, if you're using a club shaft that is too stiff for you, you'll leave your weight on your right side during the downswing in order to get the ball up in the air. Thus, subconsciously, you have introduced an error into your golf swing to compensate for a misfit club specification.

Equipment innovations include the long-shafter putter, which has helped Bruce Lietzke.

Club specification

The club specifications that have the most effect on your swing and are thus of primary importance to you as a golfer are as follows: the lie angle, club length, shaft stiffness, loft angle and weight.

Lie angle

The lie angle is measured by a line from the center line of the shaft to the ground when the club is soled correctly. There are two aspects to lie angle:

■ The lie angle that's created as the club sits unmoving on the ground as described above.

■ The effective lie angle which changes as you swing when the shaft bows downward, causing the toe of the club to get closer to the ground. This is the dynamic aspect of lie and also the reason why the irons are fitted with the toe slightly up in the air.

Note: If your lie angle is off, your divots may tell you. If the divot is toe deep, your clubs are too flat; if it's heel deep, your clubs are too upright.

The wrong lie

Lie angle that is too upright at impact causes your ball to go to the left of target. If it's too flat (toe down), your ball goes to the right of the target, assuming that, in both instances, you have aimed correctly.

With mis-fit lie angles, it is very easy to groove a swing error. If you make good golf swings and the ball consistently flies to the right of the target, it won't be long before you introduce an over-the-top move to pull the ball back to target. However, if your ball flies to the left, you will delay your hands to block the ball back to the target.

The important point here is that you may have a static lie angle which appears to fit you, but as soon as the club starts in motion, the lie angle becomes a function of how fast you swing, how strong you are, and your hand action through impact. There is only one way to tell how your individual characteristics will affect the static specification of lie and that is to experiment with it while you swing. This is part of a good fitting process and any fitter worth his salt will have the proper tools to determine in-swing lie angle.

Club length

All other things being equal, the longer the shaft, the further you'll hit the ball. However, there is a trade off because it's harder to make square contact using the longer shaft and you can lose distance if the contact isn't on the sweet spot of the club.

Besides feel, you can use impact tape or chalk to determine the centeredness of hit for each swing. To find out which length is right for you, tape each club face and try out three different shaft lengths, hitting 10 shots with each length on two separate occasions. As soon as your percentage of off-center hits is greater than 30 percent, the shaft is too long.

The club is referred to as being "flat" when the toe moves downward toward the ground; when it moves toward the sky it's called "upright." In order to get a square club face at impact, you may have to adjust the lie of your club at address. You can have your clubs either bent flat or upright in a lie machine, depending on your body and swing characteristics.

When you lengthen a club, the club head gets more upright (toe up) as you stand farther away. As you shorten the club, you stand over the ball more and the toe flattens. The rule of thumb is that adding a half an inch of length, makes the club more upright by about one degree.

1 The correct lie angle aims the club face down the target line.
2 When the lie angle is too upright, the club aims left.
3 Too flat a lie aims the club face right.

Traditionally drivers have been about 43 inches with about 11 degrees of loft. Today's driver shafts are getting longer thanks to the new, much lighter shaft materials being used. Rocky Thompson's 52-inch driver has transformed him from being a relatively short hitter into one of the longest hitters on the Senior Tour. Studies show that if you lengthen your driver by two inches you can add about four miles per hour to your swing speed, about a 12-yard increase in distance. One caveat: it's tricky simply extending the length of your current driver, because when you change one specification, it changes the others.

1 Clubs that are too long cause a rigid, erect posture.

2 Clubs that are not long enough will force excessive tilting of the spine.

Club specification *continued*

Club length *continued*

You will have balance problems when your club length is wrong because club length affects your posture, and it is proper posture that promotes good balance while you swing. If your clubs are too long you will compensate by standing too upright, and in doing so, your weight transfers back on your heels and your arms can't hang freely. Conversely, when your clubs are too short, you bend over too much, forcing your weight onto your toes.

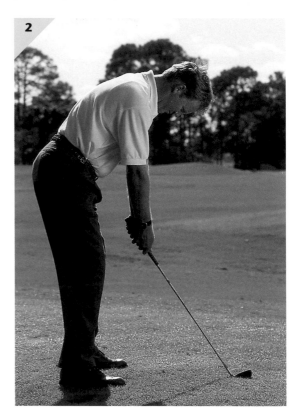

Shaft stiffness

Where and how much your shaft flexes while you swing determines your club face position at impact. If the shaft is too whippy, it's hard to square your club face at impact, whereas if it's too stiff, it won't bend enough, leaving your club face open through the hitting zone.

Generally, most golfers use too stiff a shaft. Your goal should be to swing the most flexible shaft you can handle without the ball flying all over the place. If your shots are going low and to the right, your shafts are too stiff. If your shot pattern is unpredictable, i.e. some to the left and some to the right, then your shaft is probably too flexible.

Loft angle

The non-technical description of loft is how much your club face looks at the sky, and it has a major effect on the height and trajectory of your golf shot. It's difficult to make a well-balanced, well-timed energy transfer with too little loft on your clubs because you'll subconsciously make adjustments in your swing to get the ball in the air. However, too much loft costs you distance and encourages over-swinging.

Adjusting loft from the normal is known as strengthening or weakening. You will strengthen

your pitching wedge by changing it from 56 degrees of loft to 54 degrees and consequently you'll hit the ball lower and a little bit longer. Weakening works in reverse and is used to raise the trajectory.

Weight

The total weight of the golf club is the actual scale weight or "dead weight"; for example, 13 ounces. It is important because if your club is too heavy for you, your swing gets out of control, whereas if it's too light, you can't feel the shaft.

The swing weight is the relationship between the length of the club and the amount of weight in the head. How the weight is distributed determines the "feel" of the club head. Swing weight should be the same for all your clubs to promote overall feel, but the scale weight differs for each, with your sand wedge being the heaviest.

Although there are other specifications, lie, loft, length, flex and weight are the "big five" of club specifications and if you get them right, you'll have a set of clubs that rewards balance, timing and the energy transfer necessary to get the ball to target.

Length, lie and loft

Note: Standard isn't always standard.

	length in inches	lie in degrees	loft in degrees
Woods			
Driver	43+	55	11 to 13
3	42	57	13 to 16
4	41	58	16 to 19
5	40	59	19 to 21
7	40	60	25 to 27
Irons			
1	39.5	58	17
2	39	59	21
3	38.5	60	25
4	38	61	29
5	37.5	62	33
6	37	63	37
7	36.5	64	41
8	36	65	45
9	35.5	66	49
PW	35	67	53
SW	35	67	57

Overall, the best way to determine which clubs are right for you is the "hit 'em and fit 'em" technique; in other words, be fitted by an expert while you are actually swinging the club.

The overall weight of your club is as important as how that weight is distributed (swing weight). This is because clubs that are too heavy for you can cause swing faults. One way to tell is to monitor your last five rounds of golf to see if the clubs become "heavier" as the round progresses. If you're swinging the correct weight clubs, you shouldn't notice much of a difference from your first swing to your last.

Another sign of too-heavy clubs is an overswing where you lose control at the top of your swing as your club head dips well below your shoulders pointing to the right of the target. If you can see the club head out of the corner of your eye, have your clubs checked.

It's nice to inherit a set of clubs but they may not be right for you, especially if they're men's clubs and you're a woman or a junior golfer. You should also "try before you buy," no matter how attractive the price.

Club specification *continued*

Game improvement

Perimeter weighting is a process in which a cavity is created by taking weight from the back of the club and distributing it around the perimeter. This reduces twisting when you contact the ball off the sweet spot, minimizing both the distance and directional loss that accompany off-center hits with traditional forged clubs.

This is the secret of over-size club heads, both woods and irons, and it's the new materials, such as titanium, that make perimeter weighting more effective. The lightness and strength of titanium allow club manufacturers greater versatility in shifting the weight around the club head and increasing its overall size. A typical stainless steel head weighs about seven ounces (200 grams) while the titanium version is a mere four ounces (120 grams). The club maker using titanium has

Above left: a perimeter weighted, oversize head for maximum game improvement. Center: a standard size "forgiveness", perimeter weighted head. Right: a traditional forge head offering the advanced golfer a softer feel and feedback about off-center hits.

three ounces (80 additional grams) to make game improvement changes, such as super-sized club heads and extreme perimeter weighting, that keep your drives flying straight.

Swing speed and club specifications

Club speed is the velocity of the club head as it passes through the four inches just preceding the ball. For every one mile an hour that you increase your club head speed, you can generate about three more yards in distance.

Swing speed	Shaft flex	Flex point	Golfer categories
very slow < 60 mph	very flex very soft	lowest	senior women and super senior men
slow 60 to 80 mph	flexible, "A" or senior shaft	low	amateur women and senior men
medium 81—94 mph	regular to firm	middle	amateur men and seniors/women pros
fast 95—110 mph	firm to stiff	high	long hitting amateur, golf pros, very long women tour pros
very fast 110 +	stiff to extra stiff	highest	very long tour pros, long drive competitors
Note: Companies vary in their shaft flex designations.			

Which ball?

Golf balls are available with basically two types of covers: Surlyn and Balata. The average golfer likes the durability of Surlyn whereas the top players favor Balata because of high spin rates that allow them to "work" the ball, i.e. curve it left and right, hit it high and low.

Ball construction

Two-piece balls have solid interiors and an outer cover, while three-piece balls have a liquid core surrounded by a rubber winding, covered by either a Surlyn or Balata outer shell. If you are looking for distance, use a two-piece ball with a low spin rate; it will also minimize slicing and hooking by reducing side spin.

With the introduction of Lithium Surlyn, a softer cover which gives you more feel and a high spin rate, the playing characteristics between three- and two-piece have narrowed considerably. Increasingly, golfers are choosing their balls on the basis of spin rate, i.e. how fast the ball spins around its axis.

■ For control and maneuverability, choose a ball with a high spin rate and a soft cover.

■ For maximum distance and a durable golf ball that flies higher and gets more roll, you should opt for the two-piece ball with a low spin rate.

■ For a distance and control blend, opt for a combination: a moderate spin rate with a durable cover.

Nowadays you can actually fit the components of the ball to your swing and to the type of shots that you want to make. It's like a ski racer matching a ski wax to the snow conditions.

Dimple arrangement

Back in the early days of the game, golfers learned that if you scuffed up the ball, it had a tendency to fly better and that was the beginning of the quest for the perfect dimple pattern.

The key elements are the depth, diameter, number and shape of the dimples. Manufacturers create different trajectories, distance, and spin by adjusting the dimple pattern and it's up to you to match your skill level to the appropriate pattern.

Golf balls may look very similar but their construction and inner make-up can be very different indeed. Pictured here are a two-piece Surlyn ball (left), a three-piece Balata ball (center) and a two-piece Surlyn wound ball (right). You'll improve your score when the ball you choose matches well with your swing and the conditions of play.

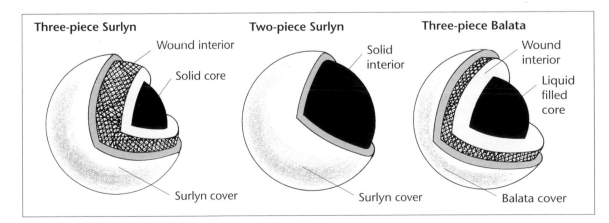

Three-piece Surlyn — Wound interior, Solid core, Surlyn cover

Two-piece Surlyn — Solid interior, Surlyn cover

Three-piece Balata — Wound interior, Liquid filled core, Balata cover

Equipment selection

Golf courses can be categorized broadly as:

1 "Driver courses" **2** "Second shot courses" **3** "Third shot courses"

Driver courses

A "driver course", which is characterized by narrow fairways and hazards bordering landing areas, demands accuracy off the tee. The greens are often large and receptive if you meet the driving conditions.

Examples of driver courses

Courses such as Royal Lytham in England, and Carnoustie in Scotland, Tryall in Jamaica, and Oak Hill in New York are good examples.

Along the seaside, or in the absence of a watering system, you'll often find the wind-swept fairways dry and firm. These "fast" conditions are a good opportunity to give your driver a rest for the day. Your three wood will get you plenty of distance off the tee, and since it produces shots that fly higher and land softer, your ball won't run off the fairway and into the rough as it might with the "hot" rolling driver.

The challenge of a driver course is to hit as many fairways as possible. A one iron, while difficult to hit from the fairway, can be an asset off the tee. With the objective being accuracy, you can count on your "driving iron" to go reasonably straight even if you mis-hit it.

Another consideration is the height of the rough. Low rough that's not much of a penalty means that the course is wider than it looks so

keep your driver in the line up. Alternatively, high rough can make the three wood or an iron off the tee the wise choice, even if the fairway is relatively wide.

Second shot courses

Greens that are tough to hit usually have generous fairways but the "second shot course" does demand that you hit your tee shot a long distance. If this is not already one of your strengths, let the longer shafted driver help you cover more ground. The longer shaft, about 44 to 48 inches, produces a wider arc, faster club head speed and increased distance but its length can make it difficult to square the face at impact so make sure that you can handle the big stick.

Examples of second shot courses

Pebble Beach in California, Firestone in Ohio, St. Andrews in Scotland and many of Jack Nicklaus's designs typify the second shot concept.

Before you strap on your spikes, check the conditions. For example, wet conditions make even the average-length course play long. The "slow" course provides little roll for tee shots and that means longer approach shots. If you're a good player (single digit), select a driver with a sole plate designed to make it easier to hit off the fairway in case you need it. And no matter what your skill level, be sure to add your strong three wood for the longer carries.

The second shot course has generous landing areas for your tee shots but be prepared for plenty of pitches, chips and bunker shots because the greens are typically small or obliquely angled and always well guarded by hazards. You may want to put a "chipper" in your bag because the weighting system for this specialty club is designed to roll the ball accurately to the hole from just off the green.

Two putters can help, if you're playing a "second shot course" where you're likely to miss a lot of greens: your regular putter for the lag putts and the long putter anchored at the top of your chest for the "knee knockers." Because of its pendulum motion, the long putter works well from short distances but the longer your backswing the more inaccurate it becomes, so unless you practice regularly, it's tough to judge the lag putts.

Third shot courses

The "third shot course" is typified by large, fast greens with severe undulations and slopes. The battle really begins once your ball is on the green. Your putting skills need to be polished and your

putting strategy must begin with your approach shot because although the greens are large, you must play to specific locations, positioning your ball on the correct tier and below the hole so that you're putting uphill. Be exact about your yardage—missing your area on a "third shot" course can mean the difference between a 70-foot putt and a ten-footer. Some architects even build "collection areas" where the ball can be funneled off the green and onto the fringe.

Examples of third shot courses

Augusta National in Georgia, Oakmont in Pennsylvania and The East Course at The Broadmoor in Colorado are good examples.

One or two *putters?*

When you're scheduled to play a third shot course where green speed varies, your putting touch will determine your success so once again consider carrying two putters. Always use a light-weight putter for the lightning fast, down-grain, downslope attempts, and a heavy putter that will help to get the ball rolling against the grain and up the steep slopes. And don't rule out the long putter as described (left).

A box head putter (left) offers forgiveness for off-center hits; the weight of a mallet head (center) helps get the ball to the hole on slow greens; a blade putter (right) produces better feel on fast greens.

Utility woods and wedges

The woods

The utility woods are fast replacing the long irons; there's no mistaking the advances in design making them easy to hit from a wide range of lies. On a tight course with narrow fairways guarded by rough, be sure to pack your five, six and/or seven woods. If you are playing a course with a lot of well-guarded par threes and you hit your long irons very low, use a utility wood to get the required distance and trajectory. And when you need a high shot that holds the green, there's nothing better than a seven wood. It goes about the same distance as your three iron but much higher.

The wedges

You can save strokes if you choose your wedges correctly. The performance of a wedge is significantly influenced by the design of the sole. The term "bounce" is used to describe the effectiveness of the club in deflecting (bouncing) off a surface of grass, sand or dirt at impact. The greater the bounce, the farther it extends below the leading edge, preventing your club head from digging into the ground.

A pitching wedge with 50 degrees of loft and about four degrees of bounce, works pretty well from tight lies as well as from the fairway. The average sand wedge has around 56 degrees loft with 11 degrees bounce to prevent the leading edge from digging into the sand. It works well in soft sand and around the greens in normal green-side rough.

The lob wedge has between 60 and 64 degrees of loft with a small amount of bounce. It works well from wet, hard sand or hardpan and, with its loft, it can get the ball up in a hurry so that it lands softly from a tight lie. Its maximum range is usually about 70 yards.

Let the conditions of play dictate the amount of bounce you select when choosing a wedge. Left: 57° with 11° of bounce (large bounce). Center: 53° with 9° of bounce (small bounce). Right: 61° with 3° lob (zero bounce).

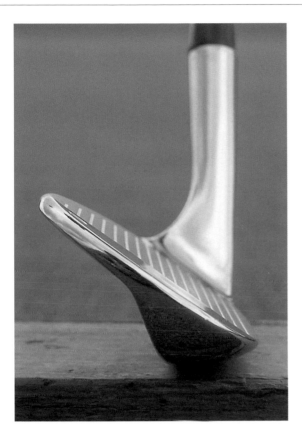

When correctly soled, only the bounce of the sand wedge touches the ground.

hit your pitching and sand wedges. Thus if you hit your pitching wedge 120 yards and your full sand wedge only 90 yards, the difference (30 yards) is too great, forcing you to either let up too much on your pitching wedge or swing too hard at your sand wedge. In our example you would adjust the loft and shaft length on your wedge to hit the ball about 110 yards.

If your bag cannot accommodate a fourth wedge, another solution to the "gap" problem is to lengthen the shaft of your sand wedge and/or decrease its loft. This increases its overall distance for a full swing and then, by simply gripping it down an inch or two, you can hit it about 10 yards shorter when you need to.

In the bunker you can save some strokes by matching your sand wedge system to the texture of the sand. When it is soft and fluffy, use a wedge with a large flange and a lot of bounce. When the sand is hard, wet or crusty, select a wedge with minimal flange and bounce.

On a "second shot course," in windy conditions or if you generally miss lots of greens, you should definitely consider an extra wedge—or two. In addition to your pitching and sand wedges, the third wedge (often called the lob wedge), is a versatile high-lofted (60-degree) club which helps you to pitch the ball high and soft from all sorts of lies.

A fourth wedge is not unheard of, especially if you face short pitches from tight, closely mowed fairways where you need a wedge with little bounce. It can also be useful as a "gap" wedge if you have a large gap between the distances you

Core set plus strategy set

The Rules of Golf limit you to 14 clubs so when you are deciding which ones to include in your bag, you may have to make some difficult trade offs. To stay within the 14 club limit carry the five, six, seven, eight and nine irons, pitching wedge, sand wedge, putter and driver or three wood in your core set. Then add your strategy clubs, depending on the course, the weather, how you feel and how well you are swinging.

Women's equipment

When choosing a set of golf clubs, you must be sure to have them tailored specifically to meet your individual needs.

Whether you're just beginning your golf career or you're a seasoned player, it's important that your equipment is well suited to your body, your swing and your playing style. In the past when women took up the game they often used hand-me-down clubs from their husbands or friends. And since a woman's build, strength level and swing speed are usually different from those of a man, these "free" clubs actually cost a woman plenty in terms of her golf swing. Clubs inherited from men are often too heavy, as well as too long and stiff for many women. These clubs become a catalyst for swing errors that become ingrained simply by the repeated use of the wrong clubs.

According to Pat Lange, LPGA Pro and founder of Lange Golf, a custom club manufacturer for women: "The biggest handicap that most women have in this game is the inappropriate equipment they've been forced to play with." And the research shows that it's not long before you learn to live with the mis-fit, although it can be a very unhappy marriage.

Right or wrong you'll adjust

Expert fitter Ross Henry's research has shown that amateur golfers tend to adjust themselves to their ill-fit equipment. "I can give you any club and you'll figure a way to hit it. If you believe the club is right and you're wrong, you'll change your swing. What always happens is that amateurs match themselves to the club they happen to have in their hand. And that's one of the big differences between amateurs and professional golfers. Professionals can take any club a manufacturer gives them and hit it a few times. When they're sure they're making their good, balanced swing, and the ball doesn't go where it's supposed to go, they throw the club away. The amateur does just the opposite. They pick a club and adjust their swing to it and say, 'Well, this club must work; I paid $500 for it.' So the perception with most amateurs is that they are the ones who are wrong, not the equipment."

As teachers we see this all the time in our golf schools. A student has a new set of "off the rack" clubs and is determined to adjust to the clubs even if it ruins their swing in the process. One woman in the school had a brand new set of clubs that were much too stiff and two inches too long for her. When told that she was mis-fit she said that the next time she bought clubs she would be

Custom club fitters can adjust each element of the club to suit your swing and body build, so that your equipment enhances your swing. Improperly fit equipment can actually cause swing errors to occur.

Right or wrong you'll adjust *continued*

custom fit. We asked when that would be and she said at least two years down the road. So for the next two years she'll play with clubs that teach her to swing incorrectly and by the time she gets the correct clubs she'll have learned to swing perfectly—perfectly wrong!

Another problem women face, especially the stronger player, is the lack of variety in women's clubs. Although it's changing, manufacturers historically have focused most of their attention on the male side of the market. Recently, as the number of women golfers has increased, variety in women's clubs is starting to arrive.

Sandy Jaskol, promotions manager at Titleist, reports that her company is clarifying the perfor-

mance needs of serious women golfers through club and shaft research projects and test opportunities. Appropriate lofts, lie angles and shaft flex options are being determined through a combination of resources, including input from Titleist and Foot-Joy Worldwide's Women's Advisory Board and Panel Members, which consist of LPGA and PGA Women Golf Professionals nationwide, computerized testing and focus group surveys and studies. Jaskol says, "Research attained from shaft flex performance preferences, in addition to shaft and club color and graphics surveys from serious women golfers, is positively influencing our current direction in customization for women through custom fitting."

Club manufacturers, such as Titleist, are now broadening their research into women's equipment. Here, their Women's Advisory Board, comprised of female golf professionals, discuss the equipment specifications for women.

General guidelines

In this chapter, you'll learn how the individual specifications of a golf club affect your ability to swing and ultimately the quality of your ball flight. There are five important features that affect performance: shaft flex; weight; length; lie angle; and grip size. You'll also learn about components such as club head styles and shaft materials.

Five important club specifications

1 Shaft flex

Incorrect shaft flex is probably the most common characteristic of misfit clubs and the most harmful to your golf swing. The shaft is often referred to as "the engine of the club," but if the shafts in your clubs are wrong for you they're no more useful to you than a car without gasoline. When your shafts are too stiff, you'll struggle to get the club head back to the ball and hang on your back foot to help the ball into the air. When your shafts are too flexible, you'll find it hard to be consistent with your direction as well as the trajectory of your shot.

A properly fit shaft does three things for you:
1 It adds a powerful kick to your shots.
2 It returns your club face square at impact.
3 It allows you to swing in balance.

Pat Lange says that she "found early on that there was not a shaft made for women that seemed to be flexible enough for a certain population of female players," so that was the first product she developed when she began her custom club making business.

Shaft flex is the mysterious element in the fitting process. The popular belief that shaft flex is determined by swing speed, which is largely dependent on physical strength, does not always hold true. Surprisingly, when all elements are taken into consideration, a tour player may need the same shaft flex as a non-athletic woman who doesn't have much strength. The point is that matching shaft flex to swing speed as the sole fitting parameter is dangerous.

Club head speed While not the only bench mark, club head speed is a good starting point for finding the right shaft for your clubs. It's defined as the speed of the head just a few inches before impact measured in miles per hour. For those who swing the club slowly (under 60 mph), the most flexible shafts should suit you best. These shafts are usually marked with an "F" for flexible. Although it's changing, "F" shafts are also known as "ladies' shafts," so sometimes you'll find an "L" on the shaft instead of an "F." They are not, however, suitable for all women and are appropriate for some men.

For golfers who swing a little faster (60 to 80 mph), the slightly less flexible "A" shaft may work best. It's commonly known as a men's "senior shaft" but here again gender and age are really irrelevant. An "R" or regular shaft is the next step up the scale, and is suggested for those who swing from 81 to 94 mph. These shafts are generally the standard for male amateurs but are commonly used by strong female golfers, especially professionals. An "S" on the shaft stands for stiff, and

In choosing your equipment it's a good idea to follow these general guidelines:
1 Whatever your choice of clubs, consult your golf teacher to make sure that your swing is matched well with the clubs that you're going to buy.
2 Don't buy anything unless you are given the opportunity to "try before you buy."
3 Go to a professional fitter and never accept a static fit. A quality fitting procedure is always dynamic, i.e. you're fit with the club in motion.

Graphite
or steel

Golf clubs have come a long way since their original wooden shafts. Now the material of choice is graphite, and with good reason. Graphite and other light-weight materials, such as titanium, have made it possible for manufacturers to move more weight into the club head for higher, more powerful shots. However, steel shafts still have plenty of appeal: they are much less expensive than graphite, and many better players still prefer them, especially in their irons, because they are more accurate. But if distance is your problem and money isn't, go for the graphite or titanium.

When clubs are too heavy, they commonly cause golfers to make too long a backswing, where the club drops past parallel. Since the club head has traveled a great distance from the ball, returning the club to the ball with power and accuracy is a struggle for most golfers.

General guidelines *continued*

"XS" for extra stiff. These are the least flexible shafts and a high swing speed is required to make them flex and kick into the ball correctly.

It's worth repeating that, while important, swing speed is only one variable in the mix. The only way to get the right fit is to undergo a hands-on fit by an expert who can interpret all the variables.

2 Club weight

One of the most common swing errors among women is the "over- swing," where you lose control of the club allowing the club shaft to drop past the proper parallel position at the top of your swing. A common cause of over-swinging is using clubs that are too heavy.

In the past, swing weight (the relation of the length of the club to the weight in the head measured in ounces/inches) was the key concept with designations like C8, D0 and D4, but now space-age computers show us that the focus should be on the club with a light "dead weight," i.e. the actual weight of the club when measured in ounces.

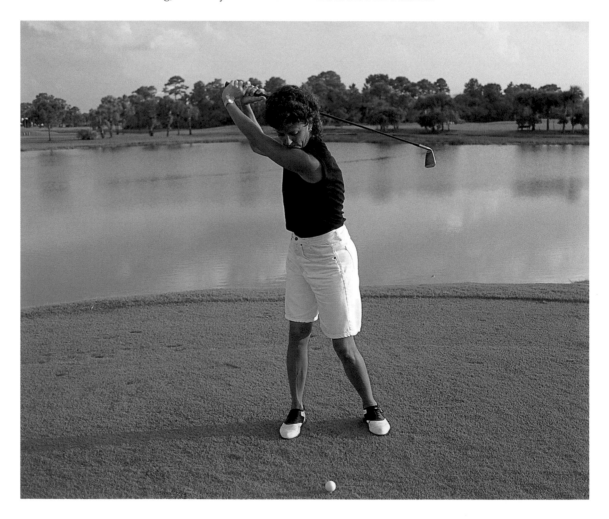

3 Length

You'll learn in Chapter 2 on set up that good posture and good balance go hand in hand. But if your clubs are not the correct length for you, you'll be forced into an unbalanced position over the ball. Clubs that are too short force an upright plane, one that's too abrupt. Clubs that are too long flatten your swing arc because you must stand too far away from the ball. If you start out of balance at address you'll struggle to regain balance throughout your swing. Since no one likes to fall over, you'll naturally be more concerned with keeping your balance than hitting the ball.

The length of the club also affects the centeredness of contact, so if you want to hit the ball squarely, producing a shot that feels light and effortless, your clubs need to be the proper length. Lange's statistics show that "for every half-inch you hit off-center with an iron you lose approximately five percent in distance, and with woods, it's anywhere from five to seven percent." The point is that you can't just add length to your clubs and expect to get more distance.

If your clubs are too short and you make a good swing, you'll make contact with the ball on the toe. If your clubs are too long, you'll hit in by the heel. Thus you can see the cycle that develops with mis-fit clubs: you make a good swing and hit the ball on the heel. The club head twists open causing a weak shot to the right. You think you've made a bad swing so on the next swing you make some changes—you might strengthen an already correct grip or you take the club more to the inside

Since the tall golfer at the rear is using clubs that are too short, she must bend excessively to the ball. The near golfer is using clubs that are too long, as evidenced by her erect posture.

Face tape can determine the area of the club face that contacts the ball. If your clubs are the right length, it helps you to hit the solid center of the club face each time.

The trend
is long

Your driver is designed to hit the ball longer than any of your other clubs not only because it has the least amount of loft, but also because it has the longest shaft. The trend these days is to make clubs with longer shafts, especially drivers, because the longer the shaft the further your club head travels during your swing and that spells power. Unfortunately, you'll reach a point where the longer the club the more difficult it is to make solid contact—a prerequisite for a powerful shot. The only way to determine how long you can go is to hit clubs of varying lengths and compare them.

Long-shafted drivers help you gain distance only if you can deliver the club face squarely to the ball. If the shaft is too long for you, you'll have trouble making solid contact, in which case your distance can actually decrease.

General guidelines *continued*

thereby ruining your take away. By the time you finish, you've gone from a good swing-bad clubs scenario to a bad swing-bad clubs situation.

As we have said, the only way you can be sure that the length of a set of clubs is right for you is to test them dynamically. Either you or your golf professional can apply a special tape to the face of the club, so that when you hit the ball it leaves a mark on the face. After 10 or 15 balls a clear pattern should develop, ideally in the center of the club face.

4 Grips

Getting the correct grip size is important for distance because the right-sized grip facilitates the releasing action of the club so that you generate as much force as possible and still control the club. When your grip is too large, it prevents you from releasing the club on time; on the contrary, play with too small a grip and you'll overuse your hands, giving your swing that flippy look.

The size of your grip should be fit to the size of your hand. To be sure you have the right-sized grip make sure that the tip of your left hand ring finger just barely touches the heel pad of your left hand when you're gripping the club properly (see page 23). If there's a large gap, your grips are too big, and if one or more of your fingers is digging into your heel pad, your grips are too small. You'll find ladies', men's and seniors grips but ignore the labels and get what's right for you.

The material in your grips affects the feel, and the texture of grips is a personal preference. Some people like a smooth, leathery feel while others like the more textured feel of a cord grip. A word of caution: if you play golf in hot, humid conditions, a textured grip, such as the cord, is less likely to slip in your hands.

Golf grips are relatively inexpensive but often golfers neglect to replace them once they wear out. Grips age rapidly, not only because of use but also due to deterioration from the extreme heat they suffer in car trunks. And unless you are conscientious about cleaning them on a regular basis,

Worn grips can make you hold your club too tightly, and this tension can actually turn a good swing into a bad one.

sunscreens and lotions build up and make them slick. All these combine to make grips slippery and difficult to control.

One solution is to keep your grips clean by washing them with warm soapy water, then rinsing and drying them. Also avoid storing them in your car where they are exposed to extreme temperatures, and, of course, have them replaced once they're worn.

Note: the markings on the grip are not guides to how you should position your hands. Thus when you take your grip on the club be sure to ignore the markings on the grip.

5 Lie angle

All clubs are built with the toe slightly in the air to account for the in-swing bending of the shaft toward the ground. The angle at which the shaft is drilled into the neck of the club depends on the individual fit. If your swing is sound but you're still troubled by off-line shots you should have your lies checked.

When your club sits properly on the ground the sole is flush, the face aims straight ahead, and the loft is correct. For this to happen, your clubs must have the correct lie angle—a specification that varies depending on the individual.

You can use a piece of sole tape to check the lie angle of your club (see page 18 for some expect advice on how to do this).

Flat and upright When you set up to the ball with good posture and the toe of your club is too much off the ground your club face actually aims to the left of the target, so you'll need to have your clubs "flatted" by lowering the toe. And if the heel is up in the air when you're in a good

Your divots
tell tales

Even if you don't have a lie board you'll know your lie angle is off from your divots. If your divots are consistently "toe deep," meaning they're deeper where the toe passed through the ground, your lie is too flat. If they're heel deep, your clubs are too upright. Instead of changing your golf swing, have your clubs adjusted to the proper lie angle so that your good swings are rewarded with good shots.

General guidelines *continued*

address position, your club face aims to the right. Your clubs should be more upright, i.e. the toe should be raised more off the ground.

Most golf professionals have access to a machine that adjusts clubs to the proper lie angle by bending the shaft near the neck of your club. To test the lie, your golf professional or club fitter tapes the sole of your club and you hit balls from what is known as a lie board. If the lie angle is correct, the tape will be marked in the center of the sole from its contact with the board, and if the lie is incorrect the evidence will be on the tape.

In addition to getting these elements of your clubs properly matched to meet your needs, you'll have other choices to make regarding the design of your club heads. These "game improvement" options can help you add distance and accuracy to your golf game.

Club head design

While there are other combinations, most simply iron club heads come in two basic styles: forged or cast. Their names refer to the process used to manufacture them; whereas the forged club head is pounded into shape, the cast is made from a mold. Forged irons are also known as "muscle backs" because their weight is focused in the center of the club face—known as the sweet spot. Cast heads are known as "perimeter weighted" because their weight is evenly distributed from the heel to the toe of the club.

Forged versus cast

The problem with forged clubs is that contact on the toe or heel doesn't have a lot of weight behind it so the ball doesn't go as far as a centered hit. These off-center hits also cause the face to twist and your shots to go off line. Perimeter-weighted clubs are far more forgiving of mis-hits because the sweet spot is actually bigger since the weight distribution allows much less twisting for off-center hits.

If you're confident that you can hit the sweet spot the majority of the time, you'll enjoy the soft feel of forged heads and the ease with which you can draw and fade the ball. If, like most golfers, you tend to hit the ball inconsistently you'll benefit from the greater margin of error cast heads allow.

Over-sized heads

Nowadays new, light-weight materials allow irons and woods to be made with over-sized heads. Like an over-sized tennis racket, you've got a larger area to contact and the lighter material allows greater distribution of weight for an even larger sweet spot.

Despite their generic name, today most woods are made of metal or light-weight materials, such as graphite and titanium. Again, these newer materials allow greater weight distribution for larger sweet spots. The trend with woods is bigger heads with game improvement features. Our experience of watching thousands of students with these over-sized heads is that they really do help them play better golf and are therefore a worthwhile investment.

Offset heads

Irons and, more recently, woods are offered in an "offset" style where the leading edge of the club is behind or "offset" from the hosel. This feature helps to get the ball in the air more easily. If you're a low ball hitter, test out the offset feature. If you already hit the ball high enough, stay with the standard design.

The driver on the left features an oversized head, whereas the driver on the right has a jumbo head. Like oversized and jumbo tennis rackets, these drivers provide you with a larger hitting area and an expanded sweet spot, thereby providing more solid contact to off-center hits.

Putting it all together

Once you have the right club specifications for your long game you're ready to choose the individual clubs that will make up your set. According to The Rules of Golf you can have up to 14 clubs in your bag. Making smart choices here can take strokes off your handicap.

Putters

Putters are made in three basic styles: the box, the blade and the mallet. The box putter features perimeter weighting, like cast irons, which give you a bigger sweet spot and, therefore, more margin for error if you hit slightly off center. Blade putters, preferred by golfers with very consistent putting strokes, have the majority of weight in the center of the club face. Mis-hits are more likely to roll off line but centered hits roll straight and true. The mallet putter often features a heavy head. Golfers who struggle with excess hand motion and have short, abrupt putting strokes find that the weight of the mallet keeps the club head swinging and helps them make more of a "stroking" motion. Mallets are also helpful on slow greens because the weight of the head tends to roll the ball firmly without excess motion.

The long putter

Pendulum putters, featuring a shaft that extends about chest high, can be found with every variety of club head. Since you can anchor the top of the long shaft against your chest with your left hand and move it with your right hand, the golfer who struggles with excessive wrist action can find relief with this style of putter. These putters tend to be especially good on short putts, because the stroke is very stable, but on long putts you may have difficulty with distance control. The key to the long putter is patience because it takes about two weeks of practice to get used to it, but once you're over the breaking-in hurdle, it can be very effective.

Note: if you play a course with severely undulating greens, stay away from the long putter—it's too hard to handle on big slopes.

You should choose a putter head that complements your putting ability and the type of greens you play most often.

Long irons versus utility woods

Old habits die hard and it's tough to imagine not carrying a three, four and five iron, but the trend is definitely toward utility woods, and not just among amateurs. Liselotte Neumann, winner of the 1988 US Open, carries a variety of woods, including a nine wood, and no irons longer than a six iron. Annika Sorenstam, 1995 and 1996 US Open Champion, also uses a nine wood.

Pat Lange says: "I think a seven wood should be in most women's golf bags. We've renamed our seven wood '911' because, in any emergency, this club comes to your rescue. We make our seven wood with a four or five wood length, but the loft gives confidence to anyone who has qualms about getting the ball airborne. Most women generally don't like hitting long irons, so the three and four irons are not even considered for most women's sets."

We predict that the day isn't far off where a nine, ten and even an eleven wood will be standard in a set of clubs. They are easier to hit, and out of the rough these woods perform much better than their iron counterparts.

Wedges

In Chapter 11 on bunker play you'll learn how a club with special features (the sand wedge) is your best choice in a green side bunker, but a sand wedge can be a stroke saver in various green side situations other than sand. Since it's the heaviest club in your bag, it cuts through thick rough much easier than your other clubs. Your sand wedge also has the most loft, so your shots fly high and land softly, a necessity in those situations when you don't have much putting surface to hit to. The lob wedge, which is even more lofted than your sand wedge, should be in every golfer's bag. Once you get comfortable with it even those treacherous green side shots over bunkers can be executed with ease.

Three wedges can add some variety to the trajectory of your pitch shots without having to modify your swing.

The set up

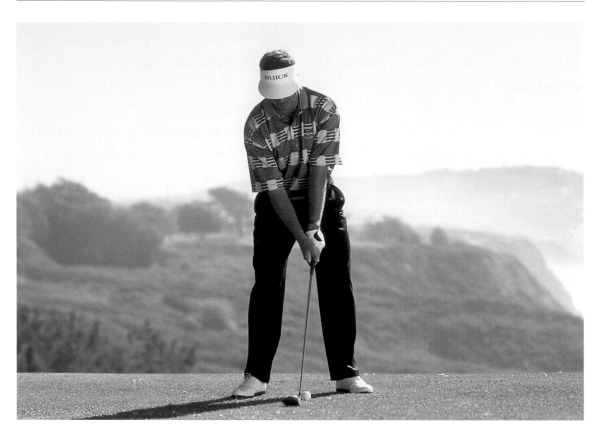

The term "set up" is a good one because that's just what this portion of your pre-shot routine does: it sets up your whole swing. Now you may not have the athletic talent of a tour player once the swing starts (few people do) but every golfer has the ability to set up like an expert so there are no excuses when it comes to getting this part of your swing perfect.

No matter what method they teach, you won't get much argument from golf instructors when you say that the correct set up is essential to a good golf swing. The set up writes the script for the performance of your golf swing. How you position your body in relation to your golf club, the ball and the target has a major effect on the quality of your golf shot. A proper set up encourages proper motion throughout

Steve Elkington's picture-perfect golf swing is founded on his precise and fundamentally sound set up. Note especially the look of relaxed readiness.

your swing; an improper set up encourages swing flaws. We estimate that over 90 percent of all swing errors are caused by an improper set up. For example, if you mis-aim too far to the right of the target (a common set up error made by over 80 percent of golfers), you must either flip your hands over at impact in order to hook the ball back to the target or you have to rotate your chest and pull the ball back to target. Either way you have introduced one error to compensate for another and you cannot play your best golf with a patchwork quilt of errors that can unravel at the least provocation.

The grip

The initial fundamental for a good set up is a correct grip. The function of the grip is to establish and maintain control of the club face, to allow the proper hinging of the wrists and to create a connection between your body and the club.

From this unusual angle, you can see the fundamentals of a good grip as shown by Lanny Wadkins. The handle is cradled In the lower palm and fingers of the left hand, and the knuckles of both hands are in a line. Notice also the beautiful firmness without tension. He has a "hold" on the club rather than a strangulation grip.

Your left-hand grip

1 Hold the club in front of you in your right hand at a 45-degree angle.

2 Place the side of the shaft across the base of the fingers of your left hand. The club will rest between the two creases (the Palmer creases) so that when you close your hand, it will be anchored under the heel pad of the left hand, thereby giving you control of the club without inducing any tension. This will also allow your wrist to hinge properly throughout the golf swing.

3 Now place your left thumb slightly to the right of the shaft so that your left wrist joint is now directly on top of the club handle. This is

important because if it is done correctly, the joints of your shoulder, elbow and wrist line up with the club face to square it up at impact.

Checking your grip pressure to make sure that it is correct is an important part of a good swing. If you squeeze the club to death, you can't cock your wrists correctly and this denies you the power source created when your left arm and your club shaft form a 90-degree angle during the backswing. If you grip it too lightly, your brain will sense it and at some point in your swing, you will have to re-grip to maintain control.

Now it is true that the "effective" weight of your club changes as the speed of the club head increases. This requires an adjustment in grip pressure as your club head approaches the ball but that's all done automatically. Fortunately, all you have to do is to start with the correct pressure and your brain will take care of the rest.

Your goal is to hold the club exerting equal pressure with both hands. Your grip pressure should be firm enough to control the weight of the club, but not so tight that movement is inhibited. On a scale of one to ten where ten is very tight, your pressure on normal shots should be in the five range.

The grip *continued*

Your right-hand grip

■ Your right hand comes in from the side with the palm facing in the direction you want the ball to go.

■ The handle is held in the fingers of your right hand with the two pads of the right hand forming a pocket to accommodate the left thumb.

■ When your right hand is closed on the club, your thumb and index finger should form a trigger. Your right thumb is to the left of the shaft.

■ With this configuration your right palm should be facing both your left palm and the target. The thumb of your left hand fits in the pocket of your right palm.

Check points

Once both hands are on the club, you can check to see if your right hand is on the club correctly by simply extending your right index finger down the shaft. If your index finger extends exactly down the side of the shaft so that the shaft is between your index finger and the target, your right hand is in a good position. You will know that your right hand is incorrectly positioned if your index finger is either on top or underneath the shaft.

An excellent check point for a correct left hand grip is the positioning of your "anatomical snuff box," the small pocket at the base of your thumb between your wrist and hand. It should be directly over the center of the club handle because when centrifugal force pulls your arms straight through impact, your wrist joint (snuff box),

1 Let your right hand approach the club from the side rather than from above or below.

2 The "V's" formed by your thumbs and index fingers are parallel and point to your right cheek.

elbow joint and shoulder joint will seek alignment. If you want a square club face at impact, those three joints need to be in alignment at address.

Ball position

The second fundamental is ball position. A correctly positioned ball is a prerequisite for square contact. The location of the golf ball affects both your shoulder alignment and the steepness of your swing. If the golf ball is too far forward in your stance (toward your target foot), your chest must turn toward the target so that you can sole your club head behind the ball. This "opens" your shoulders and because the club swings where the shoulders point, you're stuck with a slicer's swing path—steep and outside-to-in.

If you locate the ball too far back in your stance (toward your trail foot) then your chest must point to the right of the target, closing your shoulders and creating a flat, inside-to-out swing path. That's not what you want either.

1 With the ball too far forward, your shoulders align left of the target promoting a slice.

2 With the ball back in your stance, your shoulders align right of the target, the prelude to a hook.

3 Depending on the club, the ball moves about three ball widths from your left cheek, to your logo and finally to your armpit.

The bottom of your arc

With an iron, your club face contacts the ball just before it reaches the bottom of its arc. When the ball is teed with a wood, contact takes place at the bottom of the arc or slightly on the upswing. Since your left hand is higher on the club than your right hand and you are on your left leg at impact, the bottom of the arc is opposite your left armpit.

Thus for your driver, the ball will be positioned opposite your left armpit, guaranteeing that the club will travel level to the ground at impact. With your long irons and fairway woods, locate the ball off your logo and with the medium to short irons, the ball will be positioned farther back opposite your left cheek.

Ball position *continued*

Target

Left foot
flared

Not to scale

▷ Flaring your feet can distort your perception of your ball position.

Don't use your feet

Always relate your ball position to your upper body: feet are a poor reference, since most golfers use their toes to judge ball position and they can give you the illusion that the ball position is correct when, in fact, it is not.

You can see how easy it is to be fooled by trying out the following: place a ball in the middle of your stance opposite the mid-line of your body. Now when you draw your right foot back about five inches the ball appears to have moved forward. When you open your stance the ball appears to "back up" just as it does when you flare your left foot out.

Checking ball position

Once you have set up to the ball, the way to check your ball position is to straighten your spine until the golf club has been lifted to waist high and is parallel to the ground.

■ If your ball position is correct, your shoulders will be square and the club shaft will be perpendicular to the target line.

■ With the ball too far forward, your shoulders will be open, and the shaft will be angled to the left of the ball.

■ With the ball too far back, your shoulders will be closed, and the shaft will be angled to the right of the ball.

Aim and alignment

Aim and alignment are both defined in terms of the target line, an imaginary line connecting the target to the ball.

■ **Aim** refers to the direction in which your club face points in relation to the target line. When it looks to the left, it is said to be "closed"; when it points to the right, it is "open"; and when it looks directly at the target, the club face is termed "square."

■ **Alignment**, on the other hand, always refers to the direction your body faces. When it looks to the left of the target line, it is open; to the right, it is closed; and when the imaginary lines connecting your shoulders, hips and feet are parallel to the target line, then you have a square body alignment.

The key here is to begin all normal full shots from a square set up position with regard to both your club face and your body. Your shoulders determine the direction in which your arms swing, so they must be aligned correctly to ensure that your club face looks at the target at impact.

Because it is your club face that makes contact with the ball, where it is pointing at impact determines the direction in which the golf ball will travel. It is helpful to use the lines on the toe and heel formed by the grooves on your club face for aiming. It may sound simplistic but you must take

Aiming your club face

An open club face aims right of target.

A square club face aims down the target line.

A closed club face aims left of target.

What does "Square" mean?

The term "square" is rarely explained. To understand this key concept lay down four clubs as follows:

■ One club along the target line.

■ One club along your foot line parallel to the target line.

■ One club from your left heel perpendicular to the target line.

■ One club from your right heel also perpendicular to the target line.

The four clubs form a square. Your feet, knees, hips and your shoulders are square, as is your club face. Creating the square shows the relationships of the geometry between your body, the club face, the ball and the target line.

great care to aim your club face at the target.

The alignment of your hips is especially important because they dictate the amount of rotation away from and back to the ball. Open hips will restrict the backswing and cause you to open them too much through impact. However, closed hips will cause an over-rotation on the backswing and make it hard to get your hips turned back in time for impact.

In and of itself, your foot position is the least important of the body alignments, but because the position of the feet can influence the position of both your shoulders and hips, they should be in line parallel with the target line.

1 In a good set up, the body will be aligned parallel left of the target line and the club face is aimed square to the target line.

2 Use the aiming lines on your club to properly square your club face to your target.

Stance width

Finding the correct stance width provides you with a stable platform on which to swing. How you set your feet at address depends on your body build and which club you're hitting.

Foot width

The width of your stance influences your stability, balance and mobility. The widest your foot spread should be is shoulder width apart; the narrowest is the width of your hips. A good way to check your stance width for a mid iron is to turn into your follow through position and if your knees reach each other your stance is the correct width.

■ If your knees cannot reach each other, your stance is too wide.

■ If they overlap, your stance is too narrow.

Foot flare

When your left foot is flared out at address, it is easier to rotate your left hip and knee correctly as you swing through the hitting zone. To find your ideal amount of flare, experiment with hitting some balls with the left foot flared out at different angles.

■ Start with your left foot turned out about 25 degrees (a quarter of a turn) and allow the quality of your golf shots to determine how much flare you need.

■ If your left foot is flared out too much, your shot pattern will be weak fades.

■ If the left foot is too square, the shot pattern will be low pull hooks.

1 If your right knee passes your left, your stance is too narrow.

2 Your stance width is correct when your knees are even with one another.

3 If your right knee can't meet your left knee your stance is too wide.

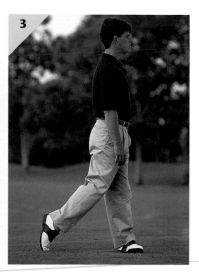

Posture

Posture affects not only your balance but also your swing plane. When your posture is too upright, you'll swing the club in an exaggerated curve around you that results in a hook or a pulled shot. When you're bent over too much, you'll pick the club up producing an abbreviated backswing that's so abrupt that it virtually guarantees sliced shots.

Knee flex

Your knees are designed to bend your body backward. Your knee flex should match the knee bend of your normal walking stride just as your forward foot flattens on the ground. This is your natural balance flex point and it differs from golfer to golfer, depending on flexibility and body physique.

The amount of knee flex is also related to the length of your arms. With proper posture, golfers with short arms require more knee flex than those with longer arms.

No matter how much knee flex you have, make sure that your weight is evenly spread from the balls of your feet to your heels and never on your toes.

Bending from the hips

Your body is designed to bend forward from the hips, not the waist. When you bend from your waist, you hunch your back and de-activate your centers of rotation. Your hip joints lock up, thus forcing your hips to move laterally, producing a slide instead of a turn.

By bending from your hips, your arms will hang, tension-free, directly below your shoulders. This also creates room for your arms to swing, and it will establish your swing plane.

Notice that when you assume the correct position, your abdomen is retracted upward and inward causing your backside to protrude. Remember that with your spine angled correctly, the weight of your head and shoulders pulls you forward toward the ball during your golf swing and it is your protruding backside that provides the counterweight to keep you in balance.

To get the feeling of the position, imagine that you are about to sit on an above-the-waist, three-legged stool. The traditional image of a regular-height stool causes too much knee bend with a squatting appearance.

Shoulders

The shoulder level check point features your arms hanging straight down from your shoulders with your upper arms adhering lightly to your body as if they were strapped on top of your chest. You're in the correct position when you can drop the club at address, relax your arms and they don't change their angle of hang.

Posture *continued*

Posture drill

1 With straight knees, place a shaft across your hips, parallel to the ground.

2 Now push the shaft backwards until your backside protrudes and your weight moves to your toes.

3 Then flex your knees until your weight is redistributed from the balls of your feet back to your heels.

Summary

Once you're in the correct posture, the top of your spine, the tip of your elbows, your knees and the balls of the feet will be in a straight line.

You will be in that universal athletic position similar to a quarterback taking a snap, a tennis player waiting to return a serve or a swimmer ready to make a racing dive. The overall set up position is one of springy readiness so that if there was a pit of snakes between you and your ball, you could leap over it without rearranging your body before you spring.

Useful tip

If you can avoid it, don't wear bifocals when you play golf because they will force you to drop your head in order to see the ball.

Pre-shot routine

The pre-shot routine is often perceived as something you do just before you swing but which does not have much relation to the golf swing. But it is part and parcel of the swing and, however personalized it might be, no expert player is without one.

The advantages of a good pre-shot routine are numerous. A good routine calms you down because you're doing the same things in the same order for every shot. This protects you against the tendency to disrupt your rhythm under stress by either speeding up or taking too much time.

When you develop a solid routine, you'll be insulated from outside distractions like noise and people moving around while you're trying to hit your ball. And as we shall see in the next chapter, once under way, your pre-shot routine is like an avalanche culminating in that special feeling called a "go" signal which allows you to pull the trigger with confidence.

The routine

Good golf shots are a combination of correct distance and direction, but you'll confuse your brain if you make it think about both while you swing. This is why you need a pre-shot routine that will separate the two, for each and every shot.

Take care of direction by aiming your club face and aligning your body correctly at address. Once this is done, forget about the direction of your golf shot and let your golf swing produce the correct distance your shot needs to travel. Design your routine so that you fix the direction first, then the distance—and always in that sequence.

1 Stand behind your ball and plan your shot. Make sure that your practice swing is a true rehearsal of the up-coming shot by taking it in the direction of the target, off a similar lie, and at the same speed as the swing you are about to make. Once you've pictured the shot in your mind and made a practice swing, take a deep breath to relax.

2 Now step into your address position with your right foot leading the way. Before you bring your left foot into position, sole your club face behind the ball, so that it points at the target. Then, keeping your club head in the same position, bring your left foot into position so that your body is perpendicular to your club face. You have now locked in your direction.

3 From this position, take one look at the target to finalize your distance calculation by rotating your head without lifting it, waggle and pull the trigger, allowing the speed of your swing to produce the correct distance.

Note:

This procedure will take only about 30 to 45 seconds and if you make it a habit, then your priorities will be correct for every shot: direction through address, distance through swing speed.

Your golf swing

In this chapter, we describe the entire swing in detail based on our belief that your golf swing will be no better than your concept of what a good swing should be. If you know what to do and this is clear and distinct in your mind, you'll be able to do it.

Whether you're a beginner, setting about building your swing from scratch, or an experienced player who needs to rebuild your swing, don't confuse comfort with correct. When you're learning something new, it usually doesn't feel right at first, and since you're accustomed to doing it incorrectly, your brain will label the correct way as wrong. We call this uncomfortable transition time an "incubation period" and in learning any motor skill it depends on how perfectly you do it and how many times you repeat it before your new skill becomes a habit.

Don't let the ball be your master

Another sound piece of advice when you're learning to make a golf swing is: don't let the ball be your master. When it is your master, you make changes in your swing based solely on how much you liked the previous shot. But when ball flight (high, low, slice, hook etc.) is your only evaluation system for how well you're learning, you'll spend most of your time tinkering with your swing to get the ball to go straight rather than learning each piece of your swing sequentially.

Remember, when you're learning a swing piece, such as the grip, your evaluation system for success is how well you're matching the model grip, not where the ball goes. You might have six more changes to make in your swing before you can expect the ball to go where you want.

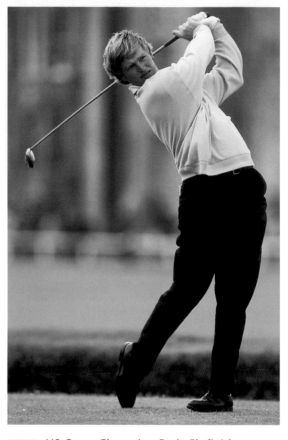

US Open Champion Ernie Els finishes another flawless swing. The balanced, dynamic finish is indicative of all that went before.

Play golf, not "golf swing"

The swing mechanics presented in this section give you the information you need to build your swing, but this information is not for thinking about while you're actually playing the game.

On the practice tee, you break your swing down and work on its parts but when it's all said and done, you need to put Humpty Dumpty back together again, forget about your swing and go *play* golf. You are now ready to develop the blueprint for your swing and we begin with several key concepts that apply to all swings, no matter how personalized.

The plane angle

The plane angle of your golf swing is the tilt or angle that your club shaft creates with the ground both at address and also as you swing the club.

Each club in your bag has a different shaft angle so if you carry 14 clubs you have 14 different swing plane angles. Your five iron, assuming it's correctly soled, creates an angle with the ground of 62 degrees, whereas your nine iron has a shaft angle of 66 degrees. This means that your swing with your nine iron will be more upright than with your five, and your five iron much more upright than your driver (55 degrees).

Thus the plane angle of each swing is established by the club you choose for the shot, and each time you change clubs, you change the angle of your swing. Don't worry about this; you don't have to consciously adjust your swing because the correct progression of shaft angles is built into your clubs at the factory. Just take your address correctly as described in the previous section and you'll at least start with a perfect plane angle—it's called being "on plane."

The trick, of course, is to stay on plane from start to finish. In essence, everything you do in terms of weight shift, shoulder rotation, wrist set and all the other in-swing mechanics is dedicated to keeping your club shaft on plane; if you can do this, you're well on your way to playing better golf.

Axis

Your golf swing is a three-axis affair composed of your spine, around which your upper body moves, and your left and right hip joints, around which, each in their turn, your entire body rotates.

While you are swinging, your goal is be "in" the correct hip socket at the correct time. Being "in" means you have established that hip joint as the center of rotation by shifting weight into it and then turning your body around it. Remember that your hip must be over its corresponding heel in order for it to rotate. Thus every good swing has a hip switch.

When your club head is moving away from the ball, weight flows into your right hip joint. When your club head is moving toward the target, pressure flows into your left hip joint.

Levers are multipliers of power. Your body and your club form your lever system, and when you use your hands and arms correctly, angles of power are created through which the energy produced by coil is increased before being released at impact.

For example, during your swing away from the ball an important power angle is created when your wrists cock forming a 90-degree angle between your left arm and the club shaft.

Another important power angle comes from the same angle that you create at the elbow to throw a ball. This is called the "Power V" and it is one of the most powerful levers in the human body. When it snaps open—in other words, when your right arm suddenly straightens during the downswing—it serves as the key multiplier of the energy generated by the large muscles of your legs and trunk.

Swing path

Coil is
a ratio

To coil correctly you must set one part of your body against the other so that torque is produced. When you turn your shoulders more than your hips during your backswing you stretch the big, banded muscles of your back, pelvis and thighs and this tautness turns into club head speed on the way back to the ball as you uncoil through impact.

Unfortunately, too many golfers are so intent on turning that they never coil. If you turn your hips and shoulders the same amount you never produce any resistance which is why we say that there's a turn in every coil but not a coil in every turn. If you turn your shoulders 90 degrees, you turn your hips about 45 degrees; if you only turn your shoulders 80 degrees, you should try for a 40-degree hip turn.

At the start of your backswing, the club head travels directly back from the ball on the extended line of the target and continues in a gently flowing arc both inward and upward. If you picture a large tilted wheel, with your neck as the hub, and the ball at the point where the wheel touches the ground, you will get an idea of the backswing path.

The path your club head takes as you swing back to the ball is underneath the backswing path so that your club head approaches the ball from inside the target line. The backswing starts the club head down the target line, and the downswing returns it inside the target line. The rotation of your body then squares the club at impact. As your body continues its turn through impact the club head will again move inside the target line. So the proper path is: **inside—square—inside**.

The most common violation of this **inside to square to inside** path occurs when you

Sequence

Even if you coil correctly, there are often times when you release your coil too early, causing power to leak out before it can be used at impact. Thus there is an optimum sequence to your swing, one that first generates, then transmits and finally delivers the power to your golf ball right on time. This sequence of moves and swing positions is called proper sequential motion (PSM) and it represents the concept that when you do something is as important as what you do.

On your downswing, let your club head follow the path of the balls to create an inside to square path.

start your downswing with your right shoulder moving out toward the target line, creating an outside-to-in slicer's path.

Impact

While you know the ecstasy of success and the emotional pain of failure, your ball knows only impact. There are five characteristics of impact that control your ball flight:

■ What the face of your club is doing through impact.

■ The path of your club.

■ The angle of approach of your club head.

■ The speed of the club head.

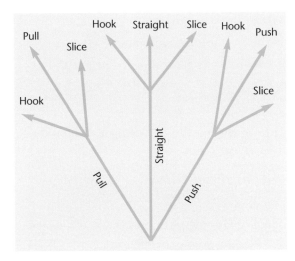

Pull / Hook / Slice / Straight / Slice / Hook / Push (ball flight directions)

■ Where on the club face you hit the ball.

With regard to direction, there are nine ball flights possible, as illustrated above.

In general the path on which your club face is moving at impact influences the direction in which your ball starts; it may start left of target (a pull), to the right of your target (a push) or go straight at the target.

What your club face is doing through impact influences both the starting direction and the spin of the ball.

■ If your club face is held open in relation to its path, your ball will curve from left to right.

■ If the club face is in the process of closing, your ball will curve from right to left.

■ If your club face is square to its path, your ball will fly with minimal curve.

Tempo

This is a key to striking consistently good golf shots and it's your hips that control your tempo. In the golf swing, the rotary speed of your hips governs how fast your arms and club head move. By turning your hips at a constant rate, your club head speed increases incrementally during your swing. Remember that as you coil you're creating multipliers of speed called levers, and these are "operated" by your hips.

To better understand how the tempo of your hip turn controls your swing, imagine a skate line at an ice show. The skaters are holding hands as the middle skater (the hub skater) begins to spin. Each skater picks up the motion from the preceding skater and adds to it, so the farther from the center a skater is, the faster she's moving and the more distance she travels as the line revolves. The hub skater controls the entire line and as she increases her spin rate, the skater at the end of the line moves faster and faster.

The hub skater represents your hips, and as you progress out from the hub, each skater represents a club in your bag. The longer the shaft of the club, the farther the club head is from the hub of your swing and thus the faster it moves. By allowing your hips to move at the same speed in both directions with every club in the bag, you can develop a swing tempo that is the same for every club. Your "hub tempo" stays constant and you produce the different distances you need to play the game by simply changing clubs. With this in mind you can see how the effortless power of the expert player is tied to good tempo.

To find your natural tempo, note the speed of your walk. If your gait is quick, your hip turn should also be rapid. If your stride is slow and deliberate, your hip turn should match it.

Club face and path, combined with the other three characteristics, dictate your ball flight, and if you know how they affect your shot pattern, you can troubleshoot your swing.

For example, if your ball slices, then the club face was open at impact relative to the path of the club. If you push the ball straight to the right of target, your swing path was too much from in-to-out with the face of your club square to the path. If you top the ball, then your swing was too vertical ("V"-shaped), causing your club head to catch the top of the ball. And if you pop up your tee shot, then you probably swung the club down on too steep an angle from out-to-in.

The swing in sequence

For analysis, your swing away from the ball is divided into two phases:

■ The backswing where your club starts back from the ball creating width and leverage.

■ The upswing where your club elevates to the top of your swing generating the height and arc you need for power.

Your return to the ball is composed of:

■ The downswing as your club moves downward from the top of your swing, retaining the angles of power developed in the backswing.

■ The forward swing during which you deliver your power at impact by releasing your club head to the ball.

Each phase is distinctly different, and an understanding of how the phases differ and what goes on in each will help you in assembling the blueprint of your golf swing.

The backswing

In the short span from address to the end of your backswing the width of your swing is established. For our purposes, width is the distance your club head moves away from the ball down your toe line.

Width is important to your swing because a good golf swing requires a certain amount of space where you can move your arms and club. Without this space, you'll be too cramped with no room for the club to travel on its proper path.

Starting your swing

1 In the section on the set up we saw that your left arm was on top of and tight to your chest. Now to start your swing your left arm simply slides across your chest until it reaches its full length and can move no further on its own without pulling your left shoulder with it. At this point you "run out of left arm" and it is the momentum of your arm swing that starts your shoulder turn by pulling your left shoulder down and away from the target.

2 At the same time that your left arm starts its move across your chest, your weight transfers into your right hip joint preparing it for rotation. Your right elbow bends slightly and moves several inches down the toe line from its original position at address. Here the shaft of your club is directly above your toe line with the face of the club matching the tilt of your spine. This position signals the end of your backswing.

The upswing

1 Once your backswing is complete, all that remains to be done is to turn your chest away from the target allowing your left shoulder to move under your chin and your right shoulder to move behind your neck. The folding action of your elbow is similar to the motion you make when you throw a ball. At this point, the weight of the club head swinging upward from the ball causes your right wrist to hinge back toward your right forearm while your left wrist remains flat. This is known as "cocking" the wrists and at this point all the important relationships have been established for your on-plane swing to the top.

2 Note that your right hip should turn over your right heel but no further. To prevent overturning your hips, keep your right knee flexed just as it was at address.

Note: During the upswing, everything moves as a unit (club shaft, arms, shoulders, chest and hips) to ensure proper coiling and prevent any independent lifting of your arms and hands.

This one-piece upswing and its companion, the one-piece forward swing, is what gives today's rotational golf swing its quiet, simple look. In the modern swing there are no unsightly angles to catch your eye and, since they move as a unit, no specific body part stands out.

The top of the swing

At address your shoulders are parallel to the target line with your left shoulder higher than your right by the same amount that your left hand is above your right on the golf club. In-swing your shoulders rotate in a circle around your neck. As you swing away from the ball, your left shoulder moves down and under your chin while your right shoulder rotates behind and over your neck. At the top of your swing and just after impact, a line connecting your shoulders would be tilted at the same angle as your club shaft. Thus your shoulders tilt as they rotate because your spine is tilted at address. Coming back to the ball, your shoulders reverse the circle as the left retraces its path back through its starting point at address to a position over and behind your neck while your right shoulder travels downward and under your neck.

1   At the top of the swing you're fully coiled with your club shaft perpendicular to the line of your shoulders and your shoulder incline matching the plane angle of your club shaft at address. Your club is supported by the palm of your right hand as if you were carrying a tray. Your elbows are level so that an imaginary line connecting them is parallel to the ground.

2   Your right leg is flexed with 80 percent of your weight supported by your right hip joint and leg. The distribution of weight in your right foot should be from the balls of your feet to the heel, favoring the inside rim of your right foot. Avoid feeling that your weight is on your toes or leaking over the outside of your right foot.

Your return swing

Just as your swing away from the ball had two distinct phases, so does your return swing. The first phase is the downswing in which your left arm drops back down your chest as your right elbow begins to straighten. Once your club is in position, your forward swing begins, allowing your turn to square the club head to the ball at impact.

Your downswing

As in everything else you do on this planet, gravity plays an important part in your golf swing. Your upswing must overcome the force of gravity but once your club reaches the top of your swing, it's poised to take advantage of the very force (gravity) that was working against it just a moment before—if you let it.

The move that starts your downswing is really two moves: one lower body and one upper body. At the same time that your left arm slides back down your chest retracing the exact route it took during your upswing, your weight transfers into your left hip joint beginning your lower body turn back to the ball. This establishes your left hip as the center of rotation, allowing your swing arc to flatten out just before impact so that you can make solid contact.

You have probably noticed by now that your downswing is just the reverse of your backswing. In both, your left arm moves across your chest as your weight flows into the correct hip: right on the backswing and left on the downswing. A good swing is therefore symmetrical both back and through.

The angle
of power

Note: There are two important points that you should remember concerning your downswing.

■ The first is that while your left arm slides down your chest and your right arm straightens, you maintain the 90-degree angle between your left forearm and the club shaft. This is an angle of power that must be held until the impact zone.

■ The second is that during your downswing, your back is still to the target, a prerequisite for preventing "over-the-top." The premature movement of your chest pulls your club head on to the target line much too early.

49

The "one-piece takeaway" used by some golfers demands that you start everything (club, hands, arms, shoulders, chest and hips) together away from the ball, but if you're not careful, you'll turn your hands and club inside your toe line too quickly, ruining your coil and fouling your swing plane. This is why we recommend a sequence of moves starting with your left arm during your takeaway and then a one-piece "upswing" where your club is elevated to the top of your swing by simply turning your chest against your resisting lower body. It is much safer and produces more coil when you get your swing under way with your left arm moving across your chest as your weight shifts into your right hip.

The forward swing to impact

Once your left arm has dropped the club into position and you have established your left hip joint as your pivot center, you're ready to release your right side. At this point in the swing you have about 80 percent of your weight on your left side ready to act as a buttress or wall of resistance against which you will hit.

The key here is that while your left side, from the knee down, stops to form the wall that you hit against at impact, your entire right side must continue its motion so that it can smack full force into that wall. This collision gives you a powerful, well-timed release. The concept that cues the right side of your body during your forward swing is that everything that is moving should keep on moving.

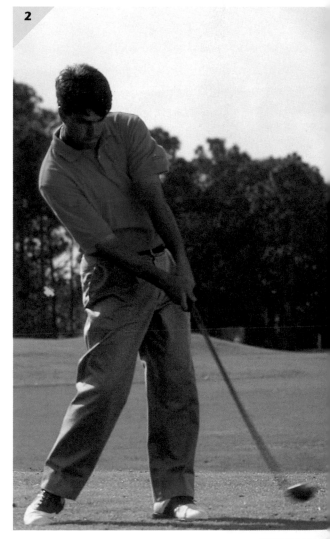

1 Just before impact your left hip has rotated behind you, increasing the pulling force on your club head. Your left arm is straight with your bent right arm under it, a position that holds your wrist cock till the very last instant.

2 Now, in a split second, your right arm fully straightens, emptying the pent-up power down the shaft and into the ball.

Follow through to finish

If you've kept your chest and right side moving as they should through the hitting zone, just after impact the force of rotation will pull both arms straight so that the club head will line up in the middle of your chest.

After impact, let your body rotate upward around your spine without any feeling of restriction in your left or right side. Allow the force of the right shoulder turning through impact to gradually rotate your head toward the target so that you are looking "under" the ball as it speeds away. In other words, allow your body to fully release through the ball, neither adding anything nor holding anything back.

1 Both arms reach full extension through impact.

2 After impact, the shaft and club head are in front of the chest.

3 The right side releases fully through the ball producing a perfectly balanced follow through.

There are four criteria for a well balanced finish:

■ Your full body weight is on your left side.

■ You are standing at your full height.

■ The front of your body including your right knee is pointing at the target .

■ You are on your right toe, using your back foot as a rudder.

Women's golf swing in detail

In order to describe the details of your golf swing it is necessary to break them down into individual pieces. Please remember, however, that your golf swing is a blending of these motions and cannot actually be executed piece by piece when you are on the golf course. They can be learned one piece at a time on the driving range but, when you play, you'll need to stop thinking in pieces and let your motion be one of a well-coordinated swing.

The takeaway

From a proper set up position, you are ready to start your takeaway—the movement of the club away from the ball.

1   To do so, let your left arm swing across your chest until it begins to pull your left shoulder behind the ball. As your left arm swings, your right arm moves away from your right side and your right elbow begins to fold.

2   Just before your hands reach hip level, you'll begin to cock your wrists. When you do, your hands remain low as your club head gets high and slightly behind your toe line.

Caution: a common error during the takeaway is to roll your hands and forearms, causing your club

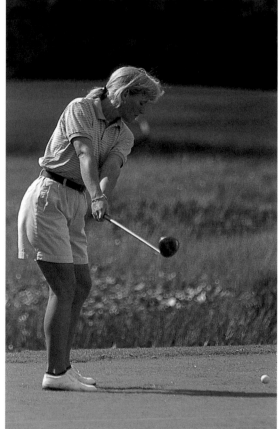

face to open (point to the sky at hip height) and the club head to get deep behind you. From this position, your only option is to lift the club to the top, thereby destroying your coil and the path of your swing.

Check your takeaway

To be sure you've made it through your takeaway correctly, check the following points.

1   Lay a club shaft on an extension of the line of your toes away from the target. From the time you start your takeaway your hands should stay on your toe line, neither moving inside or outside the line.

2   When your left arm reaches a position where it is parallel to the ground, check that your hands are still on your toe line.

3   At this point your right elbow is bent, creating a right angle between your forearm and your upper arm, with your wrists cocked so your club head is high but your hands are low. The club should now be in a very light position supported by the pedestal of your hands. The leverage of your golf swing is now set.

Check your swing plane

From a well-executed takeaway position you will start to feel coil building in the muscles of your left side, especially the back of your left forearm. As the motion of your left arm across your chest drags your left shoulder away from its address position, you'll also feel coil as your feet remain planted. At this point, you can check the plane of your swing.

The shaft of your club should form the

When your left arm swings to a position parallel to the ground, check that your hands are still over your toe line and the butt end of your club points at an extension of your target line.

same angle with the ground that it did at address, i.e. the butt end of your club points at an extension of your target line back from the ball, with your hands on your toe line. You are now ready to elevate the club to the top of your swing.

As you can see, your backswing is controlled by a combination of arm swing and shoulder turn, but there are several other important elements. Your hips play a significant role in the backswing, moving in response to the motion of your upper body. Your hips turn until your right hip is over your right heel, and no further, making their journey a short one. At the top of your swing you should feel about 80 to 90 percent of your weight in your right hip, knee, and foot, with the weight balanced from the ball of your right foot to your heel. To avoid a hip sway, keep the weight more toward the inside, rather than the outside, of your right foot.

Over the *top*

A move that gets many golfers in trouble is known as coming over the top, when your shoulders start the downswing by turning level to the ground, usually because of an impulse to throw your club head directly at the ball from the top of your swing. This may be the fastest route for your club head to get back to the ball but it is the least effective way to propel your ball to the target.

During the backswing, your club head transcribed a path gradually inward and outward. To reach the target, you must revisit this path on the way down. Throwing your hands at the ball opens your shoulders too early and pushes the club head well outside the path you established on your backswing.

To the top

From your completed takeaway position you can elevate the club to the top of your swing in one of two ways: lift your arms or continue your shoulder turn.

■ If you lift your arms, you'll destroy your coil and posture, an error that results in a loss of distance and accuracy.

■ The correct choice is to continue your shoulder turn until your left shoulder moves behind the ball. In doing so, you will build maximum coil, maintain your posture and keep your golf swing on plane.

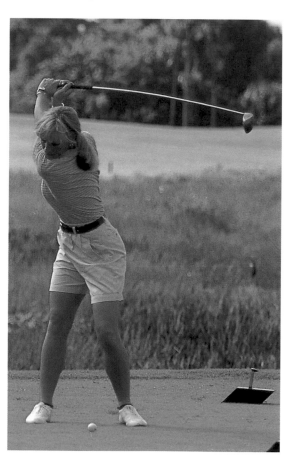

Understanding your shoulder turn

To be sure that your shoulders turn properly, you will need to keep them moving at a 90-degree angle to your spine. When you do this, your left shoulder appears to move down while your right shoulder moves up. Actually your shoulders are making a level turn but because your spine is inclined toward the ball, they appear to tilt.

To understand how your shoulders work, stand in front of a mirror and you'll notice your shoulders form a perpendicular T-line with your spine, level to the ground. Turn your chest to the right and then back to the left so your shoulders remain

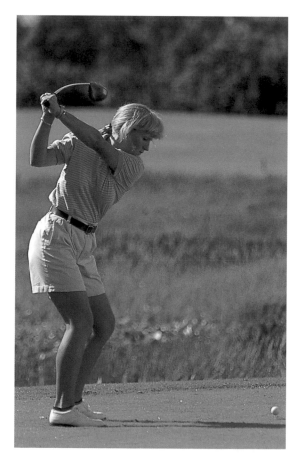

perpendicular to your spine and level to the ground. If you bend from the waist into your golf posture and turn your shoulders in the same way, you'll have duplicated the motion required for your golf swing. It is important when you swing to keep your shoulders perpendicular to your spine as they turn both back and through the ball.

The key is not to make any effort to move your left shoulder down to the ball, a swing error known as a shoulder tilt. When you tilt your left shoulder down, your weight stays on your left leg and never gets behind the ball. Another temptation is to level your shoulders to the ground as you turn in your backswing. This straightens your spine and destroys your posture and relationship to the ball.

Your downswing—it starts with a surrender

The start of your downswing requires two moves performed simultaneously: your left arm swings back down your chest as your weight shifts from your right leg to your left.

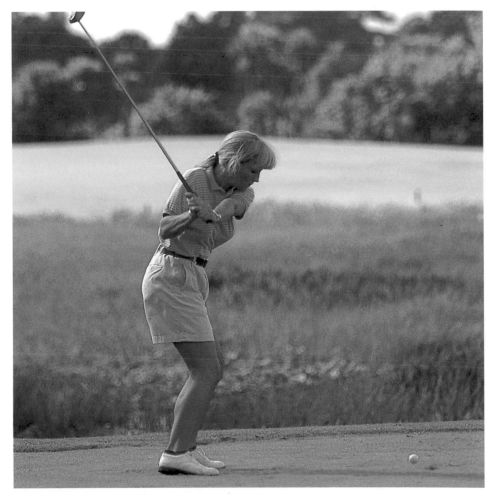

Women's golf swing in detail *continued*

Just as your left arm swung across and up your chest to begin your backswing, it reverses its path to start your downswing. Since your shoulders elevated your arms in your backswing, your left arm has a descending motion as it moves across your chest—you don't make your left arm come down; you let it come down by surrendering to the pull of gravity. Keep in mind, however, that your shoulders stay in place until your arms drag them around: the sequence starts with the arm drop/weight transfer followed by the hip turn, and lastly the shoulder turn.

The pressure shift from your right to your left is extremely subtle, but after it has been accomplished your hips take over your swing and begin

a powerful rotation, with your left hip serving as the axis for the rotation. In order to achieve this, you'll need to have the pressure of your weight on your left hip. Again, this transfer of pressure is a subtle movement which is similar to shifting your weight when dancing.

Impact

When your downswing unfolds as it should, your club head is literally on a collision course with the ball. Once your arms have moved back in front of your chest, your shoulders key your swing motion as they did in your backswing. Now your left shoulder moves forward and upward away from the ground and your right shoulder moves toward the

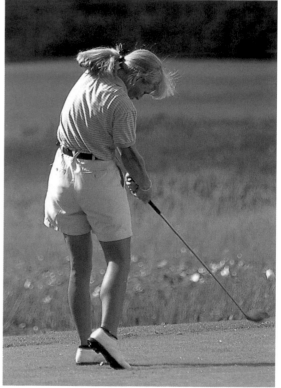

place your left shoulder occupied under your chin at the completion of your backswing. The rotation of your left hip moving behind you causes your left leg to straighten, providing a firm wall to hit against. At impact, your club face mimics its position at address.

Follow through

Although the follow through happens after the ball has gone, it is still an integral part of your golf swing. A well-executed swing is completed with the head, chest and hips facing the target and all of your weight on your left foot. Your right foot is almost completely off the ground, with the toe of your right shoe serving as a balance point on the ground. Even if the ball doesn't go where you

want it to, you should practice finishing each swing in this full and balanced position.

A good follow through is a result, but if you train yourself to go to that position after each swing, you will help improve the earlier parts of your swing. When you know where you're going, you'll use the proper muscles and motions to get you there. So if you finish incorrectly, take a moment to stand in the correct follow through position and concentrate on getting to this position on your next swing.

Blending

As you can imagine, while you are actually swinging, it would be impossible to think about even a

Sometimes, in an effort to transfer weight to their right side golfers sway rather than turn their hips. When the hips sway, they move laterally, to such an extent that the right hip slides outside the right leg. On the downswing, the left hip slides too much toward the target so that it is outside the left leg through the hitting zone. The problem is that while all this sliding is going on, coiling and the correct swing path take a back seat, so when you sway your hips, you'll hit a variety of fat and thin shots.

To be sure that your hips are working correctly, plant a shaft or an umbrella next to the outside of your right heel and cross your arms over your chest. Make your backswing motion. If you sway on your backswing, your hips bump into the shaft.

Women's golf swing in detail *continued*

A common error, especially among beginners, is an effort to lift the ball off the ground and into the air. To do so, they hang on their right side during the downswing and flip their wrists to try to get under the ball. What's worse is that their effort produces exactly the opposite of their objective: at best, a very low shot due to contact with the middle of the ball or, one of the worst shots in golf, the fat shot. The good news is you don't have to do anything in your golf swing to help the ball into the air. The loft of the club is designed to do that for you. Your objective is to drive the ball forward to the target letting the loft of the club provide the trajectory.

few of the many instructions you've learned about the golf swing. What you need to do is to evaluate the area of your swing that is most in need of improvement and then work on that one piece until it becomes a habit. Be sure to eliminate errors in your swing in the order in which they occur. For example, fix a takeaway error before you work on your downswing. Golf swings are an excellent example of cause and effect, so often you'll find that an error late in your swing disappears once you perfect an earlier part of the swing. And this follows through to your set up: most errors are eliminated once you set yourself properly to the ball.

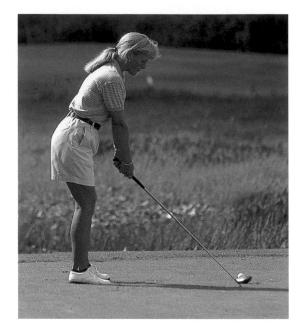

Summary

As you have probably noticed, your downswing is a reverse of your backswing motion.

1 Your left arm swings across your chest and your wrists set the club head up and slightly behind you.

2 When your arm can swing no further, your shoulders begin their rotation around your spine and, finally, your right hip turns over your right heel.

3 To start the downswing, the motion reverses itself. Your left arm moves back down your chest as your weight shifts to your left hip.

4 Once your arms drop, your shoulders will continue the motion through the ball as your left hip moves behind you.

5 To finish your swing, your left elbow begins to bend as your right arm moves past impact across your chest.

6 Your club head releases through the ball and your wrists re-hinge; this is a mirror image of your completed takeaway position.

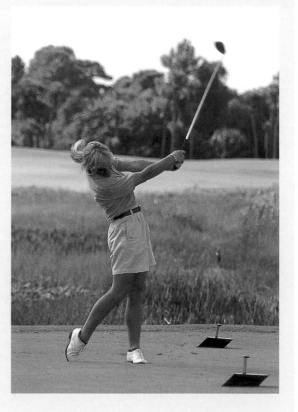

Drills

Throughout this chapter you will find a progression of drills, starting with the most basic eye-hand co-ordination, and building to more golf-specific drills. If you have never played a sport before, start at the beginning. For those who have higher levels of skill, find out where you fit in the progression and begin from that point.

Hand-eye coordination drills

The bucket drill

A simple drill to enhance your hand-eye coordination is to toss balls into a bucket. To do this you should stand six feet away from a wash bucket and toss balls into the bucket. When you can make eight out of ten, take two steps backward and repeat until you are 20 feet away.

The clap drill

Choose a partner and face each other in your golf posture—be careful not to bang heads. Each person extends their right hand so their palms are facing one another. From this position, take turns gently swinging your right arm back and through as it would in your real golf swing so that your palm meets your partner's palm at impact.
Note: once you have mastered hand-eye co-ordination move on to weight transfer drills.

Weight transfer drills

The "X" drill

■ To learn the proper weight transfer in your golf swing, set up with your feet about hip width apart and lay a club from your right heel to your left toe and a second club from your right toe to

your left heel. The two clubs form an "X" with each at a 45-degree angle to the target line.

■ Hold a third club across the top of your thighs and turn your right hip over your right heel so that 80 percent of your weight is supported by your right leg. When the shaft across your thighs

You can also use the "X" drill to check the path of your takeaway and follow through by matching the shaft in your hands to the shafts on the ground.

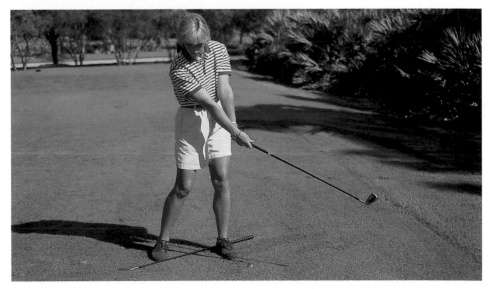

Drills *continued*

matches the one on the ground your lower body backswing transfer is complete.

■ For your downswing transfer, reverse the process and turn your left hip over your left heel until the shaft on your thighs matches the one on the ground.

Balls in pocket drill

■ Place a golf ball in both the front pockets of your pants, with the grip end of a club against your belly button.

■ Grip down on the shaft until both your arms are fully extended.

■ Now turn your body while shifting your weight to your right side (as in the "X" drill) until the ball in your right pocket is over your right heel.

■ Turn through the ball so your stomach and

club move as a unit, until the ball in your left pocket is over your left heel.

Note: once you have mastered these drills you are ready to learn the body sequence drills.

Body sequence drills

Path drill

■ Place a tee in the hole at the top of your club's grip and another in the ground where the ball would be. Put two more tees two feet behind and in front of the tee on the ground along the target line.

■ Take your grip and golf posture and set up to the center tee.

■ Extend your right index finger down the shaft and swing the club with your arms only so your club head passes over the rear tee, back over the

1 Use the path drill to learn the rudimentary part of your golf swing.

2 Once you have mastered the path drill, move on to the plane drill.

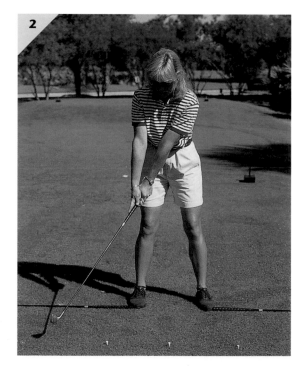

middle tee and through to the front tee. Throughout this motion, your index finger points at the line formed by the tees.

■ Once you can do this, put a ball on the tee and just let the ball get in the way. Don't try to add any force to hit the ball or you will find you change your path.

Plane drill

■ Using the same set up as in the path drill (opposite), use two clubs to mark the extension of the line of your toes—one out from your left foot toward the target and the other out from your right foot away from the target. Be sure that these shafts form a straight line and are parallel to your target line (the line of the tees).

■ From your address position, swing the club back until your right arm folds and your left arm is parallel to the ground. Your left arm and your hands should be over the shaft extending from your right foot, and the tee in the grip end of your club should point at the target line, specifically the back tee.

■ When you swing your club through, your right arm and your hands should be over the shaft extending from your left foot, and the tee in your club should point at the target line.

1 The plane drill also teaches you how to set the leverage for your golf swing.

2 When done correctly, you'll also learn how to release the leverage of your swing through the ball.

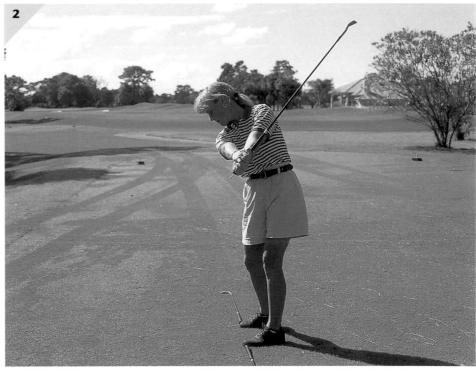

Three keys for the S swing

Distance and accuracy are perhaps even more important to the senior golfer than they are to any other. This section shows how those two vital components can be achieved by using the S—for Senior—swing.

The moving coil

The key is the "moving coil" method, coupled with the principle of "low hands, high club-head." The moving coil means your upper body moves laterally as you turn, allowing you to swing your left shoulder behind the ball as your right hip turns over your right heel. It is not, however, a sway because your weight stays on the inside of your right foot and your right hip turns instead of sliding.

Low hands, high head

You have learned to hold the club with a strong left hand grip and a long left thumb, a combination that maximizes wrist cock. This is a vital power element because your shortened swing means your hands and arms stay low to preserve your posture and coil, but your club-head swings on as high an arc as possible due to the large amount of wrist set. So you take advantage of three power sources: the club-head arc, the leverage between wrists and left forearm, and the power your muscles contribute.

The direct radius

The S swing produces accuracy by using the "direct radius" method. Your hands are on a straight line with your chest throughout the swing, and you establish the most direct route to the ball, one producing a consistent, repeatable impact position.

With these essential concepts coupled with the particulars of your set-up that you learned in the previous chapter, you are now ready to learn the S swing.

The head leaves its address position when it is allowed to follow the movement of the upper body in the back-swing.

The S swing in detail

The fundamentals you learned in the set up chapter set the stage for you to draw the ball, a powerful ball flight that starts right of the target and curves no more than about ten yards back to the target. For a senior who wants to regain distance, learning to hit a draw is imperative. If you have survived with a slice so far, now is the time to learn to draw the ball because that slice is destined to get shorter, weaker and more crooked.

Pieces for learning

Though we would never want you to think of a swing in "pieces" when you actually play the game, we have separated out various swing stages so we can describe them in detail and clarify every element. Keep in mind that while sectioning a swing into pieces is contrary to the overall concept of a golf swing, it can be helpful as a format for explanation. Once you've learned the details though, banish these pieces from your swing thoughts. Call upon the pieces only when you are having trouble with your swing and have time to go to the driving range to work on whatever element is causing the problem. To master your swing you will blend all the individual parts into a rhythmic motion known as the golf swing.

Address

As you learned last chapter, you begin the S swing from a slightly closed address position where your club-face aims at the

Once you've mastered the S swing we are certain you will hit the ball better than you have in years. But even the best swings in the world can go off track now and then. The question always is, how do I get it back? We strongly suggest that you avoid tinkering with any mid-swing elements and start with the basics.

Take your book and go to a full-length mirror. Open to the set-up chapter and use the photos and the mirror as a guide. Has your left hand grip slipped from strong to neutral? This is the most common mistake, and an easy one to make. Is your posture too erect, or is the ball too far forward? If you find the problem in your set up, and chances are you will, make the adjustment and then hit some balls to reintroduce it to your swing. Remember, every error will cause another, so give the rest of your swing time to adjust to your new set up.

If the problem wasn't in your set up, no doubt you will find it early in your backswing. Follow the same process, giving your entire swing time to adjust to the correction.

Address *continued*

target as usual, but your body also points at the target itself, rather than parallel left of it, which is the usual prescription. Remember that the corresponding ball position for the S swing is back of the standard. If you adopt the other elements of the S swing and set up, but neglect to move the ball back, you will hit pull hooks that go a long way, but are hard to find. By employing the new standards you learned in the set up chapter, you will establish your posture by bending more from your hips so you have sufficient room for your arms to swing across your chest rather than simply picking the club up without coiling.

The take-away

The take-away only lasts an instant but it is critical to the overall quality of your golf swing. To get off on the right track, use a one-piece take-away where your hands, arms, chest and the club all move away from the ball as a unit. To guide you in the initial path of your swing, use an extension of the line established by your toes. Your hands should follow this line and the rest of the members of the one-piece unit should maintain the relative positions they held at address as they move. But be careful not to force the club-head straight back along the target line. Instead, as your stance is closed, you should let it swing back inside the target line as your hands move along your toe line.

To visualize the one-piece take-away, think of a triangle where your arms serve as the sides and your chest forms the back of the triangle. The club-shaft extends down from the point of this triangle like a spire on a church steeple. As your hands travel over your right foot, the triangle moves away from the target intact, with all relationships between its faces remaining constant.

The head float

Although there should be no conscious effort to move your head during the swing, forget advice you have heard about keeping your head still. Let it move as part of the one-piece unit. Even the youngest, most supple players, like Tiger Woods, Ernie Els and Phil Mickelson, let their heads move behind the ball during the back-swing. It's a subtle move but it is a part of every good swing. Older players, and/or those with less flexibility, let their head float even more and so should you. Just make sure that you don't overdo and force your right hip to slide outside your right heel. In order for your head to move correctly, keep your neck and shoulders relaxed. If they are tight, you will freeze your head in its address position and your only option will be to lift the club to the top of the swing without coiling. This destroys your golf posture and your swing.

You should be aware of your weight moving to your right leg as you start your take-away because the mass of your body is moving behind the ball, and your hips are turning in response to the motion. Even if you are firmly inflexible, when you get to this point in the swing your left foot should be firmly planted on the ground. You may let it rise later in the back-swing, but if it is up at this point, you will inevitably lose coil and ruin your swing-path.

The take-away ends when your hands are just past your right foot. As the take-away blends into the back-swing, the heel pad of your left hand pushes down on the handle to set your wrists, elevating the club-head without you actually needing to raise your arms. Once you move away from the "pieces" of your swing and blend them into one motion, a hint of this feeling will occur almost immediately as your club leaves the address position.

1 A common error in the take-away occurs when the left arm rolls out from the chest and breaks the powerful connection between arms and body.

2 When the hands act independently they often ruin the take-away by rolling the club-face open.

The back-swing

The complete back-swing motion is a combination of arm swing and body turn, where your arms do the up and down, and your body does the around. Note that, while the arms swing up and down, you don't force them high for power. You let them swing up as your body turns until you reach your threshold of flexibility, at which point you are at full coil. For the flexible person, this will result in a higher hand position than for one with less flexibility, and this is as it should be, given the differences in physical characteristics from golfer to golfer.

As these motions occur, your left shoulder moves behind the ball and the pressure of your weight transfers onto your right hip joint. Once again, we've separated out each motion to describe it in detail but, to work effectively, you know they must be blended into one, seamless motion.

Even though your arms and hands swing up, we would like your concept to be that they swing back and away from you. This way you won't try to lift the club, going for a high arc. If we could give every senior only one piece of swing advice, we would tell you to repeat the following mantra before every swing, "it's a back-swing, not an up-swing," meaning that the club swings away from the ball and the up part takes care of itself – if you let it. This is good advice for a player at any age, but an especially wise doctrine for the less supple golfer and, if you are a senior, it is an absolute swing saver.

So the concept, the hallmark of the S swing, is that your body, mostly your upper half, turns behind the ball with no effort to get the club high above you. In other words, the arms swing as high as they will, not as high as they can.

If you have been playing golf for many years, you know that your club-head has to create enough arc for power, so you are probably wondering how you will arrive at a happy medium, somewhere in between too long and too short a swing. Though your hands stay lower than they do in a standard swing, you will set your wrists aggressively in the back-swing. This creates sufficient height and length of arc. Whatever arc you lose to a shorter swing, you will gain by swinging the club wide away from you in both your back-swing and your down-swing.

Low hands, high club-head

As you make the transition from take-away to back-swing, you begin to set your wrists as your left shoulder continues its turn behind the ball. Your goal is to keep your hands low but set the club-head high. This way you take full advantage of the powerful leverage your wrists provide. A good thought to achieve full cocking is "low hands, high club-head'. To accomplish this goal, push down on the grip with the heel pad of your left hand while your right palm applies pressure to your left thumb. This cocks your wrists correctly to their maximum.

Using this motion to cock your wrists also helps turn your body behind the ball. The pressure exerted by the right palm serves to pull your left shoulder behind the ball and also protects you from trapping the club behind your body. Pushing the club away from you prevents your left arm from collapsing. A wide swing, where your club-head is kept away from the body, is the key to power, and to keep your swing wide, you should maintain a sense of pushing the club away from you throughout your swing. Remember, if you are pushing down with the heel pad of your left hand, and out with the palm of your right, you will never have to worry about your swing getting too narrow. It is physically impossible to exert pressure away from you as described and collapse the club into your body at the same time.

So this push/set wrist action increases the gap between your hands and your chest, creating the widest and highest possible swing arc for your flexibility profile. This is a key to the S swing for several reasons:

Wrist cock produces a lever which, if saved for impact, multiplies your strength and club-head speed. It is the same concept as using a long pole to move a big rock: the lever, in this case the pole, is the multiplier. With the lever multiplying your strength, the boulder is easily moved; without the multiplier, you don't have enough strength even to budge the boulder.

The back-swing *continued*

■ it creates the maximum swing arc while keeping your posture intact,

■ it helps move your body behind the ball for power,

■ it positions the club on a direct route to the ball for solid contact,

■ it satisfies the leverage requirement necessary to multiply club-head speed.

As the back-swing unfolds, you will feel your weight move onto your right hip joint. This now establishes your right hip as the point of rotation. In your down-swing, the process will reverse itself and your weight will move to your left hip joint, which is the point around which you will find that you rotate through impact.

During the back-swing, it is perfectly alright if your left heel comes off the ground. In fact, if you are very inflexible, it is a necessity. The important point is that you let your left heel rise, as necessary, only when it is pulled off the ground by the tug of your upper body. This way you'll retain your coil while you turn.

1 To learn the "push/set" wrist action characteristic of the S swing, use the split-hand grip drill. Leaving your left hand at the top of the grip, move your right hand down to the end of the grip. The left hand can easily push down on the handle while the right hand pushes the handle away.

2 The split-hand grip drill teaches the "push/set" wrist action and ensures that the hands stay low while the club-head achieves maximum height and width.

Top of the swing

The back-swing is completed when your left shoulder is behind the ball, your wrists are fully cocked, and your weight is about 80 to 90 percent in your right hip socket. Folding your right elbow rather than lifting your arms elevates the club to its final height at the top of your swing.

When your back-swing is complete, you should feel that your left arm is parallel to the ground. Although momentum will take your arm higher than you think it is, left-arm-parallel is a key feeling that keeps your arm swing under control. This will be the hardest feeling to become accustomed to simply because it is hard to go from a long swing to a short one. Your brain thinks that height is power. When you first try shorter swings, you will be tempted to jump at the

At the top of the swing, the correct position for your right forearm is related to your flexibility and the size of your chest. Large-chested, players with low-flexibility respond to the unique wrist cock of the S swing by angling their right forearm toward the target line as the right elbow folds. This in turn produces what's known as a flying right elbow, a position where the right elbow is well away from your side at the top of the swing. If need be, the senior player who can't use other "high swing tactics" can use the flying right elbow. It fits perfectly with the other mechanics of the S swing and gives the club-head a bit more height.

Because your grip is strong, the flying right elbow also keeps the club-face from getting too closed (facing the sky) at the top of your swing. When you fly it, your right forearm slants at the same angle as your spine with the shaft pointing to the sky. If you do fly the elbow, you should expect less of a draw.

Top of the swing *continued*

ball to make up for what you perceive to be a loss of power. But in time, if you trust the concept, you will stop lunging.

At the top of your swing, the club is short of parallel, in a square or even a slightly

> Coil is produced when your shoulders turn further than your hips.

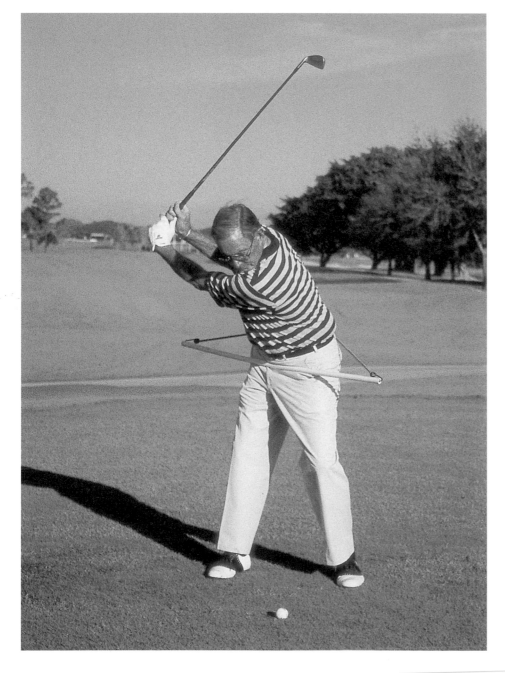

closed position (angled a bit toward the sky). Your left arm is extended away from your body and the club is in front of your chest rather than behind your right shoulder. Both wrists are cupped because of your strong left, weak right grip. If you have good flexibility, your right elbow will be bent so that your right forearm and upper arm form a 90-degree angle. If you are less flexible, the angle will be less, but never less than 45 degrees. For all players, the right forearm should be angled to the ground at the same angle as your spine.

Your shoulders should turn about twice as much as your hips. This sets your body in a coiled position that translates into power when you unwind it in the down-swing. Standard instruction calls for about a 90-degree shoulder turn and a 45-degree hip turn, producing the coil mentioned above. But remember that coil is simply a ratio. If you can't turn your hips 90 degrees – and many seniors can't – it is not a problem. All you need to do is turn your shoulders more than your hips to create the proper ratio. For instance, if you can turn your hips only 40 degrees, you can create the proper ratio by turning your shoulders 80 degrees. In this case, you would ruin your swing struggling for the standard 90-degree turn your body can no longer achieve. The point is, whether your ratio is 80/40, or 90/45, the result will remain the same: your muscles stretch to power your swing.

The down-swing

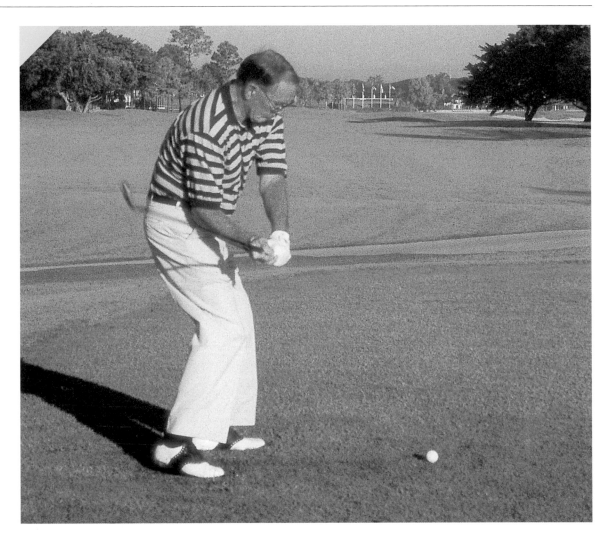

In a standard swing played from a square stance, there is a shift-then-turn down-swing sequence, where the weight shifts from the right hip to the left hip and then the body turns to bring the club to the ball. The senior swing has a turn-then-shift sequence where the upper body turn occurs first, as part of the re-set. This puts the club between the body line and the target line, a channel called the pro-slot where the club-head is then delivered to the ball from inside the target line. Once the club is re-set in that channel, the weight shift occurs. Simultaneously, the right elbow tucks back in to your side. When this happens, the right elbow is in front of, or at least even with, your right hip, a position necessary to keep the club on the correct inside approach path.

Re-set then tuck

Since your stance is closed to account for limited flexibility, you don't want to drop the club to the inside as the initial move in your down-swing. In the S swing, you move your right shoulder out toward the target line enough to re-set the club to a position between the toe line and the target line. Then your weight shifts, your right elbow tucks and you are ready to turn your hips through the hitting zone. This is not, however, the classic over-the-top error since the club-head comes onto the target line from the inside, rather than across it from the outside on a slicer's path.

In the case of the S swing, the club is re-routed out toward the target line by the upper body turn where the right shoulder and hands move together for an instant. From a square stance this move would create a swing path where the club-head comes to

71

Axis axis

In a good golf swing you will use three axes: your spine, around which your upper body moves, and your left and right hip joints, around which, each in their turn, your entire body rotates. While you are swinging, your goal is to have pressure on the correct hip socket at the correct time.

To establish a hip joint as a center of rotation, you shift your weight on to it and then turn your body around it. Remember, your hip must be over its corresponding heel in order for the hip to rotate correctly while you swing. When your club head is moving away from the ball, the weight should be flowing into your right hip joint. When your club head is moving toward the target, pressure should be flowing into your left hip joint. Even though the third axis of rotation, the spine, moves in the S swing, it still serves as the axis of rotation for your upper body turn, which is why it is known as the "moving coil."

The down-swing *continued*

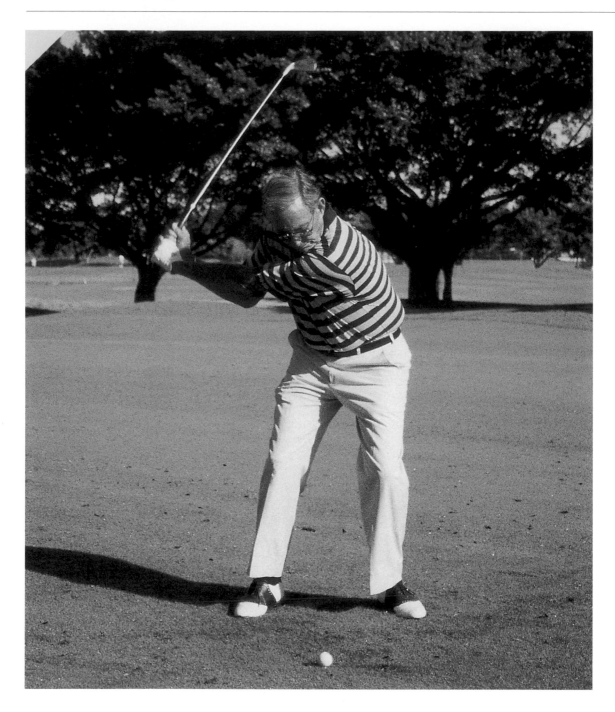

the ball from outside the target line, side-swiping the ball. This would produce one of three ball flights: a slice if your club-face is open to this path; a pull if your club-face is square to this path; or a pull-hook if your club-face is closed to this path. But because your stance is closed, and your set up is arranged to accommodate the re-set, the

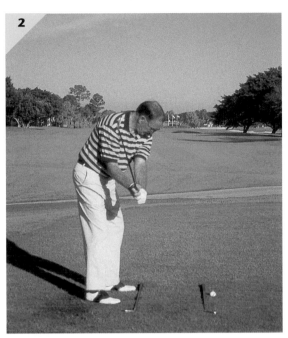

The human body is equipped with powerful levers, multipliers of power, that can be an integral part of your swing if used correctly. This leverage is produced by cocking and un-cocking your wrists and bending your right elbow to create a 90-degree angle between your left arm and club-shaft. Unfortunately, your club can also be elevated by lifting your arms or straightening your spine. This produces minimal coil, and the various benefits of leverage are substantially reduced. Cocking your wrists and bending your right elbow elevates the club and allows you to maintain your spine angle and your arms-to-body connection.

1 From a square stance, an over-the-top move creates a path where the club-head is forced outside the target line and then across it in the down-swing.

2 The senior player is allowed a slight over-the-top move, but, since the stance is closed, the club-head still approaches the ball from inside the target line.

club-head stays off the target line because the right elbow tucks into your right side.

Note that large-chested players, who have a tendency to fly the right elbow because of limited flexibility, still must tuck it back to the right side until it is even with the right hip. But they do it later than those with smaller chest size/greater flexibility, who are not as much closed at address. However, large or small, flexible or not, both types must tuck the elbow to return the club-shaft at impact to the angle it had at address – a universal prerequisite for hitting good golf shots. This move separates the good S swing

player from the poor one. When the poor player comes over the top, there's no elbow tuck, and this leaves the elbow trapped outside the right hip. The result blocks the club-head from the necessary inside path, and causes an out-to-in swing path that produces a slice.

Once the re-set is complete, the weight shifts onto the left hip, making it the axis of the down-swing. The S swing now becomes a right-sided swing, a hitting action where the right side provides the power by pushing the club to the ball in a powerful "shoveling" action as the body twirls around the left hip.

73

Impact

As you can now see, the key in the geometry of the S swing is the closed stance, so that even though you swing the club-head over your body line, you are still approaching impact from the inside. Done correctly, and with a good release of the club, this action produces a powerful draw that adds yards to your shots.

The release for the S swing allows no breaking down of the left hand. The forearms rotate in response to the momentum of the club-head so the release is full with the club-head turning toe-over-heel. This gives the S swing a "slashing arms" look because the arms release the club-head around the body. When the re-set is exaggerated, there is evidence of a blocking action where the left forearm rotation is held to a minimum. This produces a chicken wing position of the left arm, where the left elbow juts out toward the target in an effort to keep the club-face on line longer. Unless you are very strong, this action is not recommended.

During the down-swing, your head and

your swing center (located just below the throat) float back again to the original address position, then stop to let the arms swing by. This, and hitting the left wall, are responsible for the passive release of the club-head. Both heels face the ground until after impact. The right ankle rolls to the inside during the down-swing which keeps the right heel from flipping out toward the target line.

Full release

Just past impact both arms are straight for the only time in the golf swing because of the straightening of the right arm through the hitting area. Continued body rotation, combined with the force of momentum, then causes the right forearm to pass over the left so that the butt of the club slants toward the target line.

Impact *continued*

 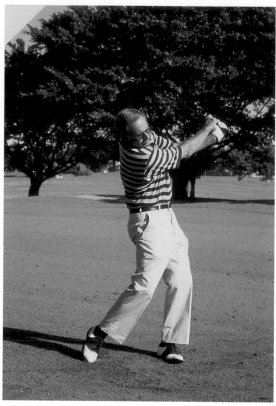

The finish

The head release

The finish should be erect with no bowing of the body because the club travels more "around" the body with your shoulders level to the ground. In the S swing, the head must release early after impact, much like Annika Sorenstam of the LPGA Tour, Brad Faxon of the PGA Tour or Jim Colbert, a Senior Tour star. This encourages you to keep everything rotating through the hitting zone, and it is also easier on your neck and back. The early head release allows you be become upright (the "I" position) much sooner, protecting your back from the damaging "Reverse C" that has ruined so many golf games. Players like Ian Woosnam, Jim Albus and Arnold Palmer finish in the "I" as do bad-backers like Rocco Mediate and George Archer.

Note that while early release gives the appearance of the head coming up and off the ball before impact, it actually does not; it releases after impact as part of the full body release as the body swivels up into the finish.

Summary of the S swing

Your S swing is cued by an upper body move away from the ball, that begins with a one piece take-away and ends in a push-down/ push-away cocking action of the hands. The left shoulder moves behind the ball as the weight shifts to the right hip. The head does not remain fixed. Instead, to allow the player to get behind the ball, there is a slight float or drift of the head as the coil is completed. Since the upper body is in control, the S swing looks more arms-orientated, with the lower body functioning as a base for stability and balance. The swing is short, with low hands, but wide as the club-head travels away from the body with the hands in the middle of the chest. The club-shaft is a bit steeper going back than it is coming down because the tucking of the right elbow during the down-swing shallows out the swing arc. The power comes from a full release of the forearms and body through the ball, a release that causes the ball to start slightly right and then draw back to target. The body is straight at the finish with 100 percent of the weight on the left side and the club horizontal to the ground.

 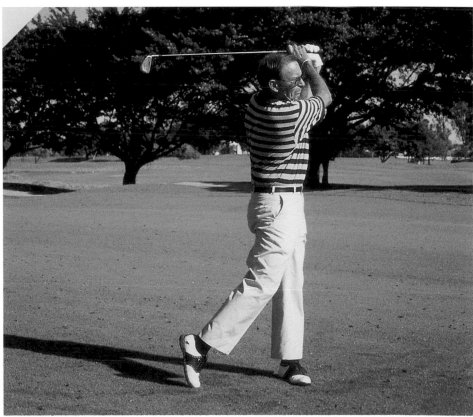

Using a long-shafted driver

If you are like most senior golfers, you've probably lost some yards off the tee and have thought about getting, or already own, a long-shafted driver with a jumbo head. You will learn all about the dynamics of these clubs in the equipment chapter but, all else being equal, a longer club swings the head on a larger arc and this translates into greater swing speed and longer drives. In addition, the larger head gives you an expanded hitting surface and a more forgiving sweet spot that increases the odds of making solid contact, another essential for long drives.

It is an interesting combination that even the young professionals are taking a close look at. Senior Tour player Rocky Thompson, once considered a short hitter, is now one of the longest hitters out there after switching to a 52-inch driver (that's a bit much for most of us). Gary Player, at 60-plus, is hitting his new bomber further than he drove it in his prime.

But while both the physics of the golf swing and actual experiments by expert players tell us this is more than just the latest golf equipment hype, there are some

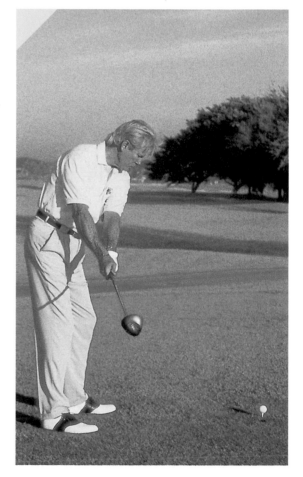

adjustments you need to make to your S swing if you are going to benefit from a long-shafted, big-headed driver.

To accommodate the increased length of the club shaft, you will need to stand taller at address. The senior player needs to bend more from the hips at address, so this can be a problem. Solve it by decreasing your knee flex and making sure you place your left arm on top of your chest, rather than dangling to the side. Because of the added length, you stand farther away from the ball and this means your swing will be more rounded.

You already have a wider-than-normal stance, so you don't have to adjust your foot-width, but you should flare your right foot a bit to allow the club to swing comfortably around you during your back-swing. You should also modify your normal weight distribution at address. Instead of 70 percent on your right foot, pre-set 80 percent there. Take care to keep the weight on the inside rim of your right foot, distributed from the ball of the foot back through your heels. This will give you a stable platform to hit from as you swing the long driver.

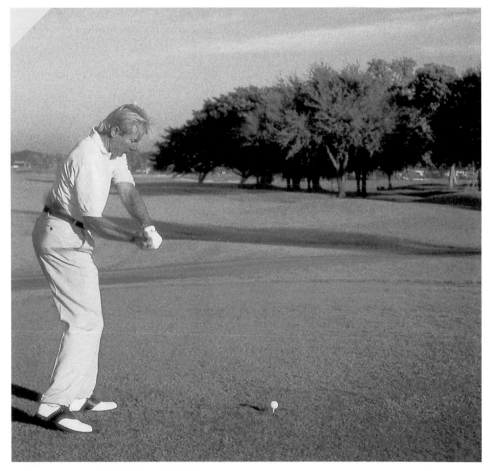

Using a long-shafted driver *continued*

When you are focusing on hitting the ball farther, be careful you don't increase your grip pressure too much in anticipation of the big hit. When you choke the club, it prevents you from cocking your wrists correctly and this defeats the whole purpose of the extra club length by shortening the swing arc. It also fouls up your lever system so you get less power out of your swing instead of more. With the light grip pressure and the longer driver, your wrists may cock a little later in your back-swing than you are used to. Don't fight it, just let your wrists set themselves in response to the momentum of your club-head as it swings back, around and up to the top of your swing.

You will find it useful to relax your neck and shoulders, making sure that your arms hang naturally from your shoulders as you bend from your hips to the ball. Natural arm hang will prevent you from reaching too far for the ball. While it may feel more powerful to reach for the ball by extending your arms away from the body, it is a sure way of losing your balance because your weight pulls you onto your toes as you swing to the top.

It is also a good idea to modify the height that you tee your ball. With the deep-faced driver the tendency is to tee the ball too low, so make sure that there is about a quarter of an inch of space between the top edge of your club and the bottom of the ball, just enough room to slip the thin shaft of a golf tee through. This will help you to catch the ball slightly on the up-swing so you can deliver maximum club-head mass to the ball at the moment of impact, thereby launching the ball at optimum trajectory.

Don't try to swing the club on a long arc because this will only lead to an over-swing. As we have already said, the squareness of contact is important to distance because off-center hits don't go as far, so don't try to hit it longer by swinging longer. Also, to make solid contact, swing within yourself and give your swing motion time to develop, starting back to the ball slowly, with gradually increasing momentum.

Basically, once you are properly fit, if you make the set-up adjustments above, the added length will get the job done. It is another case of "let" rather than "make."

Star swings

Understanding how star swings develop can help you to build your own swing. The golf swing is made up of swing elements, such as grip, posture, ball position, takeaway etc., and the question is how do you put these elements together to play your best golf? Which stars do you pick as your models and what swing elements do you appropriate from them for your own purposes?

It's obvious that the swings of, say, Colin Montgomerie and Steve Elkington do not look the same, yet they are both star players. And while categorization always does a disservice to someone, it is possible to explain how the two swings could look so dissimilar yet get such good results. To do this we can divide the star swings into two categories: the classic and the modern.

As you will gather from the accompanying chart, those golfers with a classic swing take

In an effort to gain consistency, and a lower ball flight with less backspin, Greg Norman has changed from a classic to a more modern swing.

the club away in one piece and swing it on an upright plane high above them with a long flowing arc. They exhibit a lot of lateral hip motion and their follow through is characterized by the bent spine of the Reverse C position, giving the impression that they sling the club head out from under them.

Those with a modern swing start the club away with their left arm and swing the club on a flatter plane more around them in a tight, rounded arc. Their hip turn is predominantly rotational and they enter the follow through section of their swing more erect, having unwound their coil around their spine. They whirl the club head around them.

However, as we are about to see, just when you think these distinctions are hard and fast you find a glaring divergence, such as Montgomerie, a classic swinger, adopting the ball position of the modern swing, or Alice Miller, a modern swinger, using the weak right-hand grip of the classic swinger. The existence of this cross-pollination of swing elements from one swing type to the other prompts two basic observations: the first is that good golf swings, in order to satisfy the laws of physics (which they all must do), evolve based on body type, personality, the demands of the environment, and often, although not always, under the watchful eye of a masterful teacher. Thus swing elements are assembled based on the individual differences of the player.

The second observation is that the definition of error in a golf swing is not always an objective fact carved on a stone tablet that applies to every swing mechanic and every golf swing. We believe you'll agree after analyzing our star swings that before you label a movement or a position as incorrect, and therefore set about to change it, you must show that it does not fit in with the rest of the movements and positions that make up the golf swing. The odds are that if you put a bag over his head so no one would recognize him and had him hit into a net so they couldn't see the ball flight, 95 percent of the teaching professionals would change Lee Trevino's looping, push-fade swing, thereby preserving his early career as a bag room attendant at Horizon Golf Club in El Paso, Texas.

It's fashionable to use the phrase "compensating errors" to describe any deviation from the so-called perfect, and it is usually spoken in the sad tone reserved for someone who has a debilitating disease as in "poor thing, he has compensating errors." But what would we give for the "compensating errors" of a Ben Crenshaw, a Johnny Miller or a Colin Montgomerie? As an example, Montgomerie's back ball position is not an error because it fits his golf game, producing the ball flight he needs: low and left to right. Remember that he plays worldwide in some fierce wind and if he moved his ball forward he'd hit the ball higher, exposing his fade to a wind that would turn it into a slice.

	Classic swing	Modern swing
Ball position	Forward	Back
Grip	Weak to neutral	Strong to neutral
Hips back	Tilted/back leg straight	Level
Hip motion	Lateral then rotational	Purely rotational
Takeaway	One-piece simultaneous: chest, hands and club head	Sequential: arm swing then wrist set, then shoulder turn
Backswing	High arcing/up and over	Flatter/rounded
Right foot position	Perpendicular to the target line	Flared
Hand/forearm action	Integral	Minimal
Legs	Active	Quiet
Release	Slinging action	Rotational body release
Finish	Reverse C	Straight spine

Note:
1 The elements cross pollinate.
2 In categorizing a particular player you'll find they have many features of one swing style but very few have all. The variations occur depending on the conditions of play, body build, temperament, natural tendencies and external influences. Golf swings are built by finding basic elements that fit together.

The Miller *grip*

The Miller grip has always played a big role in his success and he has coined the phrase "impact fix" to describe his wrist position: the back of his left hand and his forearm are fixed in a straight line and stay that way from start to finish. When you lose this straight line relationship, the left wrist collapses, altering the effective loft of the golf club and thereby affecting not only the direction but how far the ball goes.

In his glory years, Miller kept the relationship between the back of his left hand, forearm and the club face constant all the way through his swing, which enabled him to hit accurate irons that were often pin high. Although no statistics were kept, he, along with Byron Nelson, was probably pin high more often than any other player.

Johnny Miller The classic swing

Twenty years after his first victory at Pebble Beach, Johnny Miller stunned the golf world with a victory at the 1994 AT&T National Pro-Am at Pebble Beach. Injury to his knees prematurely ended his full-time playing career but, in his prime, Johnny Miller was unarguably the best player in the world. He won his first major, the 1973 US Open at Oakmont, in a decisive five-stroke victory with a final round 63, still the lowest score in major championship history. In 1974 and 1975, he set a blistering pace, winning 12 tournaments, posting 23 top ten finishes and two international victories. At Royal Birkdale in 1976, Johnny Miller defeated Jack Nicklaus and Seve Ballesteros by six strokes to claim the Open Championship. He was also at home in the desert where he won 13 titles, four at Tucson, and in 1975 when he won at Phoenix by 14 strokes.

1 The first impression is one of a beautifully balanced set up position; nothing is out of place here. The right shoulder is under the left by the same amount that his right hand is below his left on the club handle. In his youth his right foot was perpendicular to the line but now, to accommodate decreased flexibility, it's modestly flared. With the driver, his weight is distributed about 60 percent on the right and 40 percent on the left.

The forward ball position is an important element that controls his hip action once his swing begins. There's a dramatic flare of his left foot to encourage him to turn aggressively through the ball. With this amount of flare he must position the ball well forward in his stance to accommodate the dramatic leg drive that's characteristic of his swing.

2 Known for his early set of the angle, Miller actually sets it quickly but he does not set it early in his takeaway as indicated by the frame where his hands are on his right leg and the club head is still well below his hands. At this point his weight is already well into his right hip.

The biggest difference in Miller's swing today is that his hips and shoulders turn more level and his swing is much shorter than in his heyday. Now he suffers some bouts of wildness and off-center hitting because his level turn hip doesn't quite match the rest of his upright swing. Unless compensations are made, level hips match well with a shallow swing, while tilted hips match up with a steep swing.

3 Miller is an "up and down" swinger rather than a rotational swinger. By the time his left arm is parallel to the ground, the club head has been set well above the hands. There is not much hip turn and, as he coils into his right hip joint, his club head has moved upward rather than behind him, a relatively steep track that's perfect for iron play.

4 5 Starting down, Miller tucks his right elbow in close to his side and has a terrific amount of right knee drive, keeping his right foot planted late into the downswing. Notice the beautiful knee flex that changes just before impact as the left leg straightens. It is this that gives him the characteristic "up and out" look which is so defining of his swing even now. The upward spiral of his body is responding to the posting of his left leg and because he has bad knees he relieves the pressure by spinning his left foot out to the left of the target.

6 The finish is also a trademark: a Reverse C with high hands that end up between his left shoulder and ear, indicating that the club stayed on the target line long after impact.

Miller has always maintained that playing from a Reverse C position allows him to keep the club head going through to the target longer. With the forward ball position, a major swing characteristic is a great deal of lateral movement which also helps keeps the club face on line longer and, if done correctly, leads to the Reverse C or comma position.

John Daly The classic swing

Daly has the longest club head travel time in modern golf. He can swing back as far as he does because:

1 He's very flexible in his shoulder, hip and wrist joints.

2 He's a strong man whose body is used to swinging hard.

3 Each part of his technique (flying right elbow, high left arm, triggered index finger etc.) is perfectly suited to creating a huge arc.

Powerful as it is, his swing takes a great deal of timing to work correctly. He'll play superbly one or two weeks a year when his timing is perfect, overpowering the course and beating the entire field. When his timing is mediocre he'll be competitive and finish in the middle of the pack with the help of his beautiful short game and putting stroke. And when his timing is sub-par, he won't break 80.

John Daly rocketed to stardom after his surprise victory at the 1991 PGA Championship at Crooked Stick and since then has won on Tour every year. His super-long swing, explosive distance and mercurial personality fascinate his huge, rambunctious galleries, the size of which are reminiscent of Arnold Palmer's "Army." Lost in the shadows of Daly's phenomenal distance is his masterful touch around the greens, which he used to win his second major championship, the 1995 British Open at St Andrews. Daly remains a compelling figure wherever he plays, drawing massive galleries, even though he has not added to his two majors. In 1997, with a distance of 302.0, he claimed his sixth long-driving title in seven years.

1 At address he reaches for the ball to accommodate his large chest. He starts the swing with a one-piece move that keeps the club head lower longer than any of the modern tour players. As his left arm swings over his toe line, his hands begin to set the club very aggressively as his turn carries his club head well inside the toe line.

2 Notice that the writing on his glove is now facing the sky, indicating that as his wrists cock he's also rotating his left hand and forearm so that his club face looks upward. If his club face stayed this way, it would be dead shut at the top and he'd be a terrible hooker of the ball. But as he gets to the top of his swing the club face is pushed into a perfect position in relation to his shoulder plane by the elevation of his right elbow.

3 The angle of Daly's left arm at the top of his swing is an amazing feat of flexibility, impossible for the average person. Notice also that the trigger finger he uses helps to elongate his swing, as does his large amount of wrist cock.

4 With the club head traveling such an incredible distance the question is: what does Daly's body do in the meantime? Starting down he must find a way to slow his body to give his club time to get back in front of his body at impact. To give his club head a head start, Daly suspends

himself on his right side like a ballerina, a clever solution to the time problem. The photos show that he begins his club head's return to the ball with his arms and shoulders before he shifts his weight to his left side. In this frame he's arrived at a position that looks like a normal tour player about to begin his downswing—and yet that club head has already traveled more than a foot back toward the ball.

5 The "flying right elbow" not only gives additional arc to his swing but it also serves a very important purpose in squaring the club face to his shoulder plane. During his downswing much of his power is gained by ratcheting up the speed of the club as he slams his right elbow back tight to his body, adding extra whip to the club through the impact zone.

To pull off his big swing he not only needs time: he also needs space. Note at the top of his swing how his head is located over his right foot, but as he starts down he pivots his head back toward the ball clearing space for his right shoulder so he can bring his right arm back to his right side.

6 During his swing he uses his legs as posts to coil around—the right leg on the backswing, the left on the forward swing. Through impact he hits across his left leg as the club swings by him.

Ben Crenshaw The classic swing

Ben Crenshaw captured his second Masters Tournament in 1995 in an emotion-filled week that began after serving as pall bearer at the funeral of his life-long teacher Harvey Pennick. As well as being a player with over 40 titles to his merit, Ben is also a respected golf course architect, noted golf historian and recipient of the distinguished Bob Jones Award in 1991. Despite setbacks from illness during his thirties, Crenshaw has produced a win every year since turning forty, a tribute to the quality of his overall game and, in particular, his ability as one the best putters who ever played the game.

Getting better
with age

As Crenshaw has gotten older and his body less flexible, his accuracy off the tee has actually increased as he can no longer make those extra-long swings. Golf is probably the only game where, in some cases, you can get better as you age because as your body tightens up so does your swing. What Johnny Miller said about John Daly applies to all golfers with long swings: "When Daly is 90 his swing should be about normal."

1 At the start, his feet are wide apart, a position that brings stability to the high, free-flowing swing that is about to occur. Crenshaw has a good deal of upper body movement in his swing, another reason for his wide stance—otherwise he'd lose his balance.

He puts a classic hold on the club with both palms facing one another, ensuring that they work together rather than fighting each other for control. The "Vs" formed by his index fingers and thumbs are parallel to one another, pointing to his right cheek. A fine grip like this one is one of the great gifts an instructor can bestow on a student, the effects of which last long after most in-swing advice has disappeared.

His right foot is perpendicular to the target line to ensure that the club swings up and over him rather than around behind him. The ball position is a bit back for a high ball hitter like Ben, and when his timing gets off, this may lead to the bouts of wildness that occasionally plague him.

He begins with a one-piece takeaway using his chest to move the unit composed of his arms, hands, shoulders and club. His right elbow stays straight for a long time, giving maximum extension of the club head away from his body. He is not a large man but he does hit the ball a good way due to his extension and the high arc of his swing.

2 At the top, he's well coiled with a high left arm whose tilt or angle matches that of his club shaft soled at address. Via tilted hips and a straightened (not stiff) right leg his club head is propelled high above him. You can see that a good deal of his weight is loaded in his right

hip, and that his left foot is slightly off the ground, pulled up and back by the force of his coil.

3 He starts down to the ball with a lateral motion of his hips towards the target. This slots the club shaft behind him so he can come to the ball on an inside path. It's a much larger hip shuttle than in most players and gives the appearance that he is sliding, but this is only because his head and left shoulder have turned so far behind the ball (almost over his right foot) during the backswing. He is not sliding past the ball because his swing center, located just below his neck, stays behind the ball until well into his follow through.

4 Note that even with all the lateral hip motion, his spine stays fixed. If you draw a line from his hat to the tip of the tree in the background you can see that he turns around his neck once the downswing is under way.

5 In the impact frame of our swing sequence you can see Ben's left leg pants cuff flying forward as his lower leg plants in preparation for the release. Once again, he is a classic slinger of the club as he slams on the brakes with his left side to release the club.

6 In his finish position you see no wrinkles in his right shoe, indicating that he has fully released all his weight to the left. He appears to squeeze every ounce of power out of his swing using length of arc, rhythmically timed, as his major power source.

Colin Montgomerie The classic swing

Colin Montgomerie has won the European Order of Merit for six straight years, 1993 to 1998, the first man to do so, and finished 1998 ranked at seventh in the world with earnings of about $2 million for the year. His impressive playing ability brought him second place at the 1995 PGA Championship and a tie for second place after a grueling 18-hole playoff in the intense heat of the 1994 US Open at Oakmont. During his college years at Houston Baptist, Montgomerie was a three-time All-American. Winner of the 1985 Scottish Stroke Play and 1987 Scottish Amateur, he went on to be the European Tour's Rookie of the Year in 1988.

Hip motion

In Montgomerie's formative years, the major shaper of his swing action was his hip motion. Sliders are usually faders of the ball, while rotators are usually drawers of the ball and, as a rule, it's very hard to change your hip action. So in most cases a golf swing evolves around the natural movement of the hips. It's likely that to keep the fade out of the wind, he moved the ball back in his stance and, with the ball back, he had to be careful not to hook it, so he cupped his wrist at the top of his swing to open the face.

1 A most noticeable variance from standard is that Montgomerie plays the ball back in his stance (much like Azinger), but in this case it's linked to a vertical, up and down swing rather than a rounded one and he works the ball from left to right. His right foot is perpendicular to the line which encourages his steep swing plane.

2 At pocket high there's a straight line between his left shoulder and club head, showing the one-piece backswing that generates power through the length and height of the club head's arc. The club head lags behind his hands for the first six inches or so, a sign that he has begun his swing by turning his chest to initiate a takeaway where the chest, shoulders, arms and hands start as a unit. The danger here is that he will turn the club head too much inside as it follows the rotation of his chest. To prevent this, Montgomerie uses a rather weak right-hand grip that allows him to keep the back of his right hand to the sky for a long time during the takeaway. This, along with a straight right arm, ensures that his club is headed up and over him and not back behind him.

3 Montgomerie's right leg straightens to produce the upright swing arc and at the top of his swing his hands are fully cocked with the left wrist cupped, a key move that opens the club face and accounts for his fade. As long as his club face is open he can clear his hips as fast as he wants and he won't hook the ball. Nevertheless, for insurance, he slides his hips just a tad before they clear to prevent closing the club face.

One thing that is very apparent is the length of Montgomerie's backswing. It's longer than most but since it's the result of a large shoulder turn and very supple wrists, it's under control and therefore an asset. Note how straight (not stiff) his left arm is. The club is out of control when backswing length is attained by allowing the left arm to break down. The transition from backswing to downswing is a key part of any swing and it is a characteristic of any star player that they "own" the club at this point in the golf swing.

4 Starting back to the ball his arms drop straight down, a move that's necessary if the club head is to win the race with the body to impact. He is faced with the same problem that all the "up and downers" such as John Daly and Ben Crenshaw have. Since Montgomerie's hands swung so high above him, they have a long way to travel. He gives them the time they need with his lateral hip slide and he doesn't begin to clear his hips until his arms have dropped considerably. This is a different sequence to that of the modern swing in which the hips clear at the same time as the arms drop.

5 6 Through impact and well into the follow through, Montgomerie's in the Reverse C. This is a result of the fixed axis at the top of his spine that makes his arms sling by him as his upper spine and head rebound away from the target in response to the forces that are acting on his body through impact. Montgomerie is a big man with high hands, a high finish and a lot of talent—he's going to be a star for a long time.

Ernie Els The modern swing

Ernie Els has conquered the golf world like nobody since Greg Norman. In South Africa in 1992, he became the first player since Gary Player to win the South African Open, South African PGA Championship and the South African Masters in the same year; in 1994 and 1997 he won the U.S. Open championship; and in Europe from 1994 to 1996, he won three straight World Matchplay titles.

1 Ernie Els stands very tall over the ball with the bones in the lower leg straight up and down so that the crease of his pants is perpendicular to the ground. This shows that he's bent his upper body forward toward the ball using his hip joints. Straight lower legs also show that he's used his knees, as he should, to incline his lower body backward away from the ball, setting him perfectly in the ready-set-go athletic position which is common to many sports.

Both feet are slightly flared, the right one to allow his sizable body to make a full turn during the backswing, while the left flare grants him the flexibility to turn back through the ball.

2 With long arms and a supple back, his extension away from the ball is enormous and, just as it reaches its fullness, his right wrist begins to fold backward beginning the elevation of the club head. You can see the amount of stretch he produces by the folds in his shirt. Here he is plugging into the power of coil, setting the top of his body against his lower body.

3 Now all he has to do is fold the right forearm backward as if he were about to throw a ball. His right palm faces the sky anchoring the club in the so-called "tray" position. This is a very solid, no-nonsense position to begin his return swing to the ball. As with many of the modern stars, notice how little his hips have turned at the top of his swing for the length his club head has traveled.

4 To start the downswing, his left shoulder moves away from the chin, dropping his left arm into position. With his left arm parallel to the ground, Els' right foot is still planted but tilting in on the inner rim of his foot preventing any premature spinning of the chest and allowing him to hold his wrist cock until the last second.

5 Just before impact his shoulders are level, and just after impact his right shoulder has risen upward. If his left shoulder were to keep going toward the target his swing center would be pulled forward causing a mis-hit to the right. Note that his hands have returned to their address position and still the club head has not been released. This incredible retention of the angle between his left arm and club shaft is what is termed the "late hit," a poor use of words since there is nothing late about it. This power position is possible because Els (when he is swinging well) never tries to make anything happen—he lets it. His swing unfolds with no untidy edges and the ball just seems to get in the way.

6 His follow through position is, as you would expect, full and fluid, with both arms straight in front of him. This is a position that will bring him to a well-balanced finish.

The modern swing

The modern rotational swing favors a ball position farther back than the classic swing, and the elegant Elkington is the personification of the modern swing. With his driver the ball is played about even with his armpit. His arms hang comfortably down so if he dropped the club from this position and then relaxed his arms they wouldn't change position. His lower leg is straight up and down with just enough knee flex to give him the most solid balance position from which to make his golf swing. The common mistake—too much knee flex—pitches the body forward during the downswing, an error that causes you to straighten up just before impact to regain your balance.

Steve Elkington The modern swing

Native Australian Steve Elkington spent his college years halfway round the world at the University of Houston where he was a two-time All-American and member of the 1984-85 NCAA Championship Team. Since joining the Tour in 1987, his rock solid golf swing has produced six wins and over four million dollars in earnings. In a dramatic battle for the 1991 Players Championship, Steve bested Fuzzy Zoeller to claim the second most prestigious title of his career. The year 1995 brought a major championship victory when he won the PGA Championship at Riviera Country Club. A spectacular final round 64 forced a playoff in which he defeated Colin Montgomerie. This was Elkington's finest season: a repeated victory at the Mercedes Championship, top-10 finishes in the British Open and The Masters, the PGA Championship and the Vardon Trophy for low scoring average (69.62). Elkington must like the PGA Championship; he has finished third in 1996 and 1998, too.

1 At address, Elkington's club shaft, left arm and shoulder form an uninterrupted straight line. He flares both feet about a quarter of a turn to promote the rotational aspect of his swing, making it easier to turn his right hip over his heel on the backswing and to clear his left hip over his heel through impact.

2 His left arm movement starts his swing, setting up a chain of motion that results in a swing where the club shaft is always on the plane angle. There is some left forearm rotation during the backswing, just enough to keep the club shaft on the correct plane angle as his right wrist bends backward to create the 90-degree angle of leverage.

3 The defining element of his swing is the opposition he sets up between his upper and lower body as he moves to the top of his swing. Here he's fully coiled, having set the top of his body against the bottom by using his knees perfectly. His back knee is comfortably flexed and his hips are level. Even at maximum coil his left heel is on the ground and his knee is pointing ever so slightly behind the ball, creating the stretch that pays its dividends in club head speed.

4 Starting down, his left arm slides towards his right foot as his weight shifts to his left hip joint. There's so much down and so much around in every swing and Elkington does the down portion first, slotting the club so that his turn to the ball works for him. Too many golfers in their anxiety to hit, turn their chest (the around) before they do their down. It's an error called over-the-top and, with it, your turn works against you.

About halfway down when his left arm is parallel to the ground, his right knee begins its kick toward the target. Once again you see the simultaneous move of the modern swing where the right elbow gets closer to his body without the right foot unplugging from the ground, while at the same time the left hip turns to the left. Thus the right side resists while the left side pulls, maintaining the opposition and even increasing it just before impact. This is evidenced by the separation of the knees, creating the "straddle" or bandy leg position of the modern rotational player.

5 At impact he's nicely behind the ball. His right heel hasn't flipped up, showing that he has allowed the right side to release but hasn't twisted the right shoulder up and over the ball. He's on his left heel and the outer rim of his foot, indicating a correct weight transfer.

6 As with the rest of his swing, his follow through is perfect. You can see the spikes on his left shoe. His belt buckle faces the target as does his right knee.

Paul Azinger The modern swing

In his best year ever on the PGA Tour, 1993, Paul Azinger captured the Memorial Tournament by holing a shot from a bunker on the 18th to defeat his close friend Payne Stewart. He went on to win two more tournaments that year, including the PGA Championship, his first major. The thrill of this spectacular season ended abruptly with a diagnosis of cancer in his right shoulder blade. Azinger dealt with cancer like a true champion, using his illness as a forum to inspire others in their fight against the disease. He returned to the Tour in 1994 and while he has not been a prolific winner since then, he has earned in excess of $8 million.

The right grip

There is a tendency in some of the better players, such as Fred Couples, Bernhard Langer and John Daly, to use a strong grip, and it works out quite nicely as long as you resist the temptation to throw your hands at the ball. As a general rule, if you're a handsy player use a neutral to weak grip; and if you're a "body" player with passive hands, use a strong grip.

1 The most notable feature of Azinger's swing is the ultra-strong grip where both the right and left "Vs" point to the right of his back shoulder and the back of the left hand points at the sky. Azinger is fortunate that he has a teacher (the noted John Redman) who recognizes that his grip is not incorrect but in fact is the centerpiece of his success in that it fits perfectly with the rest of his swing parts.

He plays from a narrow stance with well flexed knees and a slightly open body line. As a low-ball hitter he positions the ball well back in his stance, a position that sets his hands ahead of the ball at address, an anti-hook defense.

2 Much of the takeaway is concerned with his left arm as the initiator, synchronizing his upper body turn with very little lower body movement well into the backswing. Note that at waist high the left knee still has not moved behind the ball, a prime characteristic of the modern swing, i.e. a weight transfer but very little lower body motion during the backswing.

3 As he reaches the end of his backswing his back leg straightens somewhat to prevent the club from getting lost behind him (a sure way to hook it), but on the forward swing he reflexes it until both knees are level as his

left arm comes parallel to the ground, a position necessary for solid contact with the ball back in his stance.

4 The key to his downswing is his lateral hip movement. Azinger slides his hips forward during the downswing, a move he must make because of his shut club face at the top of his swing. If he simply rotated his hips as he started down, he'd hook the ball off the planet. With his passive hands he keeps the leverage (the angle between his left am and club shaft) intact for a very long time, one of the prime advantages of the modern swing.

5 But his slide stops when it should and just before impact his left hip turns behind him, squaring the club face to the target. This body release gives his swing a quiet look as his arms and chest whirl together to get the job done. As an anti-hook defense, Azinger has very passive hands with hardly any forearm rotation through the ball.

6 Both his arms are very straight long into the follow through maintaining their position in front of his chest. This occurs when you rotate your body correctly through the hitting zone, allowing your right side to keep moving all the way to your finish.

Corey Pavin The modern swing

Pavin taught himself many years ago to treat his golf swing as a vehicle for getting the ball from one place to another. What does it matter if you arrive in a limousine or a Volkswagen? They're both just vehicles for getting you where you want to go. For Pavin, the golf swing, its technique and its form, is not the centerpiece of the game. Ask anyone who has been taken down by this pit bull of a competitor—Pavin is living proof of the old saying: "It's not how but how many."

Corey Pavin's 1995 U.S. Open victory at Shinnecock Hills was surely his finest moment in competitive golf. He had been a heavy winner ever since starting on the PGA Tour in 1984, but his 13th Tour win was his first major. Number 14 arrived at Colonial in 1996, but that was his last victory. Known as a shot maker and superb putter, his competitiveness was evident when at 17 he won the World Junior title. Never the longest driver, his game goes up a level in match play as can be seen by his 8–5 record in the Ryder Cup.

Pavin is a feel player. He shapes his shots kinesthetically by sensing how the club should be swung rather than thinking about the technical aspects of getting it done. By doing this he puts his body in some unusual positions and therefore, when he's working the ball, his swing sometimes looks a little odd, but don't be fooled—it's a better golf swing than it looks, as the results show.

1 Pavin sets up wide with heels spread outside his shoulders, giving a stable platform on which to turn. His shoulders are almost level at address, more so than normal. His posture is relaxed with not much spine tilt, preparing him for the flat shoulder turn that characterizes his swing. There is nice spacing between his body and the butt of the club, about a fist-with-the-thumb-extended distance away. His chin is up in the "proud" position, anticipating the arrival of the left shoulder.

Note the perfect 90-degree angle between his lower spine and club shaft as it points to his belt buckle. This maximizes his consistency because a swinging object moves most uniformly when it spins at 90 degrees to its axis.

For the driver, his right foot is drawn back to encourage the draw that gives the length he needs to be competitive. But he can curve the ball both ways depending on the demands of the course, so when he needs to fade the ball he plays from a slightly open stance.

2 During his takeaway Pavin keeps his hands inside the club head until it begins to elevate and open; then he sets the angle about waist high.

3 When his wrists cock, the club head goes higher than the hands for the first time. The left arm is on the toe line and the club head is high and behind him with the shaft through the biceps. Most importantly, with his hands on the toe line, his club head is behind the line giving him the club

head depth he needs to match his flat shoulder turn. If he allowed his hands to cross the toe line he'd be so inside that his club head would be trapped behind him. Note his eyes are tracking the ball causing even more tilting of the head as he turns away from the target.

4 At the top, the club face and the shoulder tilt match and if everything uncoils correctly, he'll arrive at impact in good shape. Also, he's maintained the flex in his knees to keep his hips level and, with his right elbow pointing down to the ground, his left arm is on the same plane as his club shaft was at address. This sets the stage for his swing back to the ball.

5 Starting down, the triangle formed by a line connecting his elbows tilts so that the club shaft moves more to the left of the target before it drops downward. This moves the shaft across his right bicep, a perfect on-plane position. Pavin's right heel remains grounded until his hands pass in front of his pants pocket, giving him a stable position to swing through to impact. His hands have returned to the toe line as has the shaft. From here all he needs to do is let the triangle swing his club head to the ball.

6 Note the results of a well-timed release where the club shaft is in a mirror position of frame 2. His head is back with the shaft coming out of his left bicep, showing that he has stayed on the plane angle.

Brandie Burton

Brandie Burton began playing golf at the age of nine and throughout her amateur career she collected numerous victories. In addition, she was runner-up at the 1989 US Women's Amateur Championship and qualified for the US Women's Open Championship three times before turning professional. In her year at Arizona State University she was ranked the number one woman collegiate golfer and won six of the seven tournaments on her schedule. Burton turned professional after that year and won Rookie of the Year honors for her eight top ten finishes in 1991. In her third year on Tour, 1993, Burton reached $1 million in earnings in record time and was the LPGA Tour's youngest millionaire ever. That year she won her first major, the du Maurier Classic, and she won this event again in 1998.

1 Brandie starts her swing from a solid, balanced position. Since she is broadly built and muscular, she flares both feet out at address to facilitate the turn of her body. Both her left and right hand are in a strong grip position and the ball is farther back in her stance than the standard driver position off the left heel.

2 She starts her motion with a gentle cocking of her wrists followed almost immediately by her left arm and chest turning away from the ball as evidenced by the movement of her shirt logo. Notice her lower body is in an identical position to frame one with her hips still square to the target line. This is the beginning of coil, i.e. turning the top of her body more than the bottom. Though a powerful woman, Brandie is already starting to set the club head up with her wrists to make use of the power of leverage.

3 Her lower body shows marked signs of responding to the motion in her upper body. Her right hip has turned back over her right heel, and her left shoulder has begun to move behind the ball. At this point, she's set the club into a fully leveraged position. Although she's turned her back to the target, her hands are still in front of her chest, pushing the club away, adding width to her swing arc. A common error among amateurs is to get their hands well behind them at this point, a difficult position from which to return the club to the ball.

4 Her lower body has completed its turn back as her shoulders deliver the club to the top of her swing. At the completion of Brandie's backswing her lower body has stabilized and her left shoulder has turned against it and behind the ball. Her powerfully coiled position is evident from the creases in the back of her shirt and the tautness of her left sleeve. Brandie gets the club to the standard parallel to the ground position at the top but, because of her body type and flexibility, she can do so only by bending her left elbow at the top of her swing. Some might call this an error but in a swing this powerful, with the club completely in her control, it's more appropriately named an "individual characteristic." The

question is, should you copy it? If you're an elite athlete who practices and plays for a living, and it works for you, then the answer is yes. Otherwise, you'd be wise to concentrate on the more fundamental aspects Brandie beautifully demonstrates.

5 To start her downswing, her right elbow tucks back to her side putting her arms back in front of her body. From the top of her swing she shifted her weight into her left hip and she now begins to turn it powerfully behind her, a move that delivers the club directly to the ball. Though her left hip is turning away from the ball, her head and neck have stayed in their position behind it, creating a reversal of the coil she built in her backswing.

6 At impact she continues the rotation of her body to bring the club to the ball. Though her arms are following the rotation, her head and neck are still firmly planted behind the ball. Here she demonstrates a position common to a good player, but uncommon to a poor player: her left arm, hand, and club shaft are in line with the lower right leg, which shows she's allowed her right side to release. Also, notice her right heel is working to the inside rather than up. When amateurs let their right heel "flip out" toward the target line before impact, it causes their club to cut across the ball. The right foot working in allows the club to be delivered more from the inside so it comes to the ball along the target line rather than across it.

7 Brandie's arms swing past her, literally dragging her up toward her finish position. She's fully released the leverage she built in her backswing as is evident from the recocking of her wrists on her throughswing.

8 Brandie's finish is a result of her right knee "getting friendly" with her left. From the top of her swing to her finish, her left knee was moving away from the right which was chasing it. At the completion of her swing, her ankle, knee, hip, and shoulder joint are stacked one on top of the other, indicating that she has rotated her powerful body fully through the ball.

Jane Geddes

Jane Geddes was a member of Florida State University's 1981 AIAW National Championship Team and she joined the LPGA Tour in 1983. In her third year on Tour she posted her career low round of 64 to finish second in a major championship, runner-up to Hall of Fame member Pat Bradley. Her first victory came at the 1985 US Women's Open, one of only 13 women to claim the Open as her first victory. Just one week later she recorded her second victory, joining Hall of Fame member Betsy Rawls as the only player to have won a tournament immediately after an Open victory. In 1987 she won five times, and by 1989 she'd won over a million dollars. Through 1998 Jane had an impressive 11 victories, including two majors and around $3.5 million in earnings.

1 Jane is similar in body type to Brandie Burton so their swings have many similarities. At address, her arms hang comfortably from her shoulders with her left arm and the club shaft forming a straight line down to the ball. Her hands are in a strong position, rotated to the right of the center of the shaft, with the ball positioned slightly back. She's bent to the ball from her hips, shown by the fact that her knees are relaxed but not excessively flexed. Her feet are slightly flared.

2 As Jane starts back, her shoulders turn and her hands push the club away from her chest, an action that begins to pull her behind the golf ball. With her left foot and lower leg serving as resistance, she's already begun to build coil, evident by the creases in her shirt. Though the motion is minimal, she's in the process of loading her weight into her right side but only in response to the motion of her upper body.

3 Before reaching the top of her swing, Jane has set the club into a full leverage position. Her hands are relatively low and the club head is high. Good players elevate the club by setting the wrists and turning the shoulders rather than just lifting their arms. Over-lifting your arms curtails your ability to rotate your body correctly. The correct rotation is evident here as Jane's right hip has turned over her right heel and her left shoulder has rotated behind the ball.

4 At the top of her swing, Jane's left foot has rolled onto its inner rim in response to the pull of her upper body turn, but it hasn't lifted. A common mistake is to let your left knee get too close to your right at the top of your swing, but Jane keeps the distance between her knees the same as it was at address to preserve her excellent coil. Her shoulders have turned well past her hips and the club is completely under control at the top of her swing, two of the main reasons why she is one of the longest hitters on Tour.

5 On the downswing, the pressure of her weight moves over her left heel, and her right arm tucks into her right side, the combination of which puts her arms back in front of her body. Every good player gets their arms back in front of their body at impact so they can deliver the club to the ball with the full force of their body.

6 At the top of her swing (frame 4), Jane's left shoulder was directly under her chin, but as she starts her drive back to the ball, that shoulder moves forward and upward, a key move that drops her right arm back to her side. At this point many amateurs let their right shoulder move out toward the target line from the top of their swing, an error known as "over the top," causing weak shots that slice to the right. In order to approach the ball on the correct path, it is of critical importance to start the upper body portion of your downswing by lowering the right shoulder and raising the left.

7 Jane has beautiful extension after impact, the only time in the golf swing both arms are straight. The club has fully released and still her head is well back and just starting to be pulled up. Good players look under the ball as it leaves and they do so because their head is behind the ball through impact. Then, as the momentum of their arm swing begins to pull them up, their head swivels with their eyes looking under the ball.

8 Jane's follow through is classic. Her head, chest, and hips face her target, and her back foot serves as a rudder. Notice there are no wrinkles in her right shoe, indicating all of her weight has completely transferred to her left side.

Jane Geddes continued

Star *profile*

In her 13 years as a professional, Jane Geddes has consistently ranked as one of the longest drivers of the ball on Tour. In 1995, she averaged 252.4 yards, which is farther than some men on the PGA Tour. Standing only five feet five inches, she produces her distance with an incredibly efficient swing. We have included a down-the-target line sequence of her swing because it is a perfect model for maximum use of leverage and coil.

1 Jane hovers her driver above the ground at address, as did the legendary Jack Nicklaus who, in his day, was also a power hitter. For some players, hovering the club in this manner allows them a greater awareness of the weight of the club head and induces relaxation in their arms and shoulders at address. If you find you're very tense over the ball, you might give this method a try.

2 As Jane takes the club away, notice how the big muscles of her body have caused the club to move. Though her hands have moved back they are still very low, down by her thighs where they started, indicating that she has not lifted the club in any way. Unlike her hands, the club head has traveled a good distance from its position at address, but it has been swung to this position, gaining additional ground through her wrists which are beginning to cock the club head up. Her lower body is showing subtle signs of responding but there is no overt action. By minimizing early lower body movement, she prevents the club from getting too far behind her body and starts to create coil early in her swing.

3 From here she'll continue the combined motion of arm swing, shoulder turn, and wrist cock to elevate the club to the top. Her lower body has moved in sympathy with her big shoulder turn behind the ball. Her weight is fully loaded onto her right leg, solidly contained on the inner rim of her right foot which is a key to her power. Jane has established her right leg as a post around which she's turning. Her elbows and hands form a triangle at the top, the base of which is level to the ground. Had she exaggerated her hip turn or whipped the club in behind her with her hands, you'd see the right elbow much lower than the left, a difficult error that causes the body to race out in front of the arms through impact.

4 The most important element to observe in Jane's downswing is that the club, specifically the grip end, is traveling down, not around. The club has moved a much greater distance relative to the movement of her body and that's appropriate since it has a much greater distance to travel to impact. You can see that Jane has transferred the pressure of her weight to her left side, which helps drop the club downward; from here she can begin her powerful hip rotation to deliver the club around to the ball.

5 Just a fraction of a second before impact, her left hip has turned well behind her and is pulling her right side into the ball. Most importantly, the club is back to the ball with the shaft on the same angle it established at address.

6 Since the club head is moving at such a high rate of speed it appears as a blur in the frame. Note though how the blur of the club head is directly in front of her chest, indicating that she's used the full force of her powerful body to deliver the club to the ball. Her shoulders are rotating beautifully around the inclined axis of her spine, a reversal of the path they transcribed in the backswing. Often amateurs have difficulty with their swings because they straighten their spine and cause their shoulders to turn too level to the ground. Make a slow-motion swing in a mirror and check that your shoulders turn as Jane's do, but any change in your posture during the critical parts of your swing will disrupt your shoulder plane.

7 Jane is gracefully drawn up and out of her impact position as a natural result of the club swinging past her. Her wrists are recocking on the throughswing in response to the unleashing of leverage through the ball.

8 Jane's finish is full and excellent, a complete representation and response to all that came before—a swing that is fundamentally a power house of efficiency.

Emilee Klein

In her first year on Tour, Emilee Klein won more money than any other rookie in 1995 and posted two second-place finishes, an appropriate transition from her sensational amateur career. She was the 1988 California Amateur Champion, the 1991 American Junior Golf Association Player of the Year, and was an AJGA First Team All American for four consecutive years. Her other victories included the 1991 US Junior Girls Championship, the 1993 Broadmoor, the 1993 North/South Amateur, and 1993 Amateur of the Year award. During her two-year tenure at Arizona State University she earned All-American status both years, was the 1994 NCAA Champion, and the 1994 Collegiate Player of the Year. In 1996, Emilee got her first two professional victories, including a British Open title, and she finished the year among the top 10 money winners.

Emilee has a unique swing due to her unusual set up position which features a very erect posture. But while it looks unusual, the analysis will show her swing adheres to the basic principles of coil and leverage.

1 Emilee is a very accurate player because, due to her set up, she doesn't have a lot of wasted body motion. Neither foot is flared and her knees are pinched in, both of which minimize lower body movement. The back of her left hand faces the target as does the palm of her right hand, a configuration known as a relatively weak grip. Her hands are set in the mid-line of her body, encouraging the more rounded swing arc that is her trademark.

2 Emilee's erect posture causes her to swing the club well away from her and then around her in her backswing with minimal hip turn. In fact, her lower body is so quiet that she appears to have a reverse weight shift, but, by frame 4, you'll see she's well coiled into her right side. She is young and very flexible in her shoulder joints, a condition allowing her maximum arm swing and minimal leg action. This flexibility is only an asset if you can find a way not to over-turn your hips and legs, a problem Emilee has solved nicely with her set up.

3 Emilee has set the leverage for her golf swing, though she does so somewhat later than most players. Her right knee has straightened (though it hasn't locked) and serves as a buttress to receive the transfer of weight so important to her coil. Her left heel has begun to pull off the ground but only in response to her upper body turning behind the ball. In a swing that is known more for its accuracy than its power, perhaps Emilee could benefit by keeping her left heel down to add a bit more coil.

4 Emilee's weight is fully loaded on her right side. Though her left heel has come off the ground, the position of her left knee shows the heel has moved more in than up, a further indication her weight has transferred fully to her right side. True error occurs when amateurs lift their heel up and the left knee juts out toward the target line, indicating their weight has remained on their left side.

5 Coming down, Emilee's hips turn marginally as her right shoulder drops and her left shoulder raises, a move that allows her to swing the club directly to the ball without cutting across it. Through impact her legs act as stabilizers and she gains power by hitting across a braced left leg. Since her left leg is already straight and her right leg is almost straight, she's generating a lot of her force through arm swing and the release of the leverage in her wrists.

6 A further indication of her dominating arm swing is that her shoulders are in virtually the same position in frames 5 and 6, showing a strong hand and arm release. With a weak grip she must have a hand and arm release in order to square the club face. Like all good players, her head is behind the ball through impact and her left hip is moving behind her rather than toward the target.

7 As Emilee swings through, her arms reach maximum extension and then begin to pull her body up into her follow through. Her right forearm has rotated well over her left, further evidence that her swing is geared toward a hand and arm release rather than a body release.

8 The creases in her right shoe indicate that Emilee's follow through is less than full because she doesn't use all of the weight of her body to hit the ball. She is primarily an arms and hands player, which is fine as long as the basics of leverage and coil are satisfied. Emilee has built her golf swing and game around pinpoint accuracy and incredible touch.

Juli Inkster

Though Juli Inkster is hardly as well known as Tiger Woods, her career began in a similar fashion after she won three consecutive US Amateur Titles. A four-time All-American during her years at San Jose State University, she joined the LPGA Tour in 1983 and captured her first victory in just her fifth event. Julie received Rookie of the Year honors, winning two major championships, the first rookie to accomplish such a feat. Her best year was 1986 when she won four times and posted her career low round of 64 on two occasions. In 1990, she gave birth to her first child and played a limited schedule, but in her next two years on Tour she won twice and earned over half a million dollars. In 1994, her second daughter was born, but she still managed eight top 20 finishes in a limited schedule. Her phenomenal career is highlighted by three major pro and three major amateur championships and 16 victories in 16 years on the LPGA Tour.

1 Juli addresses the ball with a neutral grip and excellent posture. She plays the ball a little further back in her stance than most players. Unlike Emilee Klein, her feet are flared out with her knees pointing in the same direction as her toes, giving her a solid foundation for her upright swing arc.

2 Like many long-limbed golfers, Juli's takeaway is a one-piece action, with her shoulders, arms, hands, and club all working back and away from her body as a unit rather then around and behind her. In contrast to Brandie Burton and Patty Sheehan, she doesn't fully set the club until she's near the top of her backswing. While there is a lot of arm swing it all occurs as part of coil. Julie does not "pick the club up." She "coils it up" and this is an important distinction.

3 Her lower body has turned away from the target in response to the movement of her long, one-piece takeaway but she hasn't allowed this action to cause her hips to sway, a problem for some amateurs who employ this style (right hip slides laterally outside the right leg instead of turning over the right heel). Julie's lower body has finished its backswing motion and will remain in this position while her upper body continues to turn against it, cranking up her coil. Like many players of this body type, she sets the club very late in her swing, between frames 3 and 4. The danger for golfers who don't have strong arms and hands is that a late set leaves the club in a heavy position because the club head is not underneath the supporting pedestal of the hands. But Juli is strong so she manages her late set beautifully and she keeps the club head in complete control.

4 Though her turn is full, her left foot is firmly planted. Her downswing is initiated by a shifting of her weight from the heel of her right foot to the ball of her left foot, a move that is assisted by the late set of the club. This motion drops her hands and arms down before they come around to the ball.

5 Once the left leg has accepted her weight and her arms have dropped into position, she begins a powerful hip rotation through the ball. Her left hip is turning behind her even though her right knee is driving toward the ball. Also, her right foot is off the ground very early, which is characteristic of players who swing the club in a high arc and approach the ball from a steep angle. She lets her right heel be pulled off the ground in response to the momentum of her swing. Some amateurs push off their right foot which causes a lot of thin shots.

6 Juli fully releases the leverage in her wrists and slings the club past her neck, which is in a rock solid position behind the ball. Throughout her swing, she turns her shoulders perfectly around the axis of her inclined spine. They come level to the ground only after her spine straightens at the finish of her swing.

7 Juli has marvelous extension here with her arms still straight, a result of the velocity of the club moving down the target line. And it is this velocity that pulls her up into her follow through position.

8 Her arms swing through and she finishes in a very upright position with her hands and arms over her shoulders. A beautiful golf swing.

Patty Sheehan

The LPGA Hall of Fame is commonly considered the most difficult achievement in all of sports and only 14 professionals have been able to fulfill its elite entry requirements. Early in 1993, Patty Sheehan reached this lofty goal by winning her thirtieth tournament, and added a fourth major championship to her credit later that year. After an impressive amateur career highlighted by her victory at the 1980 AIAW National Championship, she joined the Tour that same year. She claimed her first victory in 1981 and has won at least once every year since, the only exception being 1987 when she lost a major championship playoff to Betsy King. In 1983 and 1984 she won four tournaments, bettering that achievement in 1990 with five victories and over $700,000 in earnings. Through 1998 Patty won 35 tournaments, including six major championships, the last of which was the 1996 Nabisco Dinah Shore, plus the British Open title. Her earnings are in excess of $5.4 million.

1 Patty's set up features a strong left hand grip, both her feet are flared, and her knees point in the direction of her toes. Her spine is tilted a tad to the right which sets her behind the ball before she even starts her swing. Her arms hang directly downward from her shoulders, indicating that she's bent to the ball from her hips with no hunching of her back. Her left arm is on top of her chest, facilitating an unobstructed arm swing across her chest.

2 In a style typical of the "modern swing," one well suited to Patty's balanced body type, she starts the club back by swinging her left arm across her chest with an early fold of her right elbow and an early set of her wrists. At this point her weight hasn't completely moved to her right heel but it is in the process of doing so.

3 Here her right hip begins to turn over her right heel, and her left knee begins to be pulled behind the ball. She's already created a tremendous amount of coil and she'll increase it as her lower body begins to stabilize and her shoulders and arms continue to turn with her swing.

4 At the top of her backswing, Patty's left arm is swung fully across her chest and has coiled her shoulders behind the ball. Her left foot has been dragged off the ground late in her backswing.

5 Here you can see why Patty has achieved such greatness in her career. She holds her leveraged position, the angle of power, longer than almost anyone who has played the game. The club head is still behind and above her right shoulder but her arms are back in front of her chest and her hands are almost at impact, a fully leveraged position which is reminiscent of Mickey Wright and Ben Hogan. She accomplishes this because her right side holds its position as her left side turns behind her and pulls her arms down. To further assist her in this much sought after position, her left shoulder has moved out from under, and, most importantly, up from under her chin.

6 Notice the triangle formed by her chest and forearms with the shaft of the club bisecting it, an indication of a full and perfectly timed release of her arms, wrists and right side. The beauty of it is that her swing center, located just below her throat, is behind the ball as she delivers her club head, a prerequisite for solid, powerful contact. You can see the force of this momentum continue well into her follow through as the club wraps around her body in frame 8.

7 Patty continues to rotate through the ball with her lower body. She maintains her spine angle for a long time and hangs back just a little bit as both arms extend through the shot. Her left leg is still slightly flexed because she still hasn't fully rotated her hips.

8 She finishes in a perfect follow through position. You'll notice a slight wrinkling in her right shoe, indicating it's holding some weight, but since her follow through is so long and full, this is a recoil from what was a complete release to her left side. Patty's swing would easily qualify for the Golf Swing Hall of Fame, if there was such a thing.

Caroline Pierce

Star *profile*

Caroline Pierce's competitive skill began to show when she reached the semi-final round of the 1979 English Girls Championship and flourished in 1980 and 1981 when she was an English Girls International Champion. At Houston Baptist University, she continued her winning ways, earning All-American honors in 1983 and 1984. After a slow start on the LPGA Tour, she began to build momentum in 1994 with some top ten finishes and almost $85,000 in earnings. She more than doubled her earnings in 1995 with several more top ten finishes and a second place finish at the JAL Big Apple Classic. Caroline earned her first Tour victory here the following year and did so in style. She was the only player in the field to finish under par, winning with a five stroke advantage over a field of top players. The $108,750 prize money helped her finish 1996 ranked 22nd in earnings. Both Emilee Klein and Caroline Pierce stand about five feet five inches tall, with long limbs and slim bodies, so it is no surprise that their swings look similar.

1 Caroline addresses the ball with rather erect posture, which causes her shoulders to turn more level to the ground. The ball is off her left heel, perfectly positioned for a driver. This excellent ball position encourages her square address position, i.e. shoulders, hips, and feet all parallel to her target line, a strong element in her accuracy. Her arms hang comfortably with no hint of tension. Her left foot is flared out at address which helps her build coil as she turns away from the ball, a good idea since her body is the type that turns easily but has difficulty creating coil.

2 If you have a thin frame like Caroline's, you'll need to guard against taking the club too far inside on your takeaway. Her erect posture serves to keeps, her hands moving as they should, back down the line of her toes rather than in behind her as is evident from the fact that her hands and the shaft of the club are still in front of her chest. Her takeaway is a one-piece motion with a very late set of her wrists, the weight of which she controls perfectly in frame 3.

3 The function of Caroline's backswing is to get the mass of her body behind the ball. It is not very long nor does she create maximum coil since her hips have turned almost as much as her shoulders. Though her backswing is short, her hands are in an upright position as a result of her one-piece takeaway.

4 To start her downswing, her hips make a subtle move laterally toward the target while her shoulders remain in a very closed position pointing to the right of target. At this late point in her swing you now see an increase in the tension between upper and lower body, satisfying her need for coil. It's most important to note that, though her hips move toward the target to start her downswing, her head and neck have held their position behind the ball, a prerequisite for powerful contact because it's another element of coil. As she reverses the direction of her club she drops her arms back down, in the complete absence of any hitting impulse by her hands.

5 Once the lateral move of her hips is completed and her weight has transferred to her left leg, she begins to turn her left hip behind her. Caroline's arms, having dropped the club down into a perfect position, are now ready to deliver the club head to the ball.

6 She looks very stable here with her right foot remaining low to the ground. She's hitting against a firm left side, exhibiting the classic impact position of all good players with the back of her left hand facing the target and the club shaft in line with her left arm.

7 Late into her follow through she still has the club shaft pointing at her chest with her elbows in front of her, a sign that she has fully released her right side including her right shoulder. Note how the toe of her left shoe is turned up a tad, showing that her weight is perfectly distributed, starting from the ball of her foot back to her left heel.

8 An elegant finish with her weight fully posted on her left side and the club shaft across her neck. It shows she has held nothing back yet is in complete control. A good finish looks like the player could stay in that pose for a long time and certainly the comfortable and relaxed Caroline sets an excellent example.

Michelle McGann

Having joined the LPGA Tour at 18 years old, Michelle McGann's amateur career was brief but impressive: three times Florida State Junior Champion, the 1987 USGA Junior Girls Champion, and the American Junior Golf Associations Rolex Junior Player of the Year. As a teenager, she got off to a somewhat slow start in her first two years on tour, but in 1991 she earned over $120,000 and hasn't looked back. Michelle has steadily increased her earnings and scoring average through the 1990's and got her first two wins in 1995. Setting yet a higher standard in 1996 she won three times and earned almost $500,000. Michelle is one of the longest drivers on Tour, averaging just over 255 yards per drive in 1996. Michelle continued her rise, winning twice in the first half of 1997, The HEALTH-SOUTH Inaugural and the ShopRite Classic.

1 With the exception of the putting stroke and the modified swings for other short game shots, your full swing is the same whether you're hitting a full wedge or a driver. In Chapter 4, you learned some keys to Michelle's distance with a driver. In this sequence she is hitting her wedge with a full swing. Though her posture and ball position change to accommodate the club's specifications, you'll see her swing is basically the same.

Since she's hitting a very lofted club, she plays the ball back in her stance to account for the club's more vertical descent. In addition, her stance is narrow with her heels under her hips and she's bent to the ball more because of the short-shafted club.

Michelle's body features give her a natural advantage. She's tall, with a broad muscular frame and plenty of flexibility. Her swing features a big turn and a wide high swing arc but since she's very flexible she addresses the ball with her feet very straight. Less flexible players flare their toes out to facilitate the turn of their bodies back and through, but Michelle encourages her body to build coil by limiting her flexibility with the position of her feet.

2 The hallmark of Michelle's swing is a one-piece take-away, meaning her chest, arms, club shaft, and club head all move away from the ball as one unit. In contrast to Patty Sheehan who sets the club head up very early, Michelle keeps the club head low to create a huge swing arc, a key to her power. There are various ways to take the club away but, like all great players, Michelle's lower body motion at this point in her swing is a subtle reaction to the motion in her upper body

3 Late in her backswing Michelle has fully set her wrists as you can see from the 90-degree angle formed by the club shaft and her forearm. With her hands high above her, her leverage fully set and her left shoulder well coiled behind the ball, she is in a powerful position to hit the ball.

She's not as tightly coiled as some of the other players but you'll see that she increases her coil in the downswing.

4 Most of the keys to Michelle's power can be seen in this frame. Here she increases coil because her shoulders remain turned away from the target but her hips have begun their downswing turn in the opposite direction. Also, just a milli-second before impact, she still has the club in a fully leveraged position, i.e. the 90-degree angle between the shaft and forearms is identical to that in frame 4. Her feet are firmly planted on the ground, where they've been throughout her swing and where they'll stay until just after impact.

5 With her arms back in front of her chest she now begins to release the leverage of her golf swing into the ball in conjunction with the late uncoiling of her shoulders.

6 At the precise moment of impact, Michelle master-fully returns the club and her body to the position they held at address. Except for the dynamic effects of motion and her left hip turning aggressively behind her, this picture is almost identical to frame 1.

7 Just past impact you can see how her head is behind the ball and will be drawn up by the turn of her body. Both of her arms have fully extended as she unwinds her body through the ball. Again you see almost a dupli-cate of the corresponding backswing photo (frame 2) indicating Michelle swung her club in a circle and hasn't created any odd angles by lunging or lurching. Hers is an effortless power that comes from the proper use of her natural assets channeled through a technically sound and powerful swing.

8 Her finish is perfect—a full, yet smooth, release of her club and body through the ball.

Barb Thomas

In 1995, Barb Thomas had her best year ever on the LPGA Tour, winning the Hawaiian Ladies Open and posting five top 20 finishes. Early in her amateur career she was the Iowa Junior champion in both 1978 and 1979. From there she went on to an impressive collegiate record at Tulsa University where she earned All-American honors in 1980 and posted a convincing third-place finish in the 1982 NCAA Championships. She earned her LPGA Tour card at the first attempt by sinking a bunker shot on the final hole of the qualifying tournament. Barb has improved her swing consistently throughout her career and offers a fine example of strong technique.

1 Barb is a very straight driver of the ball due to her excellent set up. The golf ball is perfectly positioned off her left heel and her left arm hangs comfortably atop her chest ready to swing freely. Her feet are straight at address which will serve to increase her coil back and through her golf swing.

2 Barb's arms swing back, creating stretch in her left side, the initial element of her coil. Notice as her arms swing, her shoulders have moved only slightly to accommodate the arm swing and her lower body has maintained its address position. Each of these features adds to her early development of coil.

3 Now her right hip has turned over her right heel, establishing the right side pivot point which will serve as the lower body axis for her backswing. Her left shoulder has turned as it should, around her inclined spine and therefore appears to move downward. Though her arms are still over an extension of her toe line, her wrists have set the club head into a fully leveraged position. In doing so, her hands serve as a pedestal for the weight of the club head as it is elevated to the top of her swing. These are the takeaway characteristics of the modern, body controlled golf swing.

4 At the top of her swing, both feet are planted firmly on the ground. Barb's knees haven't moved much, yet her upper body has fully rotated as shown by the fact that her left shoulder is well behind the ball. To create coil in the modern swing three areas need attention: the shoulders and chest (upper body) turn the most; the hips (middle body) turn the next greatest amount; and the knees (lower body) turn the least. Each level produces opposition, and creating the proper ratios between each produces maximum coil. Should any of these levels turn too much the coil would be reduced and so would the potential for power.

5 Here Barb beautifully illustrates the initial movements that deliver the club back to the ball. You can see how much the club is moving down and therefore why it's called a "downswing." To do this, her left hip has turned over her left heel, yet her right side has held its position to maintain her coil. As a result her hands move downward and away from her right shoulder. Called separation, this downward movement of the hands away from the shoulder slots the club, putting it in a perfect position to take advantage of her shoulder and hip rotation which is about to occur. Now her turn works to her benefit to deliver the club to the ball. Had she turned first and left the club up high, she'd need to struggle near impact to get the club down to the ball and to do so she'd have to stop the powerful rotation of her body.

6 Barb has arrived at impact with her lower body leading the way, but notice how her left hip is turning behind her rather than sliding toward the target. Though her weight shifted laterally from frames 4 to 5, from there she began a powerful rotation of her left hip behind her. A common error among amateurs is to continue the lateral motion and neglect the rotational motion. This puts the body well ahead of the ball at impact and greatly diminishes distance potential. As with all players of her caliber, she arrives at impact with the club back in front of her body, and her left arm firmly planted against her chest to add the power of her body to the hit.

7 With the ball well on its way, this frame shows how well Barb has released her leverage and coil into the shot.

8 Her follow through shows she has delivered her energy to the ball efficiently. Her hips are fully turned, her chest faces left of the target, and she is perfectly balanced on her left foot.

Alice Miller

Alice Miller has had a prestigious career both on and off the golf course. She was president of the LPGA Tour in 1993 and that year also received the Powell Award, given annually to a player selected by her peers for her elite level of sportsmanship. At Arizona State University, she played on the 1975 NCAA Championship Team. In 1983 she recorded her first win on tour and has a total of eight LPGA victories thus far. She won four tournaments in 1985, including her first major championship at the Nabisco Dinah Shore, and finished third on the money list. She was the 1991 Bounceback Player of the Year with a victory at the Toledo Classic. Overall she has earned over $1,000,000 on the LPGA Tour.

1 To accommodate her tall, lean frame, Alice stands more upright at address. Her feet are flared out which encourages her hips to turn more. As her swing progresses you'll see how well this matches with her wide high swing arc. She employs a strong grip and matches this perfectly with a ball position that is slightly back of the standard.

2 She starts the club away by letting her left arm swing across her chest. Though her hips have turned somewhat early in her swing she avoids the error of letting this early hip movement drag the club in behind her. The club has transcribed a wide low arc and has arrived at waist high in an unleveraged position. A strong woman, Alice controls the club well at this point, and as her swing continues she avoids any temptation to lift the club to the top, a common error from this position.

3 Her big hip turn has dragged her left heel slightly inward, but her flexible upper body will make a huge turn behind the ball to achieve the proper ratio between upper, middle, and lower body. As she begins to set the leverage for her swing notice the how far the club head has traveled between frames 2 and 3 in relationship to how little her hands have moved. This indicates that her wrists are providing the elevation.

4 At the top, Alice's upper body is well coiled against her hips, and her feet and legs have stabilized to provide a solid platform. She has rolled to the inside rim of her left foot without raising it off the ground—another indication of coil. Her late wrist set has caused a long swing but it matches perfectly with her big hip turn. With her hips turned this far, she's given herself time to start her downswing before her left hip begins turning behind her. Think of your swing as a race to the finish line (impact) where your hands and arms must travel a long way from the top of your swing but your hip journey is much shorter. You want everything to arrive together and you must carefully adjust the elements of your swing in order to achieve synchronization.

5 The transition from backswing to downswing is a segment of the swing where many golfers go wrong. In a good golf swing there are some moves that occur simultaneously and others that are sequential. Starting down there can be no confusion: the left hip must clear while, at the same time, the club drops straight down toward the ground. When done together they preserve Alice's coil; if they occur separately, coil is released and power leaks away. By allowing the club to drop down Alice retains the 90-degree angle created by her left forearm and the club shaft.

6 Just prior to impact, she unplugs her right heel from the ground, which balances the movement of her head down to the ball. You'll notice other players who swing the club on an upright arc, like Juli Inkster and Emilee Klein, perform these complementary moves through impact. Their swings have an "up and down" look and the players who swing the club in a more rotary fashion, such as Patty Sheehan and Jane Geddes, look far more flat-footed just prior to impact. So what would be an error for some is not for others and having a teacher who can distinguish between the two can minimize the time you spend matching the elements of your swing.

7 Like all great players, Alice holds her head firmly in place behind the ball so the club can sling by her with maximum velocity. Her head is dragged up naturally as the force of her motion continues through the ball.

8 On her way to a full finish you can see how her hands are a mirror image of the position they were in at the top of her swing, indicating that she's fully released the club head into and through the ball. To do so efficiently, she's also fully released the power of her body in a proper rotation through the ball as she demonstrates with her excellent finish position.

The long game

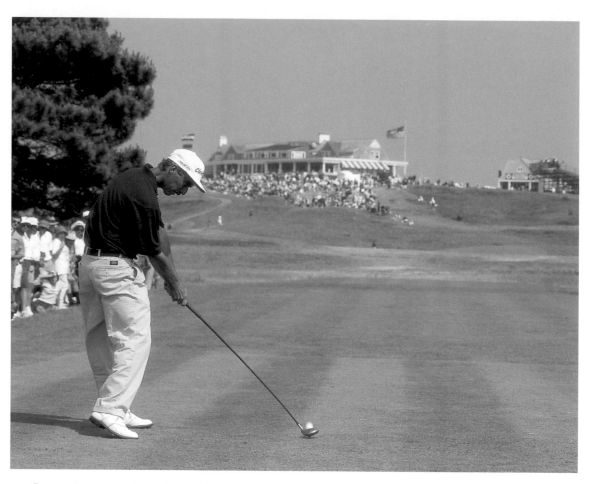

Ask some golfers how they're playing and they often say: "I'm hitting my woods great but my irons are terrible." Ask them again a week later and the response is: "I'm stiffing my irons but I can't hit my woods". In no other game do we use so many different implements, so it's no surprise that as teaching professionals we hear this all the time. This bouncing back and forth is caused by your brain fixing on one concept about the golf swing and staying with it until, out of desperation, you're forced to change it.

Think of it this way: you sweep the ball off the tee with your woods and hit down on the ball with your irons, and the good players

The crowning shot of Corey Pavin's 1995 US Open win was his four wood to within six feet of the flag stick, but that shot was set up by his well-placed drive down the right side of the 18th fairway. Whatever Pavin lacks in distance is more than made up for by his precision off the tee.

are able to cycle between these two concepts and adjust as they play.

The cycle

Let's take an example to see how the cycle operates. If you're hitting your woods well with the sweeping motion, your tendency is to use that motion on all your shots, with your ball position and stance subconsciously modified to favor your wood swing. And there's no better way to hit tops and fat shots than to swing "up" on a ball that's forward in your stance. When you do it correctly with your medium and short irons, you should hit "down" on a ball that's positioned off your left cheek.

At some point you realize that you're having trouble with your irons so you practice with them or take an iron lesson until your swing is back where it should be and, presto, you start hitting your irons much better. But then your woods go haywire and the cycle keeps running: good woods, bad irons, good irons, bad woods.

To help you avoid this cycle, we have included a special section on woods and irons so that your brain will understand "sweep versus down" and the swing mechanics necessary for both.

Your driver

With the possible exception of the long putter, the driver is the longest club in your bag. This means that you'll stand farther from the ball, making your swing more rounded. Your driver does not have much loft so it's usually teed up in such a way as to encourage you to sweep the ball off the tee for optimum launch angle.

Drivers are designed to hit the ball a long way in order to put it in position for your next shot. You probably can't win the hole or the match with your drive but you can certainly lose it if you're in the bushes. Harvey Pennick said that the "woods are full of long drivers" and that's true, but a long hitter named Sam Snead, winner of over 80 tour events, said: "I'd rather hit a seven iron from the rough then a three iron from the fairway." So somewhere between the woods and the rough there's a trade off between distance and direction. You must be long enough off the tee so that your next shot is manageable.

Overswing

Unfortunately, over-swinging with your driver is easy to do. It satisfies many of our natural urges to just whale away at the ball so the tendency is to try to kill your tee ball to get as close to the green as possible. And while it may be natural, this is an urge you must control if your score is important to you—don't be seduced into trying to hit your driver as far as you can.

Pick a route and a destination

How do the good drivers of the ball swing within themselves and put the ball in position for their next shot? They pick a route and a final destination for their driver and so should you.

Our advice is that any time you have a driver in your hand, but especially on wide open golf holes where the urge to blast it is great, choose both a route and a destination, a specific landing area for your tee ball.

Specific
targets

■ **For the route,** always aim at something on the line you want your ball to fly on. It might be a mound, a tree in the background or even a cloud in the sky.

■ **For the destination,** pick a tire track or a discolored patch of grass in the section of the fairway from which you want to play your next shot. Once you have the picture of your shot going to a specific target simply focus on making solid contact with the back of the ball.

Best driver
drill:

To learn to control your driver swing, tee up two balls side by side. Using your hip speed as the governor, hit the first one at full power and the second at three-quarter power. When you gain control of your swing you'll be able to produce the two different distances almost every time and that will help you on the course to attack with your driver when you need to, and play safe with your driver when you ought to.

The rule
of thumb

The rule of thumb is to tee your driver so that the top edge of the club head bisects the middle of the ball. If your swing speed is over 95 mph you might consider teeing your ball higher than this. Chi Chi Rodriquez, for many years one of the longest drivers pound for pound, tees his ball well above standard.

Your driver *continued*

Driver particulars

■ On all normal driver shots, tee your ball just outside the left side of your chest about even with your armpit. To make sure that your ball location is correct, lay a club shaft on the ground perpendicular to your ball and touching your left heel.

■ If you want to hit your shot higher, to take advantage of the wind at your back or to clear an obstacle, move your ball to the tip of your shoulder but be careful to move it a little closer to you since your club head will be slightly inside the target line at impact as it follows the rounded path of your swing. And make sure you check that your shoulder alignment is square because as your ball moves forward, your shoulders open.

■ Note that just because the hole is long, you may not always need a driver off the tee. Tests show that a driver and a three wood of equal shaft length go about the same distance in the air so downwind you might try your three wood for more accuracy.

■ Whatever else you do, learn to love your driver. You can bet that the guy who said "drive for show, putt for dough" was already a great driver of the ball. It doesn't help much to knock in a 30 footer for an eight after hitting two balls in the water off the tee.

Best driver tip ever:

When you need your longest drive, take it back extra slow and smooth with feather-light grip pressure.

3

4

5

6

Start with a weight distribution of 60 percent on your right side and 40 percent on your left. Your driver swing requires a flowing motion with a big turn and a significant weight transfer. At the top of your swing, you'll have 80 percent of your weight on your right side and by the time you get to impact the majority of weight transfers to your left side. At the finish, all your weight is on your left side.

Dogleg
tip

Driving it pretty well except for the doglegs? Instead of changing your swing you could carry three drivers. An open-faced driver puts fade spin on the ball; a closed driver imparts draw spin. So why not use your regular driver for the straight away holes, a four-degree closed driver for doglegs left, and a four-degree open driver for doglegs right? If you decide to try this, enlist a club maker to get the correct specifications.

Your long irons

In our view, the long irons (one, two, three and four) are not for the average golfer. Basically, unless you're an expert, they are hard to hit off the ground because they don't have much loft and the ball must be contacted perfectly to get it airborne.

Just the look of long irons can be intimidating with their small heads, straight faces and long shafts, especially if you are playing the ball as it lies and it is sitting down a little bit. Unless you make solid contact and generate enough club head speed, there won't be much of a difference between your long irons in terms of the distance your ball goes. In our experience, most golfers hit their long irons about the same distance so in actuality you may be carrying three of your four irons in the bag: one marked two, one three and one four. Unless you have a single digit handicap or you're very strong, our advice is to replace your long irons with the four, five and seven woods.

When you hit your irons from the teeing ground, the rules allow you to place the ball on a tee. But be careful not to tee your irons or fairway woods too high in this situation. If you do, you'll make contact high on the club face and hit weak shots with too much loft. The proper teeing height for an iron or lofted wood is just high enough off the ground so that the thin part of a tee can fit between the ball and the grass.

Five-time British Open Champion and the world's most dominant player in his prime, Tom Watson's upright swing gives him the ability to launch high, softly landing long irons that hold on even the slickest greens.

Long irons particulars

Although the long irons aren't for everyone, they can be a good addition to your bag if you can handle them. Since they hit the ball low and long, they're great in the wind when you need to keep the ball down.

If you know the technique and have the talent, you can really maneuver the long irons, bending them around the doglegs and curving them into pins that are tucked to the sides of green. And if you're really strong, there's no reason why you can't hit them high and soft when you have to. That's what the likes of Jack Nicklaus can do, and it's unlikely that you'd find them without their one irons, a great club on narrow driving holes.

The long iron swing

Your long iron swing is much like your driver swing in that it is a sweeping motion but because they are shorter than your driver, your swing will be a bit more upright. Still, you won't take a divot; your goal is to pick the ball off the ground.

■ Play the ball off your left breast. Start with your weight evenly distributed and make a wide backswing, avoiding the urge to pick up the club without turning your back to the target.

■ At the top of your swing, you should have about 75 percent of your weight on your right side with your right hip turned over your right heel. Start down by shifting your weight to your left hip and take care to keep your head from sliding toward the target. Long irons can put demons in your head, the most common of which is fear of hitting the ground before the ball. The "fat" long iron is a feeling you won't forget so, to shallow out your swing, keep your weight shifting and your head behind the ball.

■ About 80 percent of your weight is in your left hip at impact. Finish with your weight completely on your left side and the club over your left shoulder, indicating the fully released right side.

Your fairway woods

If they practice at all, most golfers practice their skills separately (driver, putting, chipping, etc.). Develop a "skills package" by practicing with your fairway woods in combination with your pitch shots so that you will be ready to link them when you need them on the golf course. When's the last time that you saw a golfer on the driving range alternating a three wood off the ground with a short pitch to the flag?

1 Tee a ball correctly and hit a shot with your three wood, feeling the sweeping action of your swing.

2 Drop the tee height so that the ball is just barely above the ground, and hit another shot. You should be able to hit both shots without taking a divot.

3 Hit the ball off the ground, again taking no divot. Repeat the sequence at least three times. This three-ball drill will teach you to sweep the ball off the ground with your fairway woods.

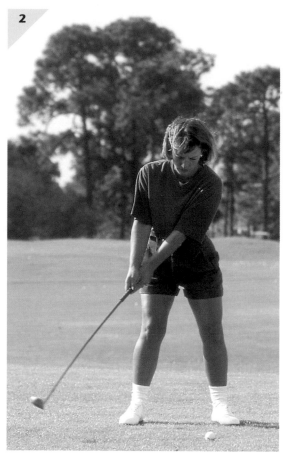

The look of your fairway woods is very different from your long irons. When you look down at address, you can see the loft on the face of the club so it registers that getting the ball airborne is not a problem. Moreover, the size of the club head is substantial enough to suggest the forgiveness a large sweet spot offers. What you can't see from address is the sole plate: the bottom surface of your club head which is specifically designed to slide through the grass rather than catch in it.

Even though these features make the fairway woods easier to hit than most long clubs,

many golfers don't realize just how important they are to playing good golf. You might not be a good driver of the ball but if you can keep your tee ball in play and then hit a solid fairway wood, it can make up for a lack of distance off the tee.

■ Look at your fairway woods as long-range siege guns which will bring you close enough to the green to take advantage of your short game.

■ Develop a good short game, combine it with a strong fairway wood game, and you'll be a match for anyone.

Most golfers play the ball too far forward off their left heel and catch the top of the ball, sending it skimming along the ground. Position your ball off your logo with your weight evenly distributed. Your goal should be to hit the ball with a descending blow that shallows out just before the bottom of your swing arc. It's a full body coil with the same weight transfer as your driver. Think of your fairway wood swing as a sweeping action and let the ball position take care of the "descending" part of your swing. There's no divot.

Three-quarter swing

The need for solid contact is why, beginning with your mid irons, your swing gets tighter and shortens to three quarters. The benchmark to shorten your swing is your left arm. Imagine you are standing inside a large clock with 12 o'clock at your head and 6 o'clock at your feet. You produce the three-quarter swing by stopping your left arm at 10 o'clock. Thus your regular top-of-the-swing position will be between 11 and 12 o'clock. **A note of caution:** As you swing your left arm to its appointed time, make sure to turn your chest along with it.

Best mid iron tip ever: The mid irons are best played with a three-quarter swing regulated by swinging your left arm to 10 on the clock.

Your mid irons

Most architects design their courses so that if you play from the tees that match your skill level, you'll hit a lot of mid-iron (five, six and seven) approach shots into the greens. Thus, in combination with your short irons, your mid irons are your scoring clubs.

The mid irons give you a combination of distance and control because their loft gives you enough backspin to stop the ball on the green. In addition to its height and stopping power, backspin also decreases the amount of hook and slice that you will get with your straighter-faced clubs, such as the driver and long irons. This is the reason why your mid to short irons will not curve as much as your woods and long irons.

A mid iron is best played with a controlled three-quarter motion and even long-swinging John Daly reduces the length of his swing and follow through for the sake of increased accuracy with his mid iron.

The particulars

Because they are shorter than your long irons, you stand closer to your mid irons, and this makes your swing more vertical—another reason why you can make your mid irons "bite" on the greens. To encourage the descending blow, position the ball off your left cheek, just forward of the center of your stance.

At address your weight distribution is 50:50 but since your swing is for accuracy, don't transfer as much weight during your swing as you do with the long clubs. At the top, 70 percent of your weight is on your right side, and by impact the majority of your weight shifts to your left side, where it stays as you rotate up into your finish position.

To be a good mid-iron player you need solid, clean contact with the ball to ensure that you get the distance and direction you expect. When you contact the ball in the center of the club face it won't twist, so the face stays square and the energy in your club head transfers to the ball. Take a shallow divot *after* your contact with the ball to avoid getting grass or sand between your ball and the club face, which would cause the ball to fly off line.

With your mid irons, your stance is slightly narrow. The ball is positioned just forward of the center of your stance, opposite the left side of your face, to encourage a descending angle of

attack. Though a three-quarter backswing is most suitable for the mid irons there is still plenty of dynamic motion through the ball and into a full finish.

The "Chicken Wing"

In those pressure situations where you absolutely have to hit your ball on the green, the "chicken wing" shot can be a valuable addition to your shot makers arsenal. It's the shot made famous by Lee Trevino and the one Nick Faldo used to win the Open.

Use one more club than normal and aim slightly left. Position the ball in the middle of your stance and take your normal backswing. Drive your right knee toward the target to start your downswing so it leads your hands and arms into impact. Since you don't want the toe of your club to pass over the heel, keep your right wrist bent just as it was at address. If you've retained your wrist angle correctly, you'll finish with your hands in front of your chest and your club face looking at the sky.

The key is to let your left elbow float up and away from your side as you clear your hips through impact. This keeps your club face square to the target line well past impact, assuring a lower than normal shot for accuracy with a left-to-right spin that stops your ball quickly.

Your short irons

Your eight, nine and wedges are the clubs that can turn three shots into two, so pay a lot of attention to them. Again, a three-quarter swing is in order for maximum control. Because the shafts are shorter, you move closer to the ball than with your mid irons, with the ball position between your left cheek and your nose. And, of course, as you would with all your other clubs, you should use the posture outlined in Chapter two.

The particulars

Of all the full-swing clubs, your swing with the short irons is the most compact with the least weight transfer. You start with 50:50, move to 40:60 at the top of your swing, and then to 60:40 at impact. There's no full-bodied movement here.

Good short-iron players have a constant arm speed, minimum hip turn and a grooved rotation rate that delivers the same force to the ball time after time. When you're 120 yards from the green, it's no time for a burst of power resulting in a 145-yard shot.

It's one thing to make a bad swing with the right club but it's often just as ruinous to choose the wrong short iron and make a good swing. Because the value of accuracy rises as you get closer to the hole, you need to choose the correct short iron. However, it is often less simple than it appears because you're in between clubs. It's too far for your normal nine but too short for your eight, and the danger is that worrying about which club to hit will cause you to make a bad swing.

When you are faced with a "tweener", take one less club and hit it harder if you're a strong-swinging, power hitter. If you're a smooth swinger with a syrupy action, take more club and hit it easy. In other words, when you match your club selection to your swing tempo you'll never have to violate your internal metronome, the personal gauge that sets your natural swing pace.

A well-struck short iron starts from a narrow stance and ends in a perfectly balanced finish as shown by Peter Jacobsen.

With the short irons, take a stance about the width of your hips. Position your ball just slightly forward of the center of your body. Since you'll be most bent over with your short irons, you should be sure to maintain your address posture during your backswing. There is a tendency to straighten up during a short iron backswing and this can turn the high, lofted shot you planned to land next to the hole into a low runner that finds a hazard behind the green.

131

Awkward lies

T he first order of business when you arrive at your golf ball is to examine your lie, i.e. the characteristics of how your ball is sitting in the grass. Your lie dictates the kind of shot you can play, sometimes allowing you to pull off a spectacular shot from 200 yards over a tall tree and at other times preventing you from getting close to the flag from 30 feet. Thus, part of being a skilful player is "reading" the lie and then being able to execute the required shot. We have outlined a variety of lies, ranging from no grass underneath the ball to grass all around it. Each of

Although it is obviously a struggle from such a severe slope, Greg Norman finishes here in balance, a necessary feature of hitting a successful shot from an awkward stance.

these situations requires that the club head should sit differently to the ball. The better the lie, the more the club is soled flush to the ground. The more buried the lie, the more your club rests on its heel, requiring you to stand farther from the ball. The tighter the lie, the more the club rests on its toe, so that you stand closer to the ball.

Difficult lies around the green

Tight lies

When there's little or no grass under your ball the first order of business is to determine exactly what is under the ball. Is it sandy soil, thin grass with dirt or the difficult hard pan lie? Each is played from a different set up that changes the length, path and timing of your swing.

From a thin lie

You're near the green with not much grass under your ball and what little there is, is patchy. In this situation, choose your sand or pitching wedge to give you the proper amount of loft you need to stop your ball on the green.

If your set up is right, you're well on your way to solving this difficult lie. The danger is that you'll hit behind the ball, snagging your club head in the ground. To guard against this, place your weight in your left hip and stand closer to the ball with a more upright spine position. This makes your club shaft more vertical and automatically tips your club head onto its toe, reducing the bounce of the club. This way, less of your club head is exposed to the ground. Your upright posture also causes you to raise your hands at address, protecting your wrists from over-cocking.

Since the heel of your club is off the ground, position the ball toward the toe of your club where you'll want to make contact. Striking the ball on the toe is not only safer but the slightly off-center hit produces a much softer shot. Once you're set up correctly, your swing is the same as it is for a normal pitch shot.

Difficult lies around the green *continued*

This sequence illustrates hitting the ball from a thin lie (above) viewed from down the line as opposed to the angle shown on page 133.

From hard pan

When your ball comes to rest on a patch of rock-hard ground with no grass to prop it up, the last thing you want is your club head bouncing into the center of the ball and causing a skulled shot that runs out of control.

To play this type of lie correctly, select a sand or pitching wedge and position the ball according to the trajectory you need:

- Forward for a high soft shot.
- Center for a standard pitch.
- Back for a low, running pitch.

As with the thin lie, move close enough to the ball so the club head is standing on its toe with the club shaft as vertical as possible. Thus you eliminate any angle in your left wrist, making sure that your club head won't drop any lower through impact than it was at address.

Set your feet according to the length of the shot you intend to play: wide and square for a longer shot, and progressively more open and narrow the shorter you want to hit the ball. To shorten the distance your shot flies, open your stance by dropping your left foot back from the target line with your club face slightly to the right of the target. For the swing, use your pitching action.

Buried in grass

When your ball is buried in the grass, your club head should rest on its heel, with the toe of the club off the ground, just the opposite of the hard pan set up. By setting the club on the heel, the bounce of the club is increased along with the potential hitting surface. This increased surface area helps your club head plow through the grass, helping you make solid contact.

When you stand farther from the ball your hands hang lower, presetting your wrists, and creating a steeper angle of attack so that the grass behind the ball has less effect on the shot. Also, by lowering your hands, your shoulders tilt more as they swing, producing a more upright backswing that adds to the cutting action of your swing—just what you need to carve your ball out of the grass. When your club is on its heel, be sure to position the ball in the middle of the club face to avoid any possibility of a shank.

The deep grass tends to grab the neck of your club, twisting your club face into a closed position at impact. This causes a pulled shot left of target so aim to the right to compensate for the pull. And of course you have to swing harder than you normally would with a firmer grip pressure that helps you retain control of your club, as it encounters the resistance of the grass.

Summary

The lie of your ball determines the set up necessary for each circumstance. An easy way to remember it is: if your lie is tight, think "up tight" (hands up for a tight lie). If your lie is buried, think "low down" (hands low for a buried lie). The amount you adjust your club on its toe or heel is determined by how tight or buried the lie is. The tighter the lie, the higher the hands; the more surrounded your ball is by grass, the lower your hands.

Blast or pick?

The sandiness of the soil is the determining factor for this awkward lie. You can play this shot like a regular sand shot where you deliberately hit the sand first or you can treat it as a pitch shot and catch the ball cleanly. It's often hard to determine the consistency of the turf under your ball: the rules don't allow you to improve your lie and so it's dangerous to poke around. The safe way is to check the surrounding area at least one club length from your ball and if there are any sandy spots similar to the one you're on, test one of them to evaluate the soil texture. If you find the sand is fluffy and powdery don't hesitate to play an explosion shot.

If there's not much sand or you're not sure what's under your ball, it's better to pick it cleanly with a pitch shot than explode your ball with a sand shot. If you make a mistake with the blast shot and there's hard turf underneath, you might end up farther away from the target than you started, whereas a missed pitch falls just short of your target.

Your putting *stroke*

In the types of awkward lies outlined here, the common themes are that the most accurate golfing stroke is one that is as level as possible to the ground, and that a major cause of inaccurate shot making occurs when your club swings vertically upward, opening the club face and imparting side spin to your ball. The problem with side spin is that you're never sure whether your ball will release (keep rolling) or trickle to a stop. Thus side spin is the enemy of roll and you should do what you can to keep your club head low.

The wood chip

When your ball lies just off the green and there's no obstacle between you and the pin that prevents you from rolling the ball, the play is a fairway wood. A seven wood is an excellent choice as it has enough loft to lift the ball out of grassy lies and its long shaft allows you a compact swing that's low to the ground. If you don't carry a seven wood you can adapt your other fairway woods by simply opening the club face a tad and moving the ball a little more forward in your stance.

To chip with a wood, use either your putting or full swing grip, assume a slightly open stance and tilt the shaft of your club until it's upright. You'll have to stand erect to accommodate the length of the shaft but be careful to keep your weight anchored on your left side so you don't sway as you make your stroke.

Now use your putting stroke, keeping the right wrist angle formed at address throughout the swing to avoid a wristy stroke. Let your club head swing through the hitting zone as an extension of your arms so it "chases" the ball to the target.

The collar shot

Every once in a while your ball stops against the first cut of rough just off the green. It's hard to judge this shot because using a normal chip or pitch, you're denied clean contact with the ball due to the intervening grass. A three wood adapted like a chipping iron is an excellent choice in this situation. The weight and mass of your three wood head ensures that the club slides through the grass to contact the ball crisply. As in chipping, raise your three wood on its toe, close the face and grip down on it with your putting grip. Assume a narrow, open stance and stroke the ball as you would a putt of equal distance. Expect your ball to hop a little and then roll to the hole like a putt.

Another solution is to choose a putter and address the ball so that the toe of your putter aims at the top of the ball. The key to this shot is to strike the ball squarely with a firm tapping stroke, keeping the toe going at the hole during the follow through.

You can also play this shot by striking the middle of the ball with the leading edge of your sand wedge. This way your club face never touches the ball so you don't have to worry about the grass getting between your club face and ball. To "belly" the ball so that it rolls with a good deal of top spin, use your putting motion with absolutely no wrist action. Just set your weight on your left side and hover the edge of your sand wedge behind the equator of the ball, then make a smooth stroke.

When your ball is just off the green, ignore the markings on your clubs and play the shot with the club that gets the job done. Your goal is to keep the ball on the ground whenever you can, so you might choose a fairway wood, a five iron, a sand wedge or a putter to get the ball close to the hole.

Full swings from awkward lies

When you face an awkward lie some distance from the green, put your course management skills on high alert. Many times you'll have to "play it safe" rather than trying a shot from 200 yards off an awkward lie. But when the rewards outweigh the risks involved and you know the proper technique, you can go for the green with confidence.

From a tight lie

Once you judge the lie to be "tight", i.e. sitting with very little grass under it, everything in your set up and swing is designed to make sure you pick the ball cleanly. It's a little bit easier to hit a short shot from a tight lie but a full swing requires attention to two additional elements: weight shift and shot shape.

Since your left hip is the turning axis of your swing, your weight shift is minimal but your turn is not restricted. You want to pick the ball off the turf or even hit it slightly thin, so your swing is an upper body one, mostly an arms and shoulders effort. For this reason, take at least one club more than normal. Remember that you're going to fade the ball with your club face slightly open at address and this costs you some distance, but it's worth it because the open club face at impact helps get your ball airborne. To encourage the fade, move the ball forward in your stance and draw your left foot back a bit.

From heavy rough

When you find your ball in deep rough you have to make two critical evaluations: "What score do I need to make?" and "How will the grass affect my swing?" If you're playing match play and your opponent is next to the pin with a sure par, the shot you'll choose is different from one if it was the second hole of a 36-hole medal play tournament. Obviously, the shot you choose depends on the circumstances and the extent to which the ball is buried in the grass.

Below: to win the 1987 US Open Scott Simpson needed a whole arsenal of specialty shots, not the least of which was the technique to power through the knee-deep rough without the club face slamming shut.

137

Full swings from awkward lies *continued*

Pine *needles*

We've chosen pine needles to discuss the awkward lie where your ball sits off the firm ground, on a mat of leaves, twigs, etc. A good practice is not to ground your club, a precaution that avoids a penalty shot should your ball be dislodged as you take your stance.

For this shot, hover your club head over the ball, open your stance and, with your weight firmly planted on your left side, pick the ball off the needle carpet. To do this, position the ball in the middle of your feet. The shorter the shot, the shorter your backswing and the less your weight shift. Around the green, it's mostly an arm swing with the firm, wristless hand action of a chip.

For a full shot you need a good shoulder turn along with your normal wrist cock but your weight stays in your left hip joint. This way you can coil your upper body around your spine without your feet slipping and sliding about. The trajectory is likely to be a low one so adjust your plan accordingly. As in the fairway bunker, think "thin before fat", a cue to pick the ball without hitting the ground first.

There are some lies from heavy rough where all you can do is take your sand wedge and hack the ball back to the fairway. It depends on the thickness and texture of the grass. Even though it doesn't appear to be as thick as some of the American grasses, the tall, wild version of fescue found in some seaside countries, such as Great Britain, is tough to play out of. It is strong in texture with enough spacing between the shoots for a ball to settle down at the base of the blades, defying extraction to all but the strongest swinger. In tropical climates, you'll often find Bermuda grass in the rough and, while it is neither as long nor as visually impressive as the tall, waving fescue, it is a gnarly grass that can smother your club head.

The bottom line is that you should know what kind of grass you are up against and adjust your shot plan accordingly. When you play a course for the first time, ask the pro or the superintendent about the grasses. And at your home course, practice out of every kind of rough you can find to see what effect it has on the distance and direction of your shot.

One thing for certain is that heavy grass, no matter what type, will rap around the neck of your club, shutting the face and producing a low pulled shot to the left of target. The harder you swing the more this effect is magnified so the distance that your shot has to carry affects how much to the right you should aim to adjust for the pull: the longer the shot, the farther right you must aim. Obviously, you can't tell for sure how much pull to allow for, so, if there's trouble on

the right, it may not be prudent to aim it there. The same goes for trouble on the left. Greg Norman was fooled on the 18th hole in the final round at Doral in 1995, when in close competition with Nick Faldo. The gnarly rough closed his club face and he pulled a six iron 40 yards into the lake to lose the tournament.

Lies that are harder than they look

Most lies are obvious in their degree of difficulty; a buried lie in the bunker, a steep sidehill lie or a ball half submerged in the water gets your undivided attention. But there are some lies that appear so benign there's a tendency to ignore the important effect that they have on your ball's flight.

Grass against

In this situation, the grass is growing in the opposite direction to your club head as it swings into the ball. The danger is that you'll catch some grass before the ball, slowing down the club head and causing your shot to come up short. In addition, the grass is liable to wrap itself around the neck of your club so that the ball squirts to the left.

The key to this lie is to make a steeper swing than usual to avoid the grass and hit the ball first. To do this, play the ball in the middle of your stance or even a little back of center. Take at least one club more, open your stance and grip the club very firmly.

To cut through the grass, your club head must approach the ball from a steep angle. To produce a steep path, move the ball back in your stance. To further steepen your swing and create the proper angle of attack, settle your weight into your left hip and leave it there while you swing. Grip down on the club with a firm hold in preparation for the control you'll need at impact. Hover the club above the ball so you can make a smooth takeaway without getting your club caught in the grass. At impact you'll need to hold your club face open as the grass pulls on the neck of your club, so let your left elbow finish horizontal to the ground with your right palm facing the sky.

As we saw with the buried lie, one of the hardest aspects of the grass against shot is aiming. The longer and more gnarly the rough, the more you must aim to the right of target, and it's hard to convince yourself to do this even though you know that you should.

Grass with

When the grass grows in the same direction as your downswing it acts as a launching pad so you can expect a flyer—a shot that goes farther than normal and won't stop well once it hits the green.

Play the ball slightly more forward in your stance than you would normally and take at least one less club (say, a six rather than a five). Open both your stance and the face of your club and make a smooth swing with a proper weight shift.

The last thing you want is to hit a pop-up by making an upright "all arms—no weight shift"

Full swings from awkward lies *continued*

swing that drives the club head into the grass before it gets to the ball. Just concentrate on making solid contact with a full follow through and let the grass be your friend.

The perched lie

This lie props the ball up as if it were on a tee. However, it isn't on a tee and the danger here is that you'll swing right under the ball and hit a weak shot that goes nowhere. Since the ball is an inch or two above your feet, if you take your normal swing, your club comes at the ball on a steep angle so you contact it much too high on the club face.

To keep your club head from sliding under a perched lie, hover it above the ball.

To prevent this there are several alterations you should make to your set up. Pull your right foot back from the line of flight and make sure that your left shoulder points slightly right of the target. This closed position encourages a more rounded swing arc that neutralizes the natural tendency toward steepness, but don't forget to aim to the right of your target to allow for the closed stance.

Move the ball forward in your stance. If you normally play this shot in the middle, move the ball opposite the logo on your shirt. If you would normally play it off the logo, reposition it off your left heel. And always choose at least one less club—you should move from a six to a seven.

The last adjustment is crucial. Hover your club head behind the ball without letting it touch the ground. There are two reasons for this. Firstly, when you sole your club head behind the ball, you run the risk of pressing down the grass and

Although it looks inviting, the perched lie can be dangerous without the proper adjustments.

dislodging your ball. And if your ball moves in this situation, it's a penalty. If you don't sole your club, you are deemed, under the rules, not to have taken your address position and there is no penalty if your ball changes position.

Secondly, hovering your club face directly behind the back of your ball gives you a better chance of making square contact at impact. You want contact with the back of the ball rather than the ground, so that's where you aim your club face.

Out of a divot

Hitting into a divot may be a bad break but recovery is not as difficult as most club golfers expect. Depending on the position of the ball in the divot, there are different shots you can play that require different techniques. If your ball lies in the front of the divot, your goal is to sweep it out with your regular swing. If it's near the back lip of the divot, you modify your swing and punch it out. Regardless of where the ball lies in the divot, always stand closer to your ball. This sets the club shaft more upright, reducing the chance that your club head will catch the edge of the divot.

Sweep the ball from the front

It may look like a troublesome shot, but when your ball is in the front of the divot with nothing between your club face and the back of the ball, you can take your normal swing. The only modifications are in your set up.

Always sweep the ball from the front of a divot.

Move the ball about an inch forward of where you would normally position it in your stance. This allows you to sweep the ball cleanly, using the divot to direct the path of your club. If the divot is deep and points left of the target, open your club face to produce a fade back to the target, then swing down the divot line. If the divot points right of the target, close your club face slightly to promote a draw back to the target and simply let your swing path follow the divot line.

141

If you're around the green and your ball is in a divot, simply use your chipping stroke with a high lofted club. However, if there's a steep front lip to the divot and the pin is at the back of the green with no hazards in your way, it may seem strange, but the shot here is a "topped putter." You'll want to hit the top of the ball so that your ball caroms off the lip of the divot, pops up into the air and hits the green with an abundance of over spin that carries it to the flag.

Move the ball opposite your right toe so your hands are markedly ahead of it. This creates an abrupt down stroke that pinches the back of the ball, causing it to pop up immediately. Hover your putter head behind the ball, even with the top third and simply make an arm and shoulder stroke with no independent wrist action.

The tendency when using a putter from a divot is to use too much force when all you need is a smooth stroke not much harder than normal for a putt from this distance. Hit a few practice shots using the "top spin putter" shot, and get a feel for how much force you need.

Full swings from awkward lies *continued*

Punch the ball from the back

When your ball trickles into a divot and rests at the edge of the back lip, you have to dig it out so plan for a low, running shot. Play the ball one inch behind the center of your stance and choose one club more than normal. Choke down about one inch and swing abruptly down on the back of the ball using an abbreviated follow through. Use a mid to short iron and don't be afraid to turn on the power for this one.

Your ball comes out of a divot low and running so aim slightly to the right of your target. And don't challenge the architect if he's put trouble in your way, especially if there's

If the ball is lying at the back of a divot, always punch it out.

water between you and the target. Remember that the goal from this lie is to get your ball into a good position for the next shot.

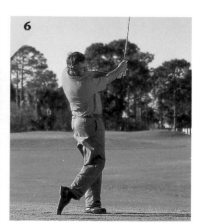

Shot from shallow water

If your ball lands in a temporary accumulation of water it's called casual water and under the rules you're entitled to a free drop on drier ground. But when your ball is in a water hazard it costs you a penalty stroke unless you exercise your option to play your ball as it lies.

When you knock your ball in a water hazard, most of the time it's too far below the surface of the water to play it. But, occasionally, when it just trickles down the bank of the hazard, you'll find it half submerged and it's possible to have a go at it.

If the ball is more than half submerged, don't try this shot but once you decide to play the ball out of the water, here's how. Take a wide stance for stability. The last thing you want is to lose your balance from this awkward position. Your swing is primarily an upper body motion, mostly an arm and chest swing with very little weight transfer. Play the ball in the middle of your stance and hit down behind it, taking as little water as you can. Your follow through should be shorter than normal, and you must take care not to move your head in anticipation of a face full of water.

Risk versus *reward*

The first consideration is how you stand in your round. Is it time to take a chance or do you need to play conservatively and take a drop? The second is how far you can expect to advance the ball. If hitting the ball out of the hazard can gain you only a few yards, opt for the drop. If you can hit your ball out of the water two or three clubs (20 to 30 yards) closer to the green, it might be worth the risk.

Uneven lies

People who don't play golf often wonder why golfers make such a fuss over the difficulty of their sport. But it doesn't take long for the beginner to realize that golf's not just another stick and ball game. Uneven lies are one of many examples where, without the proper technique, a simple swing at the ball won't do. Golf has been called the game of a lifetime and in one sense it is because it can take a lifetime to master all the skills required to play it. Once you do, you'll find that golf isn't quite as difficult as you thought, though it's never as easy as the non-golfer suspects.

The right *clubs*

Unless it's a very subtle slope, an uneven lie is no place for a long iron or fairway wood. The distance may require your three wood but your course management skills should tell you to play a safety shot back to level land and let your short game save your par. It would be a very unusual instance for the average golf player to use more than a five iron from a severe slope.

A precarious stance

Course designers build in swales, grass-filled depressions, bunkers and mounding around the course to present new challenges to your inventiveness as well as your balance. And since your body seeks to stay in balance even at the expense of your golf swing, a precarious stance can be very disruptive. When you're perched on the bank of a bunker or halfway up a mound, it's no place for a big weight shift and a lot of body motion—it's more of an upper body swing dominated by your wrists, arms and shoulders.

Maintaining your balance

The first priority when you have a precarious stance is to maintain your balance. Take your set up and after you've stabilized your lower body by anchoring your feet into the hill, swing your club head over the ball to determine the effect of your body motion on your balance. Make your practice swings identical to the real swing you are about to make, except that your club head swings over the ball instead of actually hitting it. Once you're ready, let your swing be guided by one thought—

Maintaining your balance from an uneven lie has to be your number one priority, although sometimes it's almost impossible.

you must keep your knee flex constant throughout your swing. The tendency from a precarious stance is to either increase your knee flex and hit the ball fat or straighten your knees and hit a low, bladed shot.

Ball above or below feet

Almost all the shots you hit on the driving range are from lies where the ball is at the same level as your feet. Thus your brain learns the geometry of making a level swing and adjusts your balance system accordingly. But if you've played any golf at all, you know that there are situations on the course where the ball is either above or below your feet and if you don't make the necessary adjustments, uneven lies can cause some bad shots. The trick is to understand the effects of the lie, set up to it correctly and make as close to a normal swing as possible.

Characteristics of uneven lies

Properly executing shots from uneven lies is a challenge for all golfers. In order to play effectively from these types of lies, you must first develop an understanding of the effects they have on your swing. There are four basic types of uneven lies:

1 Ball above your feet.
2 Ball below your feet.
3 Downhill.
4 Uphill.

For each of these there is a predictable ball flight pattern and simple adjustments that you can make to your set up to compensate for the effect the slope has on your body. The gravitational forces of the hill will challenge your ability to make a balanced swing, and although we'll show you how to adjust your set up to compensate for

the pull of gravity, you will be much more successful if you concentrate on making a three-quarter swing motion from these uneven lies.

Effects of uneven lies

1 The ball follows the angle of the slope.
2 The loft of the club face points in the direction of the slope.
3 You'll lose your balance down the slope.
4 The bottom of your swing arc is altered by the slope.
5 The path and plane of your swing are altered by the slope.

General adjustments

Although uneven lies tend to be opposites of each other, there are general adjustments that are standard for all of them. In every instance, make it a priority to protect your balance by anchoring yourself into the hill against the pull of gravity. Angle your shoulders to match the slope so that you can swing with the contour of the hill. The slope causes changes in your swing arc and you need to adjust your ball position accordingly. And, finally, by opening or closing your stance, you neutralize the effect of the slope by returning your hips to level.

Once you've made the correct adjustments in your set up, you need to do only two things: the first is to make a smooth, three-quarter swing for maximum control; and the second is to focus on the target.

Uneven lies *continued*

Ball above stance

When the ball rests above your feet, you're forced to swing flatter, more around your body, causing your shot to fly to the left of target usually with a right to left spin. When it's above your feet, the tendency is to pull or hook the ball, and to offset this there are several modifications you can make.

Since all good swings depend on balance the first order of business is to neutralize the tendency to be pulled down the hill. Flex your knees into the hill for balance with your weight forward toward the balls of your feet, and leave it there as you swing. Also, be sure to keep your weight on the inside of your right foot. The danger is that as your swing progresses, the momentum of your turn will topple you backwards down the hill, an error you can prevent if you are well anchored on your right side.

Take one club more and choke down so that you can stand closer to the ball. Move the ball

back in your stance because you'll reach the bottom of your arc sooner when the ball is above your feet. To account for the tendency to pull the shot, allow your shoulders to close, an alignment that will aim your club face to the right of the target. With both your shoulders and your club face aimed to the right, your swing takes an in-to-out path that offsets the tendency for the ball to start left. Once you have aimed properly, simply swing the club, allowing your set up to determine your swing path.

When the ball is above your feet, it tends to fly to the left of target.

Summary

1 Sole the club to establish your posture and the plane of your swing.
2 Grip down on the club.
3 Move the ball back in your stance from where you would normally position it for a level lie.
4 Stand more upright with knees flexed into hill.
5 Make a three-quarter motion concentrating on keeping your balance throughout the swing.

Ball below stance

When the ball is below your feet, your swing is more upright so your club face tends to point to the right of the target at impact, curving your shot from left to right. If you don't make a correction, your shot is likely to fly low and right.

Prior to arranging your feet, sole your club flush with the slope, so the shaft is more upright than normal. This establishes your swing plane and your posture at address. The upright position puts the club on its toe and aims the club face right. Since the ball is farther from you, the bottom of your arc occurs later in your swing, so to catch the ball solidly and give your club face time to square up, move the ball forward in your stance. This points your shoulders left, offsetting the tendency for the ball to start right of your target.

When the ball is below your feet, it is actually farther away from you, so stand closer, with a wider stance and more knee flex to lower yourself to the ball. Pinch your knees in and turn your feet in to minimize side-to-side motion. Settle your weight onto your heels and into the hillside to further anchor your lower body. Because the hill pulls you forward onto your toes as you swing back to the ball, you need to stay on your heels from start to finish.

Summary

1 Sole the club to establish both your swing plane and posture.
2 Stand closer to the ball.
3 Move the ball forward in your stance from where you would normally position it for a level lie.
4 Widen your stance, pigeon toe your feet and flex your knees into the hill.
5 Make a three-quarter motion concentrating on keeping your balance throughout the swing.

When the ball is below your stance, it tends to fly right of target.

Downhill and *uphill lies*

To adjust your body to accommodate the slope, visualize trying to balance a table on a slope. In order to keep it from tipping you must shorten the uphill legs to make it level. When your ball is on a slope in golf, you do the same with your uphill leg to create a level hip turn.

For downhill slopes, draw your right foot back away from the target line and increase the amount of flex in your right leg. Do the opposite for an uphill slope. Since it is your shoulders that dictate both the path and tilt of your swing, the next step is to angle them to match the slope of the hill, allowing your swing to follow the natural contour of the incline.

The amount you open or close your stance depends on the severity of the slope. For both uphill and downhill slopes, you should adjust your stance until your hips are level. For both types of lie, the ball is played in the middle of your stance.

Uneven lies *continued*

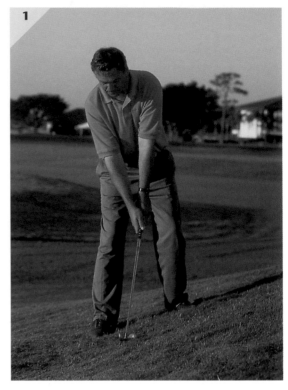

Uphill lies

On an uphill lie, your ball is higher than your right foot but lower than your left. The slope acts as a launching pad, adding height to your shot along with a tendency for your ball to go to the left. When you sole your club, the effective loft is increased because of the slope. For these reasons it's best to take more club from an uphill lie.

On an upslope, your left foot is drawn back from the target line, effectively shortening your left leg and leveling your hips. With your left foot dropped back, your weight settles comfortably into the hillside as an anchor for balance. Flare your left foot out to make it easier to get through the shot. Since you want to swing up the slope (not into it), tilt your shoulders to mimic the slope of the hill, with your left shoulder higher than your right shoulder.

In the case of a severe uphill slope, it's important to level your hips as much as possible, but when you do, you change the low point of your swing. When you open your stance, the ball in effect moves back, and when you tilt your shoulders to match the hill, the bottom of your arc moves forward. The two adjustments match perfectly when your ball is played from the middle of your stance. Your swing from an uphill lie is upper body dominated and it's important to let your arm swing follow the slope of the hill so that you finish with your hands high and behind your left ear. Once you reach this point, the momentum of your arm swing pulls you backward down the hill and you shouldn't try to stop it.

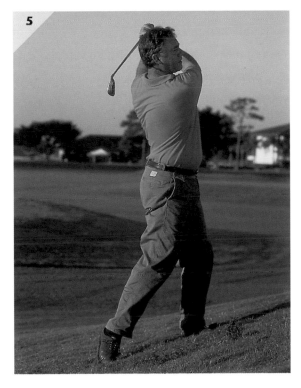

Summary
Uphill lies

1 Open your stance until your hips are level.

2 Flare your left foot.

3 Tilt your shoulders to match the slope, your right shoulder lower than the left.

4 Position the ball in the middle of your stance

5 Make a three-quarter swing and just concentrate on keeping your balance throughout the swing.

With your left foot drawn back from the target line the hips are now almost level, which helps the golfer keep his balance on a difficult slope. You can see that he has not allowed his open stance to open his shoulders; they are square to his target and angled with the slope.

Shot making

W hen you think about it, most of the golf you play is a deviation from the norm. You may hit only five regulation irons in a round of golf, while the rest, depending on your talent level, will be improvised shots, some higher than the norm to clear an obstacle, others curved on purpose to get to a protected target and still others bumped along the ground with no regard whatever for the aesthetics of the shot.

The golf course itself is a place specially designed to take us away from the norm. With its mounds, bunkers, wind and weather, it demands adjustments to the spin and trajectory of your shots. When you can make these adjustments on demand and in the proper context, you are demonstrating the art of golf—and what a true pleasure it is to be able to do this.

For the draw, your right forearm and hand are on top of your left with your right hand knuckles to the sky, indicating a full release of the hands and arms through the hitting zone with the toe of the club rotating over the heel. The club is tilted away from the target line with the club head pointing well left of the target.

To be a complete player you should know how to control the trajectory of your ball as well as how to draw and fade it (it's called "working the ball"), but even if you have not arrived at this level yet, understanding what causes your ball to spin left and right, stay low or fly high, will make you a better player and help you understand what is happening in your swing when your ball flight takes on these characteristics.

Why you need to work the ball

Usually for regular play and always for tournaments, pin placements are rotated from hole to hole so as not to favor a particular ball flight. There are some cups set toward the front of the green, some in the middle and back of the green, and some to the sides both left and right.

Off the tee there will be some straight holes, some that bend to the right and some that bend to the left.

Obviously if you can't curve the ball, they can "hide" a certain percentage of the pins from you

and you'll be going against a certain percentage of the doglegs. If you hit your shots from right to left, it's hard to get at pins which are tucked on the right edge of the green because it is dangerous to bring your shot in over the hazards that guard the greens. If all you can do is move the ball from left to right, the left pins are tough to get at, but when you can curve the ball both ways as well as control its trajectory you can get at any pin no matter how hidden it is.

The strategy for a full shot

For full swing shots, working the ball can be used to negotiate pins tucked behind bunkers and water hazards. Rather than aiming straight at the flag, and running the risk of landing in trouble with a pull or a push, aim at the center of the green, and configure your set up to move the ball toward the flag.

If your shot shape is correct, you'll knock it close; if you hit it straight, you're in the middle of the green and even if you pull your shot, the worst that you will have is a lag putt from the other side of the green.

When the flag is in the back of the green, aim for the middle of the green and bring your shot in low so it can run to the flag. When the flag is in the front of the green, aim for the center and bring your shot in high so it will either spin back to the pin or stay where it lands, giving you an achievable putt for your next shot.

For the fade, Els uses left hand control with very little forearm rotation at impact.

Imagine
your shot

Your mental image of the shot is of equal importance to the planning and technique of curving the ball. Images cue motor behavior and the more vivid and complete your image is, the more precise the cue. Great players use imagery for every shot. Chi Chi Rodriguez, a premier shot maker, explains that he "paints the portrait" of every shot in his mind before he hits it. Sam Snead, when asked how he curved the ball, said, "I just think fade or draw." Jack Nicklaus claims that he "goes to the movies" before every shot and sees the shot exactly as it should be before he swings. Seve Ballesteros and Greg Norman do much the same.

Thus rather than being paralyzed by too many swing thoughts, the great players cue up their muscles with the correct thoughts, and in no segment of the game is this more important than in the creative part of the game known as "working the ball."

The importance of the follow through

While it is important to image your swing as a whole (see it, feel it and even hear it), you should pay special attention to your follow through. While you never consciously try to curve the shot with your swing, you do need to have a very clear concept in your mind of your finish position before you swing (see the chart on page 101). For the draw finish, your club shaft points to the left of target; for the fade it points to the right. When you want a high shot, image a high finish; to keep your shot low, image a low finish.

The concept

The number one rule is that you work the ball with your set up and your follow through—not by manipulating your golf swing. First make the image of your shot, then take a practice swing which is a perfect rehearsal of the swing you want to make, focusing on your follow through.

As we've seen, what you think about your swing influences how you actually do it. If you want to fade the ball, set up for a fade and program your mind so that your swing is "on the way to a fade finish." Then, free from any in-swing manipulations, let your swing benefit from the geometry you established at address between your body, the club, the ball and your target, and simply swing through to the appropriate finish position. The same holds true for all the other specialty shots, including the draw and the high and low shots.

Shot making requires a variation from this perfectly "square" address geometry.

There are three lines you will use at address.

- **The target line**, a straight line from the target through your ball.
- The second is your **shoulder line**, a straight line connecting your shoulders.
- The third is the **intended line of flight**, a curved line that includes the line on which your ball starts its flight.

Adjust the ball position for the shot shape (see page 101) and aim your club face directly at the target using the target line as your guide. Without changing your club face aim, adjust your shoulders to the shape of the shot. Open shoulders for high, fading shots; closed for low, drawing shots. Check your grip pressure and swing down your shoulder line so your finish matches your shot shape.

The fade

To fade the ball, align your body to the left of the target with your club face pointing at the target. For your normal shots, your shoulders are parallel to the target line but for the fade they should be open, ensuring that when you swing on your shoulder line, your ball will start to the left of the target.

After starting left, your ball curves back to the target line due to an open club face at impact. This puts cut spin on your ball providing the curve you need to bend your shot. Remember that even though your club face is square to the target at address, it is open to your intended line of flight at impact. Your finish shows the effects of quiet hands and good body rotation through impact with your club shaft angled to the sky or even tilted toward the target line for maximum curve.

The draw

For the draw, everything is just the opposite of the fade. Aim your club face along the target line with your shoulders pointing right of the target in a closed position, parallel with your intended line of start.

From this set up if you make your normal swing along your shoulder line, your club face will be slightly closed at impact causing a soft draw that curves from right to left back to the target. Your finish reflects a fully released club head with it pointing left of the target.

Should you have to hit a major league slice or a hook, make only two additional adjustments. To hook the ball, instead of aiming your club face at the target, point it slightly to the left and close your shoulders more. For a slice, aim the club face to the right and open your shoulders more. With these simple adjustments you will magnify the amount of side spin you put on your ball.

The high shot

There are times when you have to hit the ball higher than you normally do. You might need to stop the ball softly on a hard putting surface or you might decide to take advantage of the wind behind you to hit an extra long drive. Most commonly, you will want the valuable high shot in your arsenal to loft your ball over obstacles such as trees or water.

As with the draw and fade, proper execution involves two elements: your image of the shot and the actual technique of setting up and finishing correctly.

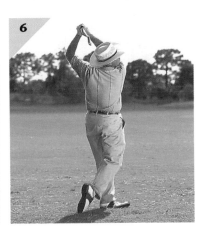

The image

For the high shot, picture your ball soaring over a tree back into the safety of the fairway. Feel the fullness of the motion in a practice swing. Hold your follow through a fraction longer to feel the high handed finish.

Finish high to hit it high

The key to this shot is a smooth swing followed by a full follow through with your hands well above your shoulders. But don't try for a longer backswing or you'll change your swing timing.

Move the ball forward about one ball width and tilt your upper body toward your back foot, feeling as if your right ear is over your right knee. With a short iron, be sure to aim straight at the target because it is tough to fade a short iron; otherwise aim to the left of your target expecting a fade. It's a dangerous shot because the ball is so far forward in your stance, making it easy to slide your body toward the target, so be sure to keep your spine stationary and turn your shoulders around it.

There's also a danger that in attempting to hit it high, you'll try to lift the ball into the air with your swing using only your arms and hands. Unfortunately, with no weight transfer your club will plow into the ground behind the ball, leaving it well short of target. Make a full chest turn away from the ball, without any lifting motion, then let the loft of your club face do its job to create the trajectory you want.

The low shot

When circumstances, such as wind or a low-hanging branch, force you to keep the ball low, the knock-down shot is the shot of choice. It produces what we call "soft distance", meaning that while the trajectory is that of a fast-moving, hard-to-stop long iron, the knock down actually comes into the target softly with some stopping power.

Play the ball one inch back of its normal position and choke down on the club. When you move the ball back, your club face and shoulders automatically align to the right of the target so open your stance to realign your shoulders to the target. This also moves your weight to your left side, and helps to reduce your backswing producing more control.

The swing itself is simply a three-quarter motion with the weight remaining on the left side throughout the entire motion. However, be sure to turn your left shoulder behind the ball or you'll slap at it with too steep a return swing, producing a higher shot than intended.

The image

To keep the ball low with control make the opposite modifications to those used for the high shot. Image the low trajectory you need as you make a practice swing that is safe and rhythmic. Avoid any images of chopping or punching. Then select two clubs more than you normally would but choke down on the club handle about two inches.

Finish low for the low shot

The general keys for the low shot lie in your swing rhythm and follow through. Most golfers hit the ball much too hard in this situation and the force of the blow drives the ball up in the air. Swing smoothly and finish with your hands, elbows and club head below your shoulders.

Grip pressures

These differ depending on the shot. Your hands control the club face, and how tightly you hold the club and the distribution of the pressure in both hands determines which hand has control at what point in your swing. Knowing how to adjust your grip pressure to match the type of shot you need is a major part of being able to work the ball.

■ **For a slice:** tighten your hold on the club in both hands but increase it the most in your left hand so you can pull your club through impact. Anytime you start your downswing by pulling toward the target with your left hand, you'll leave the club face open at impact, causing your ball to spin from left to right.

On a scale of one to ten, if your normal pressure is a three, ratchet your fade pressure up to a four in your right hand and a six in your left. The increased firmness in your hands discourages wrist action (cocking/un-cocking), and the more stiff-wristed your swing, the more likely you are to produce a fade.

■ **For a draw:** gear back to a two on your grip pressure index and loosen your left hand grip down to one. This will activate your wrists, giving them the flexibility to work the club face into a slightly closed position through the hitting zone, thereby resulting in a draw that moves away from the trouble.

■ **For a high shot:** relax the pressure in both hands and create an "oily" feeling in your wrists.

■ **To punch the ball low,** especially if the lie is bad, increase the grip pressure in both hands so that the club won't turn in your hands on contact.

SET UP	FADE	DRAW
BALL POSITION	Driver: opposite left toe Irons: opposite left heel	Driver: one ball-width back from left heel Irons: two ball-widths back from left heel
FOOT POSITION	Open: left heel 2" farther from target line than right, left foot flared out at 45-degree angle	Closed: right heel 2" farther from target line, left foot flared out 20 degrees
SHOULDER POSITION	Same as foot line	Same as foot line
CLUB FACE	Aimed at target	Aimed at target
GRIP PRESSURE	Firm with last three fingers of left hand; wrists fluid	Very soft with last three fingers of left hand; wrists fluid
SWING	Down shoulder / foot line	Down shoulder / foot line
FOLLOW-THROUGH	Club tilted toward target line	Club tilted away from target line
SWING IMAGES	Lee Trevino, Bruce Lietzke	Fuzzy Zoeller, Gary Player

SET UP	HIGH	LOW
BALL POSITION	Forward one ball width	Back one ball width
FOOT POSITION	Open	Closed
SHOULDER	Open	Closed
GRIP PRESSURE	Light / fluid wrists	Tight / firm wrists
FOLLOW THROUGH	High elbows and club head; club shaft body behind	Low elbows and club head; club shaft in front of body
IMAGE	Hitting into a cloud	Hitting under a tree limb

The long runner

Since the long runner spends a good deal of time on the ground, it is best played on a course with firm fairways and light rough so its roll won't be interrupted. Practice this shot on the driving range to get a feel for the amount of roll and learn to play it on your home course first, where you are familiar with the conditions.

When the surface of the green is hard, dry and unreceptive to even a well-struck iron, try the long runner if conditions permit.

Right: The perfect release for the long runner

When there's no obstacle, such as a bunker or water, blocking your access to the pin, the low running shot merits consideration. It has often been said that the European tour players have this shot in their bag whereas, except for a few US Tour players like Lee Trevino and Tom Watson, most Americans don't. The low runner can be played from many distances and under windy conditions it is almost essential.

You can figure that your shot will fly about half of the distance to your target in the air and roll on the ground for the other half. There is very little force exerted to hit this shot, with the club head speed coming from your body rotation and the unforced swinging of your arms.

To get the feel of the low runner, choose a mid-iron with the ball in the middle of your stance and pick a spot where you want your ball to land. Visualize it running from there to the pin and then take a practice swing that mimics the slowly paced two-quarter backswing you want for your actual swing. The end of your backswing comes when your left arm is parallel with the ground, and when you finish your swing it's your right arm that is parallel to the ground. In between, all you do is rotate back and through with no "hit" at impact.

You will notice that your right forearm has passed over your left, fully releasing your club head through impact. This action causes the toe end of your club to rotate counter-clockwise, imparting a slight right-to-left spin. The fact that you applied minimum force to the ball keeps it low, and because you've set your wrists, your ball has enough backspin to keep it airborne for half of its journey.

1

2

3

4

5

6

Caution

The long runner is a good shot to know but before you try it, make sure that it's not wet or sandy in the area where your ball will be on the ground. The other condition to check out is the direction and thickness of the grass in front of the green. If it's against you and a little shaggy, it will be too tough to judge the roll so opt for a shot with a higher trajectory that carries over the problem area.

161

The bump and run

When you're playing to an elevated green with minimum room between the pin and the edge of the green, instead of trying to loft the ball to the pin, you may have to use the bump and run if you want to get your shot close to the flag.

The technique

Position the ball about an inch back of center and use a seven iron, placing your hands ahead of the ball so the butt of the club is about even with the inside of your left thigh. Keep your weight on your target foot throughout and reduce your wrist action to almost zero, making your swing mostly with your arms and shoulders. Your goal is to hit the ball into the hill with a low trajectory that causes it to bounce upward, slowing its pace just enough so that it runs forward onto the green.

Granted that it's a tricky shot to judge but when you have to get your ball close under these conditions, it is the bump and run that should be the shot of your choice.

Move the ball back in your stance for the bump and run.

Use minimal wrist action to increase the accuracy of this shot.

1

2

3

4

5

6

The lob shot

The lob is last in the sequence of shot options that runs: "Putt it first, if you can't putt it, chip it, if you can't chip it, pitch it and only when conditions eliminate all of the others do you lob it." But even though the lob shot is the hardest of the short shots to judge, there are some situations where you have to play a high, ultra-soft shot to get to your target.

You can use this pitching technique from around the green when you want your ball to go up in the air for most of its flight so that it clears the trouble (bunkers, rough etc.), lands softly, and settles next to the pin with not much run. The lob requires a full-body motion much the same as your regular swing except that you cut way back on the power.

The
shoulder line

There is often confusion when the golfer is instructed to swing down the shoulder line from an open stance. As your shoulders rotate, your club rotates with them so that your club is always swinging on your shoulder line. In a misguided effort to follow this advice, many golfers simply take the club away on their shoulder line but fail to turn their shoulders. This forces them to chop down on the ball in a cut across motion. Or they snatch the club inside the shoulder line too quickly and force it to the outside on the downswing. Either way you are sure to shank the ball.

The lob *continued*

The loop

1 The key to the softness of the lob is that your power comes from the length of the arc. Your club head moves to the outside of the target line during the backswing, then back to the inside on the downswing on a looping path. When you swing your club back on your toe line, using mostly your arms, your club head will move to the outside of the target line because your body, including your feet, is aligned open to the target.

2 As you near the top of your swing, the momentum of your arm swing pulls your left shoulder toward the ball, rerouting your club head back toward your body so it can approach the ball on the shoulder line during the downswing.

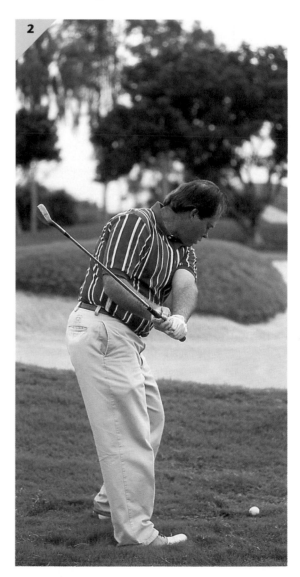

The lob shot technique

The image word for the lob is "syrupy" and your concept of the shot should be "full motion with minimum power." The key is to make a silky, flowing swing, moving the club face with the rotation of your body, with no manipulation by your arms or hands.

Since your body leads the way throughout your swing, your club head stays trapped behind you and is still open at impact exposing the bounce on the bottom of your sand wedge. Thus your club head has no other choice but to slide softly under the ball as you swing to a full finish.

Use a sand wedge or, if you carry one (and you should), a lob wedge. Aim your club face slightly to the right of your target to put both height and stopping spin on the ball. Position your hands even with your golf ball at address and play the ball off your left heel with the majority of your weight on your left side, distributed about 80:20. Once your club face is in position, align your body a bit left of the target to allow for a tad of left-to-right spin toward the hole. For increased height and spin, open your stance more and swing more aggressively down your shoulder line.

Remember this shot calls for a long, lazy swing so you don't have to concentrate on cocking your wrists—just relax your wrists and momentum will give you just the right amount of wrist set.

During your backswing, keep your weight in your left hip joint as your upper body rotates away from the target. On the downswing, the rotation of your body is led by your right knee as it leads your club head to the ball.

Your left shoulder moves toward the ball to some degree, i.e. your chest turns and your shoulders close relative to the target. Therefore to swing the club correctly on your shoulder line, your club must follow your shoulders as they turn during your backswing.

This is why your set up is so important. Your shoulders must be aligned left of the target (open) with your club face pointing at the target. This way your ball will start slightly left of the target with a soft, left-to-right spin.

"Long to long"

Your high arm swing results in a high finish emphasizing the fact that you are actually swinging your club from "long to long" when you hit the lob shot. A common mistake is to swing the club using a long backswing and a short, decelerated follow through. This "long to short" action either dumps the ball in the hazard you were trying to carry or you skull the ball over the green.

Because it's such a short shot your brain rebels at the idea of such a long swing—this is one reason why many golfers make a short, quick swing that ruins the shot. With this type of pitch the idea is to control the distance of your shot by the speed of your body turn, rotating both your upper and lower body at the same "easy does it" rate. To get your brain used to the timing of the shot, hit bunches of high, soft pitches on the driving range. Once you add this shot to your arsenal don't forget to hit a few before every round that you play.

Pitching

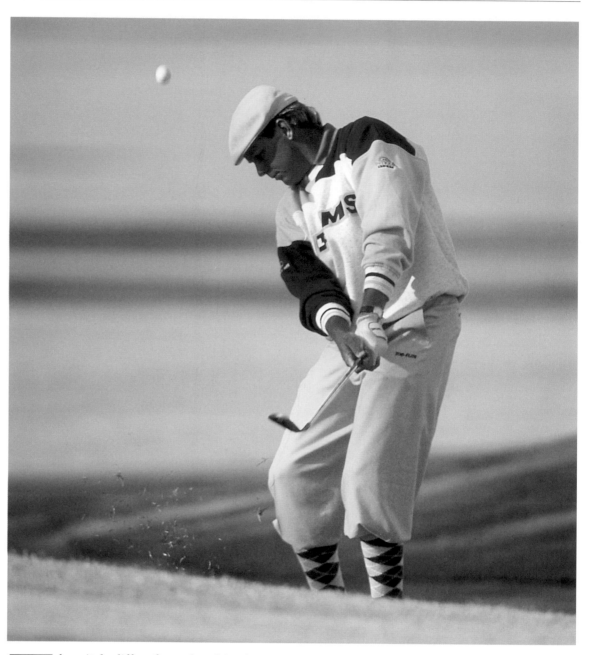

The pitch differs from the chip shot in that it requires more air time than ground time. While the chip is a stroke similar to the putt with no lower body action, the normal pitch is a swing, much like your full swing. The keys to good pitch shots are:

1   To set up correctly.
2   To allow the adjustments in your set up to

Two-time Major winner Payne Stewart shows a compact pitching motion with quiet hands, which are the key ingredients for a stylish, well-executed pitch.

dictate the shape and length of your swing.
3   To make a smooth rotating swing, which allows you to swing down your shoulder line.

The four absolutes for pitching

The first absolute

■ **Your club face always points at the target**

At address your club face must always point at the target. Note that there's a difference between body *alignment* and club face *aim* when the terms open and closed are used. For example, when your shoulders are open they point left of target, but when your club face is open, it points to the right of target. In this case, if your club face were pointing in the same direction as your shoulders (to the left of target), you'd pull your shot.

There are times in pitching when you need to either open or close your shoulder alignment and, since shoulder alignment affects club face aim, you should check your club face to make sure it's correct. When you open your shoulders your club face points to the left of target (closed) and for your pitch shot to go straight you need to adjust the club face until it points directly at the target. When your shoulders are closed, your club face points to the right of target (open) and you should close it until it looks directly at the target. It's only when your shoulders are parallel to the target line that your club face needs no adjustment because it already points at the target.

The second absolute

■ **The butt of the club points at the center line of your body**

At address the butt of the club should point toward the center line of your body. With the underhanded throwing motion of the pitch, the only way you can contact the ball on the center of your club face is to position your hands in the

middle of your body so that your club face "beats" the neck of your club to the ball. By keeping the butt of the club pointing at the center line, the effective hitting area of your club face is increased.

Unfortunately, too many golfers set their hands well ahead of the ball at address, unintentionally taking loft of the club face and losing the height they need for their pitch. Hands ahead also cause other problems with your pitch shots. They cause your club face to sit on its leading edge, making it impossible to use the bounce of your sand wedge correctly to slide under the ball.

You also run the risk of the necked shot because the neck of your club head is positioned ahead of the club face at address, "exposing" the hosel so that even a small error causes the dreaded shank.

▶ At address, the butt of the club points to the center of your body.

Distance
control factors

The distance you hit each shot is determined by three adjustments to your address position:

1 The length of the club (how much you grip down on it).

2 The width of your stance.

3 The openness of your stance.

How you arrange your body at address will determine how far you can comfortably swing the club back and through in balance and it is this motion that modifies the distance your ball travels.

The four absolutes for pitching *continued*

The third absolute

■ **The swing is of equal distance back and through**

How far you swing the club back determines how far you swing it through. The length of your backswing and throughswing should be a mirror image of each other. Maintaining the same length on both sides of the ball keeps you from adding any extra hit to it through impact. Acceleration of your club head takes place naturally due to the leverage created during your backswing and this combines with the effects of gravity and centrifugal force, give you the club head speed you need. That's why good pitchers of the ball look so smooth as the club swings back and through; they don't seem to "do" anything except get results.

What you don't see is the exercise of leverage supplying the power for a matching arm swing on both sides of the ball. Any time you try to add or subtract speed during your swing your balance is disrupted, making it hard to square your club face to the target at impact.

The fourth absolute

■ **The club swings along your shoulder line**

Your club should always swing along your shoulder line. Your body is designed so that, unless you prevent them, your arms follow the route taken by your shoulders as they rotate and, since your hands hold the club and are attached to your arms, the chain of movement that controls the club face is dominated by your shoulders.

When your shoulders swing to the left of target so will your club. When your shoulders are square to the target, your club swings down the target line, and when your shoulders are closed, the path of your club is to the right of the target line. On a normal pitch shot, with the ball in the middle of your stance, your shoulders should be parallel to the target line, regardless of the length of the shot. As you move the ball forward for a higher trajectory, your shoulders open, promoting an out-to-in club head path. As the ball moves back in your stance for the low shot, your shoulders point to the right of target, ensuring an in-to-out club head path.

An underhand throwing motion

When you throw a ball a short distance, your stance is narrow, with your hips facing the target. Your throwing motion is upper-body oriented with your arm swing in control generating the distance. As you need to throw the ball farther, the positioning of your body adjusts automatically to accommodate the length and velocity of your arm swing. These are the same distance principles that apply to the pitch shot.

Narrow, open and gripped down

The shorter the shot, the closer your feet are to one another. Any time you narrow your stance, your swing becomes restricted and more upper-body oriented, and this shortens the distance your ball flies. You should also open your stance to reduce the length of your backswing.

In addition to a narrow open stance, you shorten the distance of your pitch shot by choking down on the handle of your club.

Summary

To be a good pitcher of the ball apply no conscious "hit" to the ball. The pitch is made with a smooth swing, the force of which comes from the constant acceleration of your club head due to the length and leverage of your backswing. And the best way to control the length of your backswing is to make the following three key adjustments: change the length of the club by gripping down on it, open and then narrow your stance.

Thus, assuming that you don't over swing, a narrow, extremely open-foot configuration produces a very short shot. As you widen your stance and make it less open, you increase the length of your backswing, producing a longer shot.

Trajectory control

The trajectory is controlled by three factors:

1 The force of the blow to the ball.

2 Ball position.

3 The squareness of your club face at address.

How hard you hit the ball is determined by the length of your swing, with no attempt to create distance through manipulation of your hands and arms. The longer your swing, the faster your club head moves through impact, increasing the height of your shot.

The farther forward (toward your left foot) that you position the ball in your stance, the higher and softer the shot will fly. The farther back you position the ball, the lower and more rolling the shot will be. So to hit a high soft shot you must position the ball forward in your stance; to hit normal shots the ball should be positioned in the center of your stance; and to produce low, running shots, you move the ball back in your stance.

Opening your club face increases the loft and bounce of the club, producing high trajectories. Closing your club face has the opposite effect.

Choosing the right trajectory

To choose the trajectory you need for your shot, analyze the relationship between the amount of fairway or rough you must fly the ball over versus the distance between the edge of the green and the hole. If the area you need to fly the ball over is less than the amount of green you have to work with, then your shot should be low and running.

If the area you need to fly the ball over is greater than the amount of green you have to work with, then the shot is more lofted. If they're about equal, your shot selection is a standard pitch.

Always choose the least lofted shot possible because a rolling ball is easier to judge.

1 For a higher trajectory, move the ball forward in your stance and open your club face.

2 For a lower shot, position the ball back in your stance and close your club face.

Trajectories

Low trajectory

$^1/_4$ $^3/_4$

Standard trajectory

$^1/_2$ $^1/_2$

High trajectory

$^3/_4$ $^1/_4$

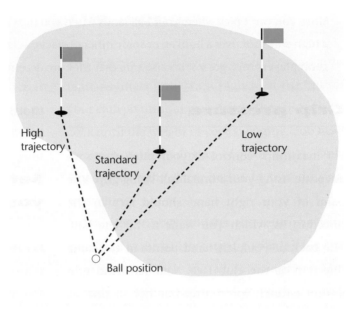

High trajectory

Standard trajectory

Low trajectory

Ball position

	Standard trajectory Ball centered	**High trajectory** Ball forward	**Low trajectory** Ball back
Short distances ■ Narrow stance ■ Open left toe even with right heel	 Target line Heel line		
Medium distances ■ Medium stance ■ Open left toe even with right arch	 Arch line		
Longer distances ■ Wider stance ■ Open slightly. Left toe even with ball of right foot	 Ball of foot line		

Chipping

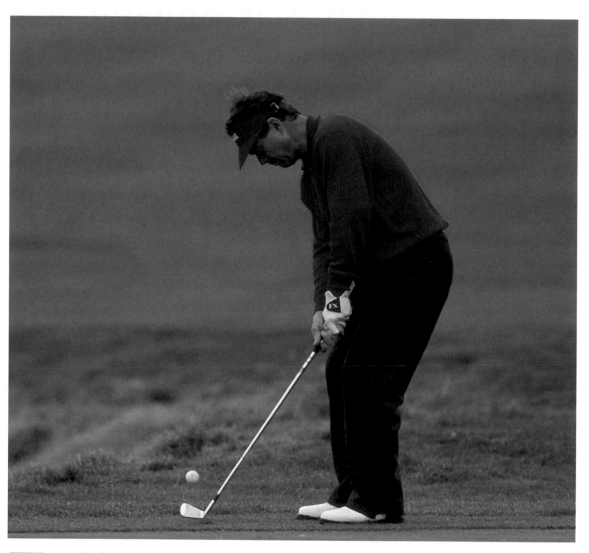

E ven the best pros in the world miss on average about six greens a round yet they manage to shoot par or better, so it's obvious that how you handle the close shots from just off the green plays a major role in how well you score. Here's the rule of thumb for these sometimes awkward little shots. Ask yourself two questions: first "Should I use my putter?" and "If not, can I use my putting stroke with another club?"

Obviously you shouldn't use your putter when the conditions are against you, e.g. if the grass through which your ball must roll is too long or

Tom Watson's low club head and firm left wrist throughout the stroke are keys to good chipping.

if there is a hazard in the way. That's a judgment call and your scores will reflect the quality of your decision. However, if you can roll the ball smoothly, without having to take too big a backswing with your putter, do so. The reasons for this guideline are two-fold. Firstly, it's easier to judge the distance of a rolling ball than a ball that spends most of its time in the air.

Secondly, problems with accuracy increase as the club head rises during the backswing, i.e. swings vertically upward, because the higher the club head, the harder it is to return it correctly at impact. This is why it's not always a good idea to use your wedge on short shots or your putter on the long ones.

A properly executed putting stroke (with any club) keeps the club head low to the ground, and with this predominantly horizontal path in relation to the ground, you increase the chances of making dead center contact at impact. The advantage of contacting the ball on the sweet spot of your club face is that solid contact minimizes twisting of the club face, giving you an accurate roll.

While you can't always use your putter due to the length of the shot and/or the terrain, your next choice is to chip the ball using the club with the least loft so that it lands safely on the green. This allows your shot to hug the ground and take advantage of the accuracy of a rolling ball.

The concept

The key concept for chipping is that a chip shot is merely a putt with a lofted club. The chip, as an extension of your putting stroke, is an offensive weapon that can keep your scores from soaring even though you're missing the greens. A chip shot played correctly provides an opportunity to hole out and, if you don't, you should leave yourself an easy putt.

The chip shot is used from five yards and in from the edge of the green. It's a low running shot with minimum flight time and maximum roll that lands about one yard onto the green and rolls to the hole like a putt.

In this chapter, you'll learn the flight-to-roll ratio that gives you the correct club for every situation, depending on the amount of flight and roll required for each shot. Regardless of the iron selected, by adapting it to function as much like your putter as possible, you can use the same pendulum motion for chipping that you do when putting.

▶ For effective, accurate chipping, you should turn your iron into a putter.

The concept *continued*

Turning an iron into a putter

There are three adjustments you should make that allow an iron to perform like your putter.

1   Raise your club on its toe to make the shaft upright like your putter. Just as in putting, this moves you closer to the ball with your eyes over the target line. However, raising any club on its toe aims the face to the right so to offset this, turn the club face in slightly until the top line of your club is perpendicular to the target line. This "toed in" position not only squares the club face to the target but also minimizes the destructive side spin that an open face imparts at impact.

When your club head is on its toe, use a pendulum motion for chipping to keep your club on the target line. Another advantage is that there is less surface on the bottom of your club head to catch in the grass so the club face remains square even if you hit a little behind the ball. If your club was fully soled, you'd pull your shot because the heel would dig in, twisting your club face to the left.

2   Grip down on your club until it matches the length of your putter. It is likely that you'll grip all the way down on your long irons and progressively less on the shorter irons to keep the length consistent with your putter. This not only allows you to bend until your eyes are over the line but also promotes maximum control. Your "chip grip" is actually your putter grip with your palms facing each other and the club handle positioned high in your palms to discourage wrist hinging.

3   Once you have turned your iron into a putter, use exactly the same type of stroke: a pendulum-style, shoulder-controlled motion, with minimal lower body movement and no wrist action.

The set up

The goal of your set up is to reduce side spin and excessive loft, both of which are the enemies of roll. The optimum chipping motion is one that creates over spin for a shot with minimum side spin and maximum roll. In this regard, one of the most important adjustments to reduce side spin and keep loft consistent is a grip that takes your wrists out of the stroke. The correct grip allows your arms to swing freely from the shoulder joints so your club moves down the target line with no opening or closing of the club face, and no addition of loft. Thus to be a good chipper, the loft you had at address is the loft you arrive with at impact.

Quiet *hands*

Producing the right distance is much easier with quiet hands. Any time that wrist action is involved in the stroke, you add a speed producer and that affects your touch.

1

2

The hands stay quiet back and through the chipping motion (left). If your wrists flip (as shown below), you'll add loft to the club head and inaccuracy to your chip shots.

3

Finish like *you start*

Perhaps the most common fault in chipping is stopping the left arm just before impact. No matter how good your intentions are to have quiet hands as you chip, your hands become activated as soon as your arms stop. On the way back to the ball, your club head gathers momentum and, unless you keep your arms moving, the force in your club head pushes it past your hands, causing your left wrist to collapse. This changes the effective loft on the club face, so you could start a swing with 48 degrees and finish with 52 degrees, not a good technique if getting up and down is the game plan.

The set up *continued*

Stance width

In order to produce the necessary loft to carry the ball over the fringe you'll need to make some adjustments to your set up. Since the stroke motion requires no lower body action, your stance width is narrow. As in putting, not only is lower body movement unnecessary to the stroke motion but it is also detrimental. You won't have time for a weight transfer and you certainly don't need the power it provides.

Open stance

In chipping, you want to hit the ball with a descending blow, so place 80 percent of your weight on your left foot. Drop your left foot back from the target line and let your weight settle naturally into your left hip. This distribution anchors your lower body and encourages your weight to start, stay and finish on the left side.

Ball position

The ball is played opposite the inside of your right foot, with your hands positioned off the left thigh. With your weight on your left side, you easily produce the proper angle of attack, a naturally descending motion, without trying to "hit down" on the ball. With the ball so far back in your stance, your shoulders close, so draw your left foot back from the target line (opening your stance) until your shoulders arrive at the necessary square address position.

Distance from the ball

While the distance you stand from the ball depends on your body build, you should stand close enough so that your eyes are over the target line and your arms hang freely, straight down from your shoulders. The ball is played close to your feet, generally about six inches away. This puts the club's shaft in a vertical position that promotes a pendulum stroke. Set your hands well ahead of the ball, inclining your club shaft until it points to your left shoulder.

The stroke

Once you've set up correctly, your backswing is all shoulders and arms, without any hand or wrist action. Your shoulders control the stroke in both directions just as they do in the putting stroke. Throughout the chipping motion, your lower body stays quiet but not rigid. Actually, on longer chip shots you will need some turn so your arms can swing freely without bumping into your sides, but what movement there is should be reactive.

The proper chipping motion should be quite similar to your putting stroke: a wristless, shoulder-controlled motion with minimal lower body movement.

Even though your ball is in the chipping zone (inside five yards from the edge of the green) don't automatically assume you should chip the ball. The position of the hole relative to your target line may require you to pitch the ball. You may be two steps from the nearest part of the green but if you walk along your target line in the direction of the hole, the landing area may be nine steps from your ball. In this situation you'll need to pitch the ball to get the necessary loft and height to stop the ball quickly.

Flag A: although the ball is only a couple of yards off the green, you cannot chip to the flag because the landing area is 8 yards away, a pitch shot.
Flag B: 2 over 6 reduces to 1 over 3 (1 part flight and 3 parts roll); 3 from 12 is a nine iron.
Flag C: 2 over 10 reduces to 1 over 5 (1 part flight and 5 parts roll); 5 from 12 is a seven iron.

The advantages *continued*

The two variables

In addition to the two constants, there are two variables: the distance the ball flies in the air and the distance the ball rolls to the hole. To determine the club for the shot, calculate the ratio (or proportion) of flight to roll.

The flight-to-roll ratio

Once you've determined the line of your chip shot, you've automatically identified your first constant because your landing area is always on that line, one yard from the edge of the green. Now pace off the number of steps from your ball to the landing area. This determines your first variable: the amount the ball flies.

Keeping your stride width consistent, next pace off the distance from your landing area to the hole to determine your second variable: the amount the ball rolls. You now have enough information to calculate the flight-to-roll ratio using some simple arithmetic. All you do is create a fraction with your flight time on the top and your roll time on the bottom. Then reduce the fraction to 1 over the appropriate number. For example, the ratio of 5 steps of flight time over 15 steps of roll time, reduces to 1 over 3, one part flight and three parts roll.

The next step is to subtract the denominator (3) from the constant "12" to identify your chipping club, which in our example is a nine iron.

If the ratio isn't easily reducible, adjust the denominator to the nearest number that gives you a ratio that's easy to calculate in your head. Thus 3 over 13 would be adjusted to 3 over 12. You should also adjust the club depending on the slope of the green:

■ Chipping uphill: add roll by choosing a five rather than a six iron.

■ Chipping downhill: subtract roll by going from a six to a seven iron.

Keep in mind that the object of walking off the distance of your flight and roll is not to come up with an exact measurement. You are simply trying to find the proportion (or ratio) between the amount your ball needs to fly and the amount it needs to roll. Rarely will a situation present itself where, for example, your ball is precisely three yards from your landing area and then exactly nine yards to the hole. The proportion between the two is what's important, and that concept should guide you as you use your logic to adjust the numbers.

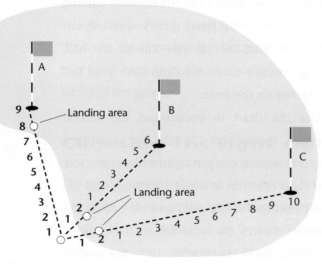

The three stages of learning

This method may seem complicated at first but with a little practice it becomes second nature. We've taught thousands of students, with excellent results, and you learn it in three stages.

■ In the first stage, you actually walk off the distances and do the calculations.

■ In the second stage, you've become so used to measuring the distances that your eyes take over and you no longer have to walk off the distances. You see every chip as one part flight and so many parts roll, and the ratio is automatic, based on your experience and practice.

■ In the last stage, all the calculations as well as the club selection are done subconsciously, so you simply evaluate the shot and reach for the correct club.

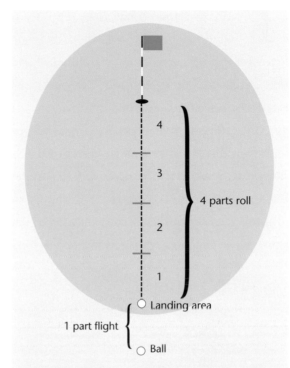

4 parts roll

Landing area

1 part flight

Ball

Eventually, you'll see every chip as one part flight with so many parts roll, and simply subtract the roll from 12 to get the correct iron.

Standardize *your stride*

Although your step doesn't have to be exactly one yard in length for our method to work (they must be consistent in length though), it's a good idea to match your stride to a yard, or a meter, since you'll be pacing off distances all over the course to determine your distance from the green. Use a tape measure and lay out ten yards. Then, using your normal stride, count how many steps you take within the ten-yard area. If you count twelve steps, for instance, a 20 percent error, adjust the length of your stride by making your steps longer until it matches the measurement of ten yards. That's your "golf stride" and it's usually longer than your normal stride.

Chipping drills

1 Path

Chip between two shafts to keep the path of your club head straight back and through. Lay two shafts parallel to each other to create a four-inch wide pathway to the green. Place a ball in the center of the path and practice hitting chips to the green. Make sure that the club head travels down this pathway in the straight back, straight through motion of the proper chipping stroke.

2 Wrist

Place a three iron under your left arm with the club head in the air and the grip end pointing toward the ground. Join the three iron grip to the grip of a five iron that you'll be chipping with, and hold both clubs with a putting grip. Chip a ball, and if your wrists are inactive the three iron shaft will finish away from your body. If you stop your arm swing through impact and use your wrists to hit the ball, the shaft of the three iron will hit your ribs, giving you feedback about your improper technique.

3 Weight

Using your right toe for balance only, hit chip shots with your right heel raised off the ground and the majority of your weight on your left side. Keeping your weight on your left side ensures that contact with the ball is made with a descending motion. If your wrists are too active, then check your finish position. If your weight is on your right side, you're forced to flip your wrists in order to get your club head "under the ball."

Putting

The key to scoring in the game of golf is your play from inside 100 yards. This is where 64 percent of all golf shots are taken yet it is probably the most overlooked and under-practiced part of the game. The short game is often perceived as boring and not as "macho" or as exhilarating as giving the ball a hard whack with your driver. However, a good short game is the great equalizer, giving players of all abilities the opportunity to save strokes. By learning and utilizing a few fundamentals, and knowing which shots have the highest percentage of success in each situation, you can become a "scorer" as well as a player.

It is not an exaggeration to say that the majority of golfers prefer practicing with their driver instead of their putter even though, during the average round of golf, you employ your driver about 14 times while the putter is in your hands over 40 percent of the time. There is no question that the quickest way to lower your scores is to hole more putts.

Putting seems easy: the ball sits on what appears to be a finely manicured surface, with no obstacles, such as bunkers or water hazards, in the way. The hole is 4.25 inches wide while the ball is only about 1.68 inches around its circumference, so there's plenty of room for it in the cup. And the stroke itself is relatively short and simple, making physical strength a non factor. Thus the putting green is truly egalitarian, a place where players are separated only by their talent and their grit. However, whereas putting is an art that almost defies analysis, there are fundamentals that can make you a better putter.

The fundamentals of putting

By simply clapping your hands in front of you, you will learn three very important things about putting.

Although many styles have been successful, the modern pendulum motion keeps the putter face on line well past impact. Here Ernie Els demonstrates why he is a world-class player.

1   When you clap your hands they come together as a unit with your palms facing one another—it's the same when you grip the putter. Even though your hands are separated, your palms face each other so that your hands work as a unit—where the palm of your right hand faces so also does the back of your left hand. When your right palm points at the target, your putter faces down the target line.

2   When you clap your hands you also learn where the ball should be positioned in your stance. Since your hands meet naturally in the center of your body, all you have to do is grip your putter and bend from your hip joints until your putter head touches the ground. You'll find that in this position, the handle of your putter points to the center of your body. For the correct ball position, simply locate the ball just in front of your putter head and you will have identified the bottom of your swing arc.

3   And lastly, when you clap your hands you learn about the putting stroke itself. Note that in order to arrive together in the middle of your chest, each hand moves at an even, *pendulum-like* pace. This balance is what you want in your putting stroke so that your putter travels back and through without any attempt to increase or decrease its speed.

Putting technique

Once you are committed to the principles of the pendulum stroke, the first step to a consistent putting stroke is aiming your putter face correctly and properly aligning your shoulders and eyes to the target. How your club face is angled at impact determines the direction in which the ball deflects; where your shoulders point controls the direction in which your arms swing and therefore the path your club head follows; and it's your eye alignment that influences the path of your shoulders.

The set up

1   Set your putter directly behind the ball so that it is square to the target.

2   Next align your shoulders parallel left of the target line. A closed position at address (your shoulders pointing to the right of the target) causes your putter head to swing on an inside-to-out path that results in a putt pushed to the right. When your shoulders are open at address, your path is outside-to-in and the ball rolls to the left of target. Ideally, in the correct stroke, your putter moves along the target line as long as possible, both back and through the ball.

3   When you grip the putter, allow your hands to hang down comfortably so that they are directly below your shoulders. This puts your arms and hands in position for a straight back and through stroke. When your hands are positioned incorrectly, either outside or inside your shoulders, they try to get back under your shoulders as you swing, disrupting the path of your putter. When your hands are too close to your body, you will cut across the ball because your putter path is outside to in. When your hands are too far away from your body, your club head moves back inside the target line with the face open, closing on the through stroke. It is square for only an instant.

Eyes over *the ball*

Bend forwards until your eyes are directly over the ball. To locate the target, you need only rotate your head instead of disrupting your eye line by lifting your head. Since your visual system is a strong determiner of how your muscles move, your putting stroke follows your eye alignment—in essence, you putt where you look. How you position your eyes at address affects the alignment of your putter head.

■ With your eyes outside your target line, you will see the hole as being left of where it really is and you'll miss a well-stroked putt to the left.

■ With your eyes inside the target line, you'll mis-aim to the right, leaving a correctly putted ball to the right of the cup.

The putting stroke

There are two motions in golf: a swing motion and a stroke motion.

■ The swing motion is lower body oriented with plenty of wrist action, both of which combine to produce power. This motion is used for long shots.

■ The stroke motion is upper body oriented and does not use any wrist action. This motion is used in putting and chipping where accuracy is at a premium and only minimal force is needed. Therefore, in the stroke motion you grip the club in a way that quietens your hands.

Set your hands on the club with your palms facing each other, square to the target line. Place the grip of the putter in the life line of your left hand to eliminate wrist action. The back of your left hand and the palm of your right hand face the target with your thumbs on top of the handle. You gain feel from your thumb and index finger so, by putting your thumbs on top of the shaft, you put your "feelers" in position to work for you.

The stroke motion

While your hands move as a unit you can understand how each one coordinates with the other as follows: to feel the correct motion of your left hand take your normal putting stance, then place your right hand on your left shoulder. With no backswing, simply push the ball toward the hole using only your left hand to operate the putter. This drill will help you understand the relationship between the back of your left hand and the putter face because you must keep the back of your left hand facing your target throughout the stroke for the ball to roll accurately.

After hitting a few of these "push putts", add your right hand to the club but keep your fingers

open and extending down the shaft so that your palm faces the target. Use your right palm to push the ball toward the target, focusing on how your right palm exerts energy through the face of your putter in the direction of the target. As in other sports (for example, dribbling a basketball), the direction in which you exert energy is always the direction your palm is facing.

> **Note:** there's a key angle created when you place your right hand on the putter. Your right wrist bends backward slightly toward your forearm. Many successful putters keep this angle intact through impact to prevent over-use of their hands.

The stroke itself

Your stroke utilizes the top of your spine as the anchor point around which your shoulders rock. This point remains stationary as the triangle formed by your shoulders and arms moves like a see-saw. The triangle must maintain its shape throughout the stroke with the distance between the elbows constant, ensuring that the bottom of the putting arc also remains constant.

The stroke itself is very similar to the swinging motion of the pendulum in a grandfather clock. This stroke works well on all types of putting surfaces and is most effective with a center-shafted putter.

Greg Norman's shoulders have rotated around the top of his spine, which is the basic fundamental of the modern putting motion.

Your *forearms*

In addition to quiet hands, you should arrange your forearms so they operate as a unit. Your left forearm should be directly in front of the putter shaft and your right forearm directly behind it. Your forearms are level with neither forearm higher nor lower than the other.

Your *knees*

Bend your knees until your weight is on your heels, pinching your knees toward each other to eliminate any lower body movement during your putting stroke. One of the differences between a stroke and a swing is that in the stroke, there's no lower body action.

Your *feet*

Position your feet equidistant from the target line and parallel left to that line. Your stance width varies according to comfort and your body build but at least 60 percent of your weight should be solidly on your left side and it should stay there as you putt.

The
pendulum stroke

The principles of the pendulum stroke as follows— acceleration without effort, force without manipulation. Never add or subtract any energy from your putting stroke. As in the full swing, you'll do your best putting when there is more of physics and less of you involved in the stroke— more let and less make.

The best way to putt is to forget about trying to manipulate the putter and simply let the principles of the pendulum putting stroke work for you. With the correct pendulum motion there is no conscious "hit" yet your club face is accelerating at impact with the face square to the target line. If you let the image of the pendulum be in control, where the arc on one side of the low point is equal to the arc on the other, your putting stroke naturally finds the correct length and force.

The putting stroke *continued*

The pendulum stroke

A lot has been said about accelerating the putter head through impact. While it is true that your club head is moving faster at the lowest point of its arc due to gravity, when you try to add speed to your putter, the heel beats the toe to the ball, leaving the club face open. The opposite happens when you force yourself to make a long and stylish back stroke. The odds are that you will over-do it and swing back too long, forcing you to slow down your putter as it approaches the ball, which tends to shut the club face, allowing the toe of your putter head to pass the heel.

The basics of putting

1 Hold your club in the life line of your left hand with your palms facing each other, square to the target.

2 Aim your club face square to the target, and sole your putter head directly behind the golf ball.

3 Align both eyes down the target line. Position your dominant eye over the ball.

4 Align your shoulders parallel to the target line.

5 Position your hands directly beneath your shoulders.

6 Set your feet parallel left to the target line, pinching both knees toward each other with your weight on your heels.

7 Maintain your forearms on the same plane parallel to each other.

8 Point the butt of your club at the middle of your spine.

9 During your takeaway, allow your left shoulder to work under as your right shoulder works up so that your shoulders control the stroke like a see-saw.

10 Maintain a constant distance between your elbows while you putt.

11 Keep your head still while you putt.

12 Maintain the angle of your right wrist throughout the stroke.

Putting strategy

Preparation plays an important role in the success or failure of every putt. On the greens, you must first study (read) your putt to determine the amount of break, the slope and how much speed you'll need.

Reading the greens

Always make your initial read from behind the hole looking back down the target line to your ball. From here you will see the general direction of the break. Give special attention to the area around the hole because the effect of the break is more pronounced as your ball slows down. Also check your line for ball marks, pebbles and anything else that might knock your ball off line.

Once you have established the dominant break, move to the low side of the putt to determine the amount of slope and its inclination. When you stand on top of a mountain and look down at the valley, it looks flat but when you stand at the base of the mountain and look up, you can see the slope and inclination. Take care to stand equidistant from the ball, target line and the cup in order to maintain your perspective. This triangulation gives you a much truer reading.

Your final read is from behind the ball. Here, determine your line and select the spot (as in bowling) to roll your ball over. Also, in lining up behind the ball, stand on the line on which you want your ball to start. For straight putts, this is the target line, but to give you the proper perspective for a putt that curves, stand on the curved line or arc of the putt—not on the target line.

The drill below develops the see-saw motion of your shoulders. Place a club shaft under both arms just above your elbows. If your stroke is correct, the shaft works up and down like a see-saw, parallel to the target line. If your stroke is incorrect, the shaft works around your shoulders and points well left of target upon completion of the stroke.

Putting strategy *continued*

Reading the greens

Good putting also requires reading the grain. The direction in which the grass grows, or what is commonly referred to as grain, affects the distance and direction of your putt.

When you are practicing, you can test the grain by lightly dragging your putter across the grass. If the grass stands up, you've scraped your putter against the grain; if it stays down, you are with the grain. When you're playing, the rules of golf don't permit you to test the green in this manner, but you can test the collar or apron of the green without penalty. Just make sure it's the same kind of grass as the putting surface before you include the information in your reading.

Grain affects both the curve and speed of your putt. Putting directly against the grain slows your putt down; putting with the grain adds speed. If the grain runs across the line of your putt in the same direction as the slope of the green, it increases the break as the ball slows down. Note that side-grain slows down your putt almost as much as putting straight into the grain.

Tropical climate grasses, such as Bermuda, grow westward toward the setting sun. The characteristically thick, coarse Bermuda grows in an upward swirl and its grain is strong and influential on the speed and direction of your putts. The finer-leafed grasses, such as Bent, lie down and grain is not a major factor. This type of grass is common in cooler climates and what little grain it has often grows toward the natural water supply.

When the sun shines on a green you can judge the direction of the grain by the appearance of the grass. If the grass looks dark and dull, the grain is growing toward you. If the grass looks shiny, the grain is growing away from you.

Which type of putt?

Now that you have read the green, you are ready to decide which type of putt is called for. There are three ways to make a putt.

- You can "die" the ball into the cup, so that its last roll barely carries it over the edge as it falls into the cup.
- You can "send" the ball into the cup at the optimum speed. Here, the ball contacts the backside of the metal cup about halfway down.
- You can "firm" the ball into the cup, where every putt is played as a straight one and the ball strikes the dirt on the back of the hole, just above the metal cup.

One advantage of the "dying" putt is that there are "three entrances" that your slowly moving ball can use to fall into the cup: the front of the cup and the two sides. Another advantage is that if you miss, your ball always finishes next to the hole. However, there are also some disadvantages. With a slight miscalculation, the dying putt won't get to the cup. And, because of its slow speed, the break is increased and the ball is easily knocked off line by the imperfections in the green. The "dying" putt is best utilized for long putts, putts with a lot of break, downhill putts and/or when the greens are so fast you must "cozy" your putt up to the hole.

When your ball rolls across a putting surface the major influence on its direction is the slope of the green. Sometimes any contours are difficult to see but an understanding of how an architect designs a putting green helps you to evaluate the effect of slope more accurately. A well-designed putting surface has drainage patterns that draw water off to the sides away from the center of the green. In general, you can expect swales to channel the water away from the bunkers and toward the ponds and lakes. Changes in grass color surrounding the green and damage from past accumulations of water are also clues to how the drainage flows.

The advantages of the "firm" putt are that it eliminates the break and, because of its speed, it holds its line despite imperfections on the green. The disadvantages are that the size of the hole is effectively reduced because the ball is moving too fast to sneak in the sides of the cup and, if it misses the hole, you'll have some work left on your next putt. This type of putt is most effective on short uphill putts.

The "optimum speed" putt does not have any disadvantages. The hole is its true size, the break and imperfections are minimized, the ball always gets there and, if it rolls by the hole, you get information about your next putt by watching the break. If you miss the optimum speed putt, the ball only travels a short distance past the hole.

The optimum speed as calculated by Dave Peltz, the American putting expert, carries your ball about 17 inches past the hole. Remember that the tour professionals who offer the advice to "die" the ball in the hole, play on perfect greens but for most amateurs, the greens are bumpy, the cups are crowned and located on slopes. If you hit a "dying" putt under these conditions it can be knocked off line or mis-directed by the crown of the cup.

Short putting

On short putts, the "never up-never in" theory applies. You should keep this philosophy in mind on any putt that you feel you can make, and it should be a normal, built-in part of your putting strategy. Being aggressive on these putts not only assures that your ball will reach the target but also makes it less susceptible to the effects of spike marks and foot prints around the cup.

When you can see into the hole from your address position, pick a spot on the back of the cup liner and putt to it. This increases your accuracy by forcing you to focus on a smaller target, one you can miss and still make the putt.

191

Avoid making unnecessary changes in your putting stroke just because you miss some putts. A high percentage of your misses are due to imperfections on the putting surface, such as footprints, spike marks, etc. Research shows that over the course of a year, the average tour professional misses 53 percent of putts from six feet. This tells you two things:

1 Keep your expectations realistic in order to preserve both your putting stroke and your self image.

2 Get the ball closer than six feet with your chips, pitches and lag putts.

Most good lag putters don't use the "three-foot circle" theory, and we don't recommend it. Good putters try to hit the ball into the hole, not three feet from it. From a long distance it is easy to leave your putt three feet short of where you want it to stop and, if you miss the three-foot circle by that much, you are six feet from the hole.

Lagging

Lagging a very long putt into one-putt range is a special skill. Conventional wisdom advises golfers to aim their approach putts into a three-foot circle around the cup, but when the pin is on a slope, as is often the case, not all "three footers" are equal. If you have played any golf at all, you know that three footers from above the hole or from a side slope can be score wreckers.

With this in mind, try to make it, but if it does not go in, your approach should be directly below the hole so you can confidently stroke your next putt straight back up the hill into the cup. When your task is to lag your ball down in two, where you putt from on your second putt is as important as how well you stroke it.

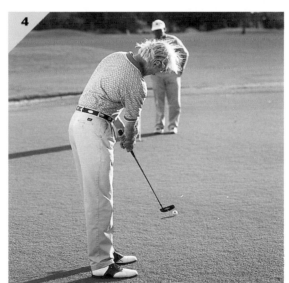

Find the sweet spot on your putter and mark it, because good putting requires solid contact and this comes from hitting the sweet spot. Note that a putter's sweet spot is not necessarily in the exact center of the blade. You can find it as follows: using only your thumb and index finger, suspend your putter so that it hangs vertically. Tap the face of the putter with a golf ball so that it swings back and forth. When the blade goes straight back with no side-to-side movement or twisting, that's your sweet spot. Then mark it with some paint.

For long putts, have a friend attend the flag stick so that you're not searching for the hole when you take your last look at the target. You'll have better depth perception if he stands behind the hole.

Tip: a tip that will help your lag putting is to strike the ball solidly by concentrating on a dimple on the back of the ball so that your head stays *still* until your ball is well under way. Off-center hits leave you that "nettlesome" six-foot distance, so after you've figured out the distance and the break, focus on solid contact.

Pre-shot routine

When you have chosen your line and decided on the type of putt you're going to hit, take a practice stroke next to your ball, looking at the hole, to program your mind for the distance of the putt. By doing this your eyes register the distance to the target and your brain calculates how much energy is required. For an uphill putt, take your practice stroke further from the hole than your ball lies to account for the added force you'll need because of the slope. If it is a downhill putt, stand closer to the hole to program hitting the putt easier.

Next, take another practice stroke, this time looking at the ball, and then slide your putter forward so that the sweet spot is directly behind the ball.

Set your feet in position and look down the line to the hole counting one; bring your eyes back to the ball on two; draw the putter back on three; and through to the ball on the count of four. Your goal, using the count of one, two, three, four, is to eliminate any need to think about putting mechanics. Once you ingrain this routine, your stroke will be automatic.

1

2

3

Putting drills

The purpose of doing drills is to repeat the feeling of the skill you're trying to learn and, once the new motion is perfect, to over-ride old habits through repetition and reinforcement. Here are some drills that will help you to perfect your putting stroke once you know what you should be doing when you stroke a putt.

Look at the hole drill

Take your stance and simply stroke your putt while looking at the hole instead of your ball. This will help you to stay focused on your target instead of thinking too much about the mechanics of your stroke.

Three shaft drill

Place three shafts on the green at ten-foot intervals from your ball. Putt your first ball to the shaft furthest from you, approximately 30 feet away. Putt the second ball to the middle shaft, 20 feet away. Putt the third ball to the shaft closest to you, about 10 feet away. When playing, you're always faced with different distance putts and this drill helps you to adapt quickly.

Ladder drill with tee

Mark your starting position with a tee 12 inches from the hole and hit three putts. If you hole all three, move away from the hole another six inches so you're 18 inches from the hole. As long as you make three out of three putts at each tee, progress in increments of six inches farther from the hole. If you make fewer than three out of three, return to the previous tee. Having to make all three putts before you advance simulates the pressure of putting out on the course.

Square club face drill

Find a flat area on the putting green about 10 feet from the cup. Position a ball with a stripe around its equator so the stripe points directly down the target line. Stroke the ball to the hole and observe the rotation. If your putter face is square to the target line and you've made a good stroke the stripe will revolve end over end with very little wobble.

Ladder drill

The object of this drill is to develop your feel for distance. Place five balls on the putting green. Putt the first ball five feet and, without looking up, putt the second ball 10 feet. Continue with the remaining balls, spacing them five feet apart. Doing this drill helps you to feel the amount of shoulder motion you need to create each distance.

Pendulum driver drill

Place the grip end of your driver against your stomach about four inches below your sternum. Slide your hands down the shaft to match the length of your putter and align your forearms with the grip end of the shaft. Bend from the hips until your driver soles on the ground. Make your putting stroke keeping the butt of the grip in your stomach and feel your arms and shoulders stroke the ball without any flipping of your wrist. This drill is great for eliminating wrist action.

Ball curve
drill

This drill teaches you how to control distance and direction and how to read breaks. Choose a putt about 15 feet long which has a noticeable break. Putt one ball to get the line of your putt. Then position seven balls along the line of the putt, each two feet apart. Putt the closest ball into the hole and work backward, putting each ball over the spot where the previous ball lay.

Sweet spot
drill

Rub some chalk on your putter face so that when you stroke a putt, the ball leaves a powdery mark, indicating where you made contact. Start with some short putts, and when you make perfect contact five times in a row, extend your distance by 10 feet.

Bunker play

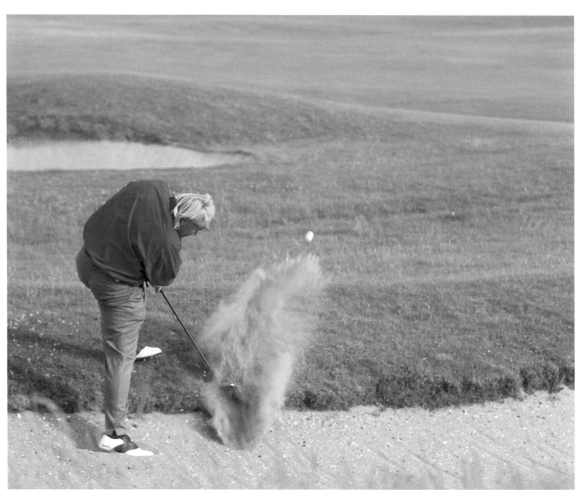

Most people call them "traps" revealing how they feel about hitting into the sand, but you won't find the word trap in the rules of golf—the hazards filled with sand are termed bunkers and good bunker play starts not only with the right club but also with the right attitude. Having the right attitude, a positive and confident one, comes from knowing the proper technique which makes bunker play relatively simple. Remember that rule number one in the bunker is always to get out on your first attempt.

The correct club is a sand wedge, specially designed to make bunker play easy. It was

John Daly's strength and length are negated by the lie of his ball in this fairway bunker. The best he can do in this circumstance is to wedge it out to the safety of the fairway.

invented by Gene Sarazen, who soldered lead on the bottom of his pitching wedge, or what was then known as a "niblick," so its leading edge wouldn't dig into the sand. So effective was his invention that he kept a towel over his bag to prevent his opponents from copying his secret weapon. They soon caught on, however, and Wilson Sporting Goods made popular what is now a staple in every golfer's bag—the sand wedge.

Green side bunker shots

There are two types of green side bunker shots depending on the lie of the ball.

■ The first situation is a good lie where your ball sits nicely on top of the sand.

■ The second lie is not good because your ball is buried in the sand.

Each type of lie requires a different technique: when your lie is good, you'll use the splash shot; and when your ball is buried, you'll hit an explosion or blast shot. One clue to the technique is in the image words used to describe the shot—"splash" for the good lie, "blast" for the bad.

Splash shot particulars

When your ball sits on top of the sand you'll use the splash shot, where your goal is to contact the sand before you hit the ball. One way to think about it is that the sand shot is one of the few shots in golf you try to hit fat. All that is required is the displacement of sand at the back of and beneath the ball, which lifts your ball into the air so it rides to the green on a cushion of sand.

Unfortunately, some golfers attempt to pick the ball off the sand, clearly a dangerous technique

Mechanics of
the splash shot

1 Position the ball forward in your stance.

2 Open your club face and then take your grip.

3 Open your stance until your club face aims to the target, keeping the butt of the club at the center line of your body.

4 Stand further from the ball and dig your feet into the sand to lower the bottom of your swing arc.

5 Make sure that your head is directly between your shoulders, not tilted.

6 Swing down your shoulder line and keep your weight on your left side throughout your swing.

The sand wedge: designed to work in the bunker

As described in our equipment section, your sand wedge is a high-lofted club with a flange underneath its face to displace sand, thereby enabling your club head to slide through the sand rather than digging down into it. The idea is to take a thin strip of sand with measurements similar to those of a dollar bill, rather than the "bucket" of sand that most golfers think they need.

The unique feature that allows you to shave the sand is called bounce. Look at the sole of your sand wedge and you'll notice that it is lower than the leading edge. Bounce is a correction factor which allows your club to skim through the sand rather than dig. As you'll see, maximizing bounce is essential to the proper execution of the splash shot, whereas reducing bounce is the key to the proper execution of the explosion shot.

■ Flange is a term used to describe the area of the sole from the leading edge to the back of the club.

■ Bounce defines the angle from the leading edge to the back of the club.

The Quadrant
method

In your practice draw two perpendicular lines in the sand and number the quadrants clockwise from one to four. One line points to your target, the other to the ball of your left foot. Place your golf ball where the two lines meet This ensures that the ball is positioned well forward in your stance and encourages you to hit the sand first. Open your stance and be sure to swing your club head into quadrant three on the backswing, then along your shoulder line into quadrant one on your through swing. Note that your club at no time enters quadrant four as it would if you were set square to the target line.

Your three-to-one swing path promotes a cut-across swing action that allows the bounce of your sand wedge to slice through the sand to give you the soft-landing splash shot you need.

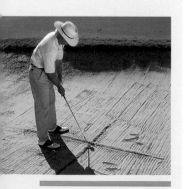

Green side bunker shots *continued*

that often leads to thin, bladed shots that travel much too far. Other golfers have the idea that the ball must be "blasted" out of the bunker so they take too much sand, producing shots that travel too short a distance and often don't get out of the bunker.

With skulled shots that fly over the green and muffed shots that stay in the bunker, it's no wonder that the average golfer approaches the bunker shot with trepidation—yet, as we shall see, once your technique is correct, the sand shot loses much of its intimidation.

Fundamentals of the splash shot

For the splash shot, always open your club face to maximize the bounce. The shorter the shot, the more open your club face. And be sure to always open the club face before you finalize your grip on the club. Do this by hovering your club head above the ball using only your right hand to aim the club face to the right of the target. Then take your grip with both hands, keeping your club face in place. The problem with taking your grip first, then rolling your arms to open the club face to the ball, is that doing it this way, your arms roll over through impact, returning the club face to square or, worse, closing the club face.

Secondly, with the butt end of your club pointing at the center line of your body, open your stance by pulling your left foot away from the target line until your club face aims to the target. By opening your stance, you effectively shorten the length of your left leg and plant your weight in your left hip. This provides a stable platform that encourages you to hit down and through the shot. To execute the splash shot properly your club swings along your shoulder line, so you should position the ball forward in your stance off your left heel. This opens your shoulders, producing an outside to in swing path that carves the ball out of the sand.

In taking your stance, work your feet into the sand for stability. With your feet below the ball it guarantees that you'll hit behind the ball, a necessary feature of the splash shot. It also allows you to test the consistency and texture of the sand—information that you need in order to calculate where to contact the sand and how hard to hit the shot. However, take note that when you dig your feet in, you effectively move the hosel of the club closer to the ball, so adjust by standing farther from the ball. For every inch you lower yourself into the sand, move back an inch from the ball.

The final set up key involves the position of your head and spine. It's vital that you hold your head in the center of your body with no spinal tilt toward the left or, the more common error, toward your right shoulder. The weight of your head is significant so if your head and spine lean toward your right shoulder, the rest of your body weight does also, tilting your entire body out of position.

The swing itself is upper-body oriented because your weight starts, stays and finishes on your left side. Your arms swing fully allowing the club to move along your shoulder line.

With your weight fixed on your left side, the swing is dominated by your upper body, primarily your arms and shoulders. Notice that while there is minimal lower body action (hips and knees are very quiet) during the backswing, the down-swing exhibits an active lower body that allows the club head to slide under the ball using the bounce rather than the leading edge.

The short
splash shot

Occasionally you'll be faced with a very short bunker shot, one you need to land softly next to a pin tucked near the bunker. You'll play this shot in much the same way as a regular splash shot using your low-gear swing speed, except that you'll open your stance until you're almost facing the target. But with such an open BASE be sure that your ball is positioned off your left heel, because unless you adjust, the open stance moves the ball back in your stance—too far to the rear for the high shot you need.

In addition to your stance, open the face of your club until it points well right of your target. By opening the face, the loft of your club is increased, causing the ball to fly higher and shorter.

One mistake that's often made in this situation is to forward press the hands until they're ahead of the ball. This takes loft off your shot and moves the hosel dangerously closer to the ball, so take care to keep the butt of the club at the center line of your body to create the high shot you need.

Green side bunker shots *continued*

Face, base and pace: controlling the distance

You can become a bunker ace by utilizing an easy to remember system called "face, base and pace" that will help you to set up correctly and to control the distance of your splash shots.

■ The first part of the system, FACE, refers to the club face, which is the first distance control determinant. The more you open the club face, the higher and shorter the ball travels. So first determine the amount of loft necessary to clear the lip of the bunker and then assess the total distance required for the shot, opening the club face the appropriate amount.

■ The second part of our system refers to your BASE. Open your stance (your BASE) to a point where your club face readjusts from its open position to aim directly at your target. Next determine how far you want to hit behind the ball. You learn this by practicing but, in general, the farther you hit behind the ball the shorter your shot; the less sand you take, the longer the shot.

■ The third control feature of our system is the PACE of your swing. The shorter the shot the slower your pace; the longer the shot the faster your pace. You limit the length of your swing by opening your BASE and alter the distance by adjusting the FACE and PACE.

Once you know the FACE and the BASE, controlling the distance that your shot travels is much like the windshield wiper system that maintains three separate speeds, each with a constant speed back and through.

■ For the long bunker shot your entire swing is on high.

■ For the medium distance it's on medium speed.

■ For the short distance it's low speed.

The board drill

Bury a painted 2 x 4 inch board, about 16 inches long, in the sand so that the four-inch side of the board is level with the sand. Without a ball, address the middle of the board and swing your club as described above, allowing the bounce of your club head to hit the board. Check your club head—if the leading edge has paint on it your swing was incorrect; if the bounce has paint on it, you're using the flange as you should.

Now place a pile of sand on top of the board and, using the same motion, let the bounce hit the board causing the sand to fly onto the green. Next, place a ball on top of a pile of sand and once again simply allow the bounce of your club head to hit the board. Both the ball and the sand will fly onto the green.

You'll feel the correct motion of the splash shot because the board will force you to swing correctly. Once you get the feeling of your club head bouncing rather than digging, place a ball on the sand next to the board and reproduce the "splash" feeling while hitting a sand shot from a normal lie. If you have trouble, go back to the board until you can hit the splash shot correctly every time.

The buried bunker shot

Playing from a buried lie is quite different from playing a ball that's sitting nicely on top of the sand. Since your ball is below the surface, you want your club to make a deep cut into the sand to dig the ball out. To accomplish this, position your ball halfway between the middle of your stance and your right foot, then close your club face to square it back to your target. With the leading edge exposed and the bounce eliminated, your club plows into the sand and, by using a combination of hands and arms, you can swing abruptly up and down, creating a descending blow behind the ball. This descending blow, along with the closed club face, allows your club to dig deeply into the sand causing the ball to pop out.

Unlike the splash shot, don't try for a follow through; if you do it correctly you'll leave your club head in or very near the sand at the completion of your swing. With a shot like this you produce minimal back spin so your ball comes out low and running. Too often, golfers try to lift the ball out of a buried lie and end up hardly advancing it at all. Proper technique eliminates this problem. However, be careful; even the pros have trouble controlling this shot, so know your limitations and just get the ball on the green.

Mechanics of *the blast shot*

1 Position the ball back in your stance.
2 Close the club face until it is square to the target.
3 Using a combination of arms and hands, strike a descending blow just behind the ball, without trying to follow through.
4 Allow for very little back spin, a lower trajectory and more roll.

1 Drop your left foot back to level your hips and set your weight into the slope.
2 Because of the necessary steep angle of attack, your club head makes a deep cut into the sand and causes limited follow through.

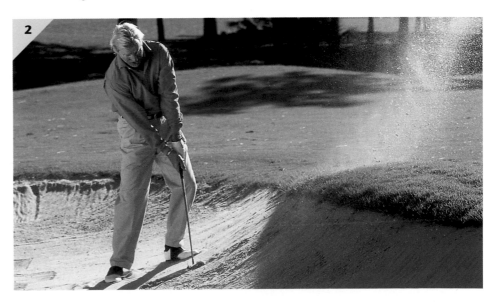

Fairway bunker shots

Fairway bunker shots rate among the most difficult in the game for the average player. This is because most people don't know how to plan these shots or how to execute them.

The "three Ls" of club selection

In assessing a fairway bunker shot your first consideration is the conditions of play. Before making your club selection, be sure to check the "three Ls":

- The *lie* of the golf ball.
- The *lip* of the bunker.
- The *length* of the shot.

The lie of the ball determines the type of shot that you can play. The lip determines which club you'll need to produce the necessary trajectory to clear it. And your last consideration is the length of the shot.

■ If your ball sits beneath the level of the sand, regardless of the length you want to hit the ball, you may have to take a sand wedge and dig it out.

■ If you have a good lie, where the ball is resting on top of the sand and can be hit cleanly, check the lip of the bunker. You'll need a club that gives you sufficient loft to safely clear the lip of the bunker. Since proper fairway bunker technique shortens the standard distance you hit an iron, you'll need to hit one more club, so include that in your calculation of sufficient loft if the lip allows.

You can only consider the length of the shot if the lie and the lip conditions allow it. If you need to hit a four iron to get to the green but the lip requires the trajectory of a seven iron, you'll have to go with the seven. When the lie and lip are favorable, only then can you consider the length of the shot.

The set up

The last outcome you want is to leave your ball in the bunker so, unless you're an expert, the guideline is never to use more than a four iron in a fairway bunker. With the long irons and fairway woods it's hard enough to get the ball airborne from a good lie in the fairway, so leave them in the bag when you have to contend with the sand and the lip of a bunker.

Begin your address proceedings by choking down on the handle of your club about an inch. This allows you to make a more controlled swing. Play the ball in the middle of your stance to help you pick it cleanly off the sand. Stand a little farther from the ball than you normally do and reach for it by stretching your arms away from your body—this helps prevent hitting the sand behind the ball, the most common mistake in a fairway bunker.

It also helps to widen and open your stance, anchoring your left foot with 60 percent of your weight, and wedging your right foot into the sand with your right knee angled in toward the target. Your shoulders should be square, even though your feet and hips are open.

Determining *the loft*

If you're unsure how to determine the loft an iron produces try this technique. Pick a club that you think may be right. Lay it down in the grass, adjacent to your position in the bunker, with the butt end of the club pointing in the direction you want your ball to fly. Step on the club face and the butt end rises up. This angle is an indication of the approximate amount of loft you can expect from that iron. Remember that you can't let your club touch the sand so don't try this in the bunker unless you're just practicing.

The swing itself: think "pick"

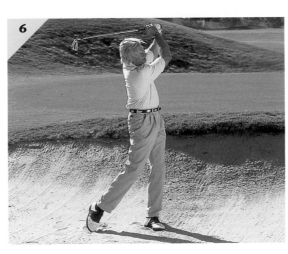

The controlling concept for the fairway bunker shot is to pick the ball off the sand, so if you make a mistake it's much better to hit the ball thin than fat. Some golfers even try to catch it a little thin to protect against hitting the sand first. Once you have the concept (think pick), keep your lower body relatively quiet during the shot. The swing should be a three-quarter motion with most of your weight remaining in your left hip throughout your swing. By reducing weight transfer, you decrease the risk that you'll sink into the sand at the top of your swing—a sure way to hit sand before you contact the ball.

The inner game

What separates the three levels of golfers: those that can't play a lick, those who can play when it doesn't really count, and those who can play no matter what's at stake? Well, as you can imagine, this is a complicated question with an even more complicated set of answers but one difference is this: the poor player is hardly ever committed to the shot; the good player is committed to the shot before he hits it; but the great player is committed to the shot while he is swinging!

Most golfers aren't committed because they never get the shot they need to play clear in

Fuzzy Zoeller's care-free style and "whistle while you work" attitude is the envy of any golfer who has ever struggled with his composure on the golf course.

their mind. They're worried about *not* doing something—"Don't hit it left; don't hit it in the water." Playing by "don'ts" won't get it done because no commitment is possible and with the fuzzy set of instructions to "don't do something," your brain is a poor commander in directing your army of muscles to swing the club correctly.

Playing by "do's" won't do either

Some golfers play by "do's", usually the mid-level player who has a brain full of information—"keep the right arm tucked; stay down; take it away low and slow." This is the DO-DO system and it puts your brain on alert that it needs to get consciously involved in a complicated motor activity (your downswing) that takes less than 0.05 seconds. This is not a good plan because if you're still calculating what to do while you're doing it, your chances for a good swing are drastically reduced.

Get committed to play your best golf

Great players decide on the shot they want to play and then stay with that decision while they swing. One way to keep your commitment from start to finish is to use images that are so compelling that they rivet your attention on your plan. If your image of the shot is strong and clear, all your resources are dedicated to making it a reality.

The power of imagery

Your mental images are created as you process information about your world and these images then cue your motor responses. When you're late, you run after a taxi; when you're scared you run away from the tiger. How your muscles get the job done—the technique of running—is done by unconscious competence; you don't have to think about it as you do it. If you did, the chances are you'd be late—or would get eaten!

But when you swing a golf club the urge to think about it while you do it is very strong. This puts your conscious mind in control and in the less than half a second it takes for your swing back to the ball, you don't have much time for conscious instructions. You're "in your own way". That's why Ben Hogan said that "the downswing is no place to give yourself a lesson".

An example of getting out of your own way is Terry Larson, who played a round of "speed golf" on the run in just under 40 minutes, shooting 75. The day before in his practice round he spent three-and-a-half hours playing the course and shot 77. He offered this explanation: "When you play sports like baseball or tennis you react to the target. In golf the ball just sits and you can end up thinking too much. In speed golf you run up to the ball, find the target and hit it."

Now if you haven't learned to swing your club correctly then reread the appropriate sections of this book or see your teaching professional, because imagining your ball tight to the hole won't help much if you don't know how to hit a seven iron. However, once you learn the basics of how to swing the club, to play your best golf you need to step aside and let imagery take control.

So if you're not thinking about swing mechanics while you swing, what are you supposed to think about? The answer is to occupy your mind with images by using your imagination.

Dr. Rod Borrie uses flotation tanks to help his patients' image. He says: "The conscious brain can process only about seven bits of information at one time, but complex movements such as athletic movements are made up of far more than seven bits of information." Thus to play your best golf, turn the complicated movements of your golf swing over to your unconscious competence.

Playing by images serves two purposes:

1 Images occupy your mind while you are swinging, leaving no room for the paralyzing "do this—do that" swing tips.

2 Images set the stage for motor responses, i.e. when you imagine something, your muscles are cued up to get the job done.

How imagery works

While you use all your senses to figure out the world, most people have a dominant sense system in which they are most comfortable when they process information and plan responses to their environment.

■ If you're a visual person, the image might be aiming the golf ball at a cloud and picturing it dropping out of the cloud next to the pin, or seeing your ball taking off up a ramp with smoke coming out of it, or imaging the ball spouting a parachute as it drops softly onto the green.

■ If you're an auditory learner the imagery might be developed using image words such as "syrupy", and "feather", or phrases such as "grip it and rip it", or "finish high and let it fly".

■ If you're a feel player, many of your shot-making images will be cued by using a special waggle or taking practice swings that exactly mimic the swing you need to pull out of the shot.

The root images are as varied as the shots you are called on to play, and the ability to match images to the demands of the moment is the creative part of the game. Thus the power of imagery is the defining element in the "golfer as artist." First, you imagine the shot in your mind, then you create the shot with your swing.

When you get to the point where you produce a vivid, multi-sensorial pre-play before each shot, you have added the full *power of imagery* to your catalog of golfing resources. This is a big league addition, and the essential prerequisite of a good player.

How some of the great players describe their imagery

Seve Ballesteros

"In order to gain confidence I must be able to 'see'—clearly visualize mentally—a line all the way from the ball to my actual target, both at the start of the set up...and, equally importantly, at the end of my routine. ...Once everything checks out A-okay, my entire body responds by swinging the club almost reflexively in response to the picture in my mind's eye."

Greg Norman

"...You do want to file the good ones (shots) away for future reference. That way you'll be able to bring them back as part of another reinforcement technique—visualization.

"You envision the ideal shot...in detail. Then you recall successful similar shots from your past and draw confidence from those earlier successes. I can think of favorite shots for every situation I face and I call them forth each time I play."

Jack Nicklaus

"I never hit a shot, even in practice, without having a very sharp, in-focus picture of it in my head. First, I 'see' where I want it to finish. Then the scene quickly changes and I see the ball going there. Then there's a sort of a fade-out, and the next scene shows me making the kind of swing that will turn the previous images into reality."

How do champions play?

Nowhere in the accounts featured here of what the great players think about as they swing do you find any "right elbows or left knees." The point is that it is not a good idea to play the game by conscious manipulation—trying to do something while you swing. This is probably the biggest mistake made by golfers, i.e. they overwhelm the playing of the game by conscious attention to it. To play the game well you need to do just the opposite; you must develop an unconscious competence.

The question is, if they don't play by "don'ts," and they don't play by "do's," how do champions play? The answer is they play by targets. Every shot is a target/player loop or interaction; you are connected to the target by your *senses*.

Champions focus on the target

When you're connected, or plugged into the target, your senses trigger feelings, seeings, rhythms, cadences, etc. and these are translated automatically into motor responses; in other words, your body moves to create the correct distance and direction necessary to send the ball to the target based on the data from your senses.

Play in a flow of go

Your conscious mind/brain is impulsive; it focuses on "doing." It's short term. What's on your mental screen is the momentary goal, your micro-agenda for action. The sentence that best describes your conscious mind/brain is "I'm ready, let's do it."

Your subconscious mind/brain contains all your personal experience. Thus your subconscious is composed of an extensive data base of "silent knowledge." It is contemplative; its focus is evaluation.

Your subconscious mind/brain is long term. It makes value judgments about your capabilities and the appropriateness of your response to the challenges of your environment. It's the arbitrator of motor behavior and the seat of unconscious competence. Your conscious mind/brain needs its approval to get things done effectively. The sentence that best describes your subconscious mind/brain is "Let's wait and evaluate."

When your conscious and subconscious mind are in agreement, all your systems (muscular, neurological, visual etc.) are on the "same page." This total mind/brain/body congruence is expressed as a GO signal.

Getting a GO signal doesn't mean you'll always hit a good shot but it does give you your best chance to play good golf. A constant stream of GO signals is what consistency is all about. A stream of GO is the current that carries you along in the "zone," that super-performance state where you place your golf swing under the control of your unconscious competence, take your hands off the steering wheel and just go along for the ride.

How do champions play? *continued*

It's wise to remember that many golf course architects practice visual intimidation. They design courses that present to the average player a scary array of bunkers, mounds, water, humpback greens, collection areas and, of course, railway ties. Euphemistically called "challenges," they are arranged to strike visual fear into the golfer's heart. And they do. In the words of course designer Robert Trent Jones Jr. "...the designer may position a tee so that it is exposed to wind and weather in an attempt to distract you and cause you uncertainty. ...Some tees are positioned with the psychological element in mind. For example, some tees are positioned to...create a certain intimidation factor for the golfer. ...Designers love to use this technique to create indecisiveness about your club and shot selection."

Science measures the NO/GO signals

Dr. Richard Lonetto conducted recordings of heart rates to determine how golfers perform under stress. There were two different patterns of heartbeats: one associated with good shots and one associated with bad shots. The subjects were 15 tour players and 15 amateurs with handicaps ranging from two to 23.

The good shot pattern

The heart rate profile for good shots corresponded with the subjective reports. When the players were over the ball they reported that their mind was "quiet" with no internal chatter; they felt decisive about their plan, and were completely committed to the shot they had chosen to play. There was an excitement, but it was the anticipation of something good. There were stomach "butterflies" but they were all flying in formation.

Golfers used terms such as solid, balanced, in tune, and in sync, to describe the signals they were getting from their subconscious. These are golfers in conscious-to-subconscious congruence and their feelings are the essence of GO signals.

The bad shot pattern

When the subjects were playing badly, there was also a distinct pattern related to the heart rate which was very different from the "good shot"

heart rate. They described being anxious, with lots of negative internal talk; they were not sure they had the right plan and as such weren't committed to the shot. They were anxious about a bad outcome. The butterflies were dive bombing!

These are the messages from your subconscious that poke their way up into your consciousness as NO signals, and if you ignore them and try to play through them, you will never reach your golfing potential no matter how good your swing.

The best way to defeat NO signals is to focus on the characteristics of the target to the exclusion of everything else. Turn your mind outward toward

Bad shot profile

Good shot profile

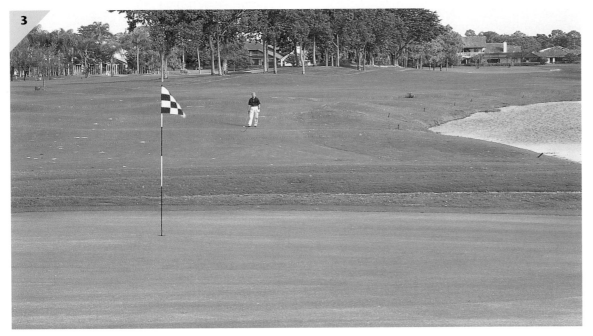

the target, rather than inward toward the consequences. Become a receiving station for the stimuli coming from the target. Occupy your mind with checking out the wind, the distance, the location of the hazards etc.

The key to creating a stream of GO signals—a flow to go—is to gather enough information to pick the shot that best matches your strengths, so that when your subconscious reviews your plan and matches it against your personal strength and weakness profile, it finds everything in order and gives you permission to execute the shot.

A common question is: "Why can I hit it well on the driving range but not on the golf course?" One answer is that there aren't any NO signals on the driving range whereas on the golf course designers have built in a series of NO signals calculated to create a mental havoc that ultimately reverberates down through your pre-shot routine and into your golf swing.

Practice

Goals drive human performance so it's important to practice with a goal. Beating balls with no specific intent is not only wasteful but could be damaging to your game because when it's not engaged in a goal-directed activity, your mind wanders, making it easy for you to tinker yourself right out of a good golf swing. The old saying is true: "Practice does not make perfect, only perfect practise makes perfect." There are four types:

1   Warm up

2   Fundamental building

3   Target orientation

4   "Practice like you play"

Your practice session might contain all four or it might focus on just one, two or three of the different types. The structuring of your program depends on your needs at the time but, whatever the specific content, the key is to have a clear-cut practice plan and to follow that plan.

1 Warm up

All practice sessions, even short game, should begin with a warm up, the purpose of which is to get blood flowing into your golf muscles. A warm up routine also puts you in the mood for what is to come, allowing you to put aside your non-golf concerns so that your mind will be free to focus on your practice session. You should personalize your warm up routine depending on your body profile (strength, flexibility etc.) but, in general, it should include three stages:

■   A stretching program that works all the major muscle groups.

Tom Kite, a player known for his long practice sessions, doesn't consider practicing hard work, and perfecting his techniques, including putting, has made him one of the all-time leading money winners in the game.

■   A continuous series of dry-run swings without a ball, where your club never stops moving.

■   A ball-striking progression, starting with partial swings, that builds up slowly over 10 balls, to full swings.

It's a good idea to get to the course in time to hit a few balls before you play, but take care not

1 At the start of every practice session, loosen your muscles with some stretching exercises. Concentrate on your turning motion, starting out slowly and working up to the normal pace of your swing.

to turn your warm up into a swing overhaul session. Don't search for a swing just before you go to the course. The best way to get ready to play is to do your stretching, then program yourself for solid contact.

There is nothing quite so disheartening as hitting two inches behind the ball on your first warm up swing, so to remove the distraction of the lie of the ball, tee all the balls while you warm up. There is something about the feel of a well-centered hit that programs your brain with good expectations, so your major goal when you warm up is solid contact regardless of where the ball goes. As we have seen in the Inner Game section, with off-centered hits your brain is confused and in doubt, the two centerpieces of NO signals. Square hits, on the other hand, produce a stream of Go signals, just what you want to begin your round.

2 To ensure that your swing is built on a solid foundation much of your practice is focused on grip, stance, posture, correct ball position, aim and alignment. We have found that about 80 percent of all swing errors result from an improper address position, so always use alignment clubs to build a practice station.

2 Fundamental building

All golfers should work on their fundamentals: beginners need to learn them one by one, mid-level players need to integrate them into a coherent whole, and experts need to tweak them now and then to make sure slippage from the perfect form has not occurred. And it's on the practice tee, either on your own or under the direction of a competent golf coach, that you isolate the pieces of your swing for specific attention. But remember that when you're doing "piece work" your evaluation system is not the ball flight but how well you performed the fundamental you're practicing.

Warm up routines *continued*

When you work on target orientation, be sure to go through your pre-shot routine, first stepping behind each ball to look down your target line.

3 Target orientation

The third part of your practice session is called target orientation. In this phase you work on hitting shots to a designated target, focusing only on the target. For each shot, go through your entire pre-shot routine using your power of imagery as the moderator. This is the vital link that helps you take your game from the range to the course.

Switch targets with every shot so your practice will be more realistic. Choose one on the left side of the range, one in the middle and a target on the right side. Change clubs as necessary and don't think about your swing while you target practice. In target practice, the ball flight gives you information and you adjust accordingly. If, while working on target orientation, you begin to hit the ball poorly, abandon target practice and return to fundamental practice. To keep the types of practice distinct in your own mind, remember to announce to yourself that you're switching your practice type.

In general, when you're taking target practice don't be concerned with your swing, and when you're working on your swing don't use a target.

4 Practice like you play

There is a saying that the longest 100 yards in golf is from the practice tee to the first tee. Something seems to happen to your swing along the way so that it's not unusual for a golfer to hit the ball beautifully on the range but poorly on the course. One reason, as we saw in the Inner Game section, is that there are no NO

Next time your round of golf is interrupted by light rain, don't hurry to leave the course. Instead, put on your rain gear and learn to adjust to the bulk of your clothing, wet grips, and the difficult course conditions.

signals on the driving range but there are plenty of them on the course.

Another is that on the course there's a one-ball success rate—you get one try and your brain knows it. Yet most golfers practice a multi-ball success rate by hitting ball after ball with the same club on the driving range. Our suggestion is to devote a major portion of your practice time to gearing up your brain for the one-ball success rate you need to play the game—in other words, practice like you play.

You can actually play a round of golf right there on the practice range, using your imagination to lay out the course, going through your pre-shot routine and hitting the shots required given the situation you have created. Place your bag next to your practice station with your entire complement of clubs therein (avoid bringing just one or two clubs when you're practicing as you play). The hole you're playing should have a specific yardage: it might be an actual hole you've played, one you've seen or heard about, or its outline could be purely your own creation.

A sample hole

Say it's a 400-yard par four that's a slight dogleg to the right. You choose your driver and attempt to hit a fade; you catch it solidly but it drifts just outside the boundaries of your imaginary fairway, coming to rest in the right rough. You have 140 yards left to the green but you have to hit the ball high over the trees that guard the dogleg.

A seven iron does the job and you finish high and let it fly—right over the trees but just short of

From this difficult uphill lie, with his golf ball resting on a thin lie, Corey Pavin needs to make several adjustments to his set up as outlined in the section on Awkward Lies. You can be sure that he knows the necessary adjustments and has spent time practicing from these difficult situations.

the green. You're left with a medium trajectory pitch shot of about 20 yards which you hit to four feet and make it for your par. Next is the dogleg right, 540-yard par five with water in the driving area on the right side. Practicing like this is an easy and enjoyable way to get in a quick 18 holes.

Adjusting to the conditions

Learn to adjust to the conditions. Unless there's lightning in the area, the next time your round of golf is interrupted by rain don't be in a hurry to leave the course. Instead, put on your rain gear and tough it out for a few holes, learning to adjust

213

Mental practice

The 17th hole at TPC Sawgrass, surrounded on all sides by water, is one of the most visually intimidating holes on the PGA Tour. But great players like Greg Norman prepare for challenges like this by mentally playing the hole before they even set foot on the course.

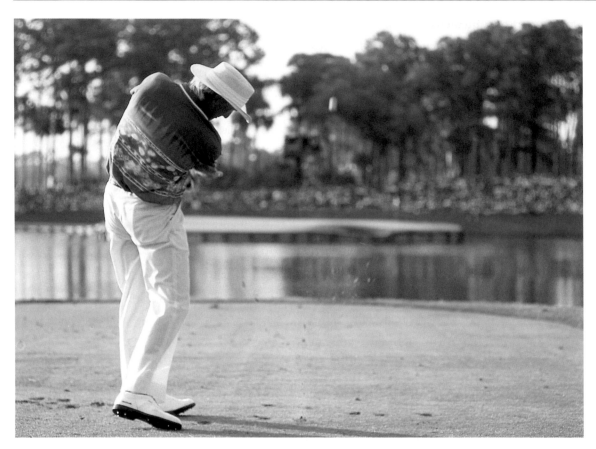

Not all practice is done on the driving range. One of the best ways to work on your game is away from the golf course using a combination of full body relaxation plus imagery, a technique similar to those the Eastern Europeans have used for years in some of their Olympic training programs. You can easily learn to summon a deep state of relaxation and then imagine practicing or playing a round of golf, shot by shot.

This type of mental practice is a great way to stay sharp, especially when the weather keeps you indoors. The first step in this technique (the relaxation part) was popularized by the Harvard heart specialist Herbert Benson. In his best-selling book, *The Relaxation Response,*

Benson described the ability of patients to lower their blood pressure by using the same highly effective, but very simple, relaxation procedure that with minor modifications can be adapted to improve your golf game.

1   Find a quiet place where you won't be disturbed. Assume a sitting position with your legs folded in front of you and your spine straight, resting against a support, such as a wall. It helps if you use earplugs because it's easier to isolate the sound of your breathing, a key element of the procedure.

2   Inhale through your nostrils so that your breath fills your stomach. Once your abdominal cavity is filled, continue your breath and fill your

216

upper chest cavity. This method gives you a full exchange that re-oxygenates your blood and expels harmful carbon dioxide.

Once your body is aerated using this low to high technique (first abdominal, then thoracic), force the air out through your mouth using your stomach muscles. Place your hand on your abdomen to feel it swell as you breathe in and contract as you breathe out. Once you get the rhythm, relax and focus on the sound of your breathing to the exclusion of all else.

3   Continue as in step two until you're in a complete state of relaxation. At first, it might take you 15 minutes or more to elicit the Relaxation Response, but as you become more adept, you can do it in less than a minute.

4   Now it's time to play a little golf. Let's say you need some practice hitting your driver. Imagine yourself addressing the ball. Feel, see and hear everything about the scene: the solidity of your stance, the gracefulness of your backswing, the controlled power of your downswing, the squareness of contact, the flight of the ball and, of course, where your ball comes to rest. The more precise you make your image, the more effective your mental practice becomes. And after you practice, you can play a few holes using your power of mental imagery. Many of golf's greatest players—from Ben Hogan to Jack Nicklaus to Greg Norman—have used mental techniques to maximize their performance.

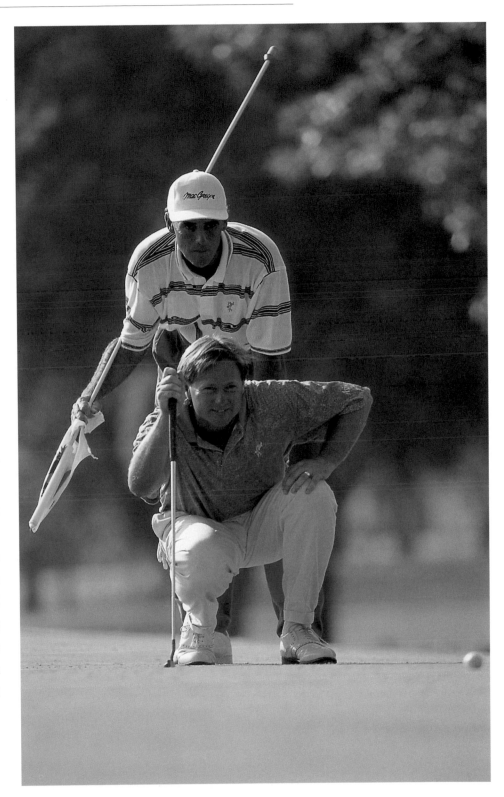

John Cook and his caddy focus on the task at hand, visualizing the putt breaking into the hole.

Key rules

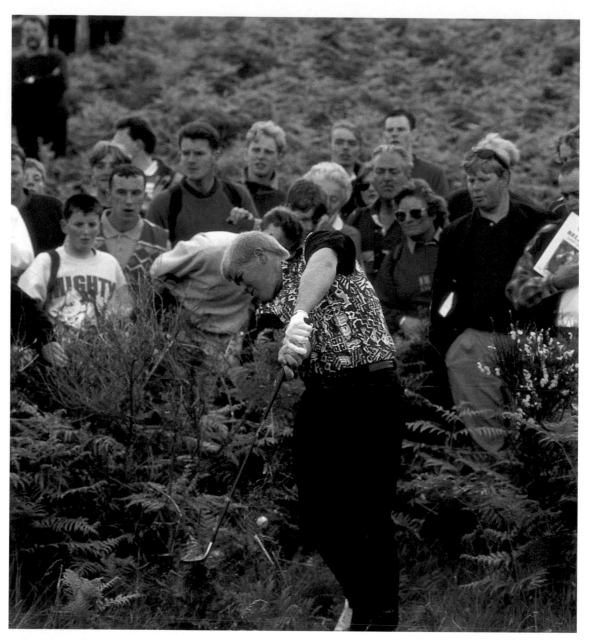

Even the awesome power of John Daly is not a solution for every problem. From an impossible lie, it is prudent to take a penalty stroke's relief and play on safely from there.

You can knock a ball around a golf course with no regard for any pre-scribed procedures or regulations, not counting swings and misses, taking mulligans or do-overs and you can even put down a four when you actually made a seven. However, although this may be some other kind of stick and ball game, it's not golf. If you want to learn to play the game of golf, you need to know not only how to hit the ball but also the rules that define the nature of the game.

The rules of the game

Play is governed by a body of rules, approved by the United States Golf Association and The Royal and Ancient Golf Club of St. Andrews, Scotland, and because golf is a game where you, the player, are obliged to act as your own referee, it's well worth taking the time to become familiar with the rules and procedures.

Match and medal

There are two styles of competitive golf: stroke play (also known as medal play) and match play. You'll win at stroke play competition by taking the fewest number of strokes. Match play competitions are decided by the number of holes you win over your opponent. Each hole is a separate contest with the hole either won, lost or halved. A hole is halved or tied when you and your opponent make the same score. The rules and their penalties are often different, depending on whether it's match or medal, and it is a good idea not only to read the rule book from cover to cover at least once a year but also to carry one in your golf bag for easy reference while you play. The following is a general overview of the rules you are most likely to encounter.

Play the ball as it lies

In general, you can't advance your golf ball except by striking it with a club. The ball may be marked and lifted once it reaches the putting surface, and in some other instances, but for the most part you play the ball as it lies. If you accidentally cause your ball to move, it costs you a one-stroke penalty. It also counts as a stroke when you swing and miss unless you move the ball accidentally while preparing to tee off; then it can be replaced without penalty.

Teeing off

According to the rules, the teeing ground is the area inside a rectangle formed by an imaginary straight line connecting the tee markers. The sides are parallel lines from the markers extending to a depth of two club lengths. You can use any club for the measurements. The back boundary of the teeing ground is a line connecting the sides of the rectangle (see below). You can tee

Knowing the boundaries of the teeing ground allows you to maximize your strategy off the tee.

Etiquette

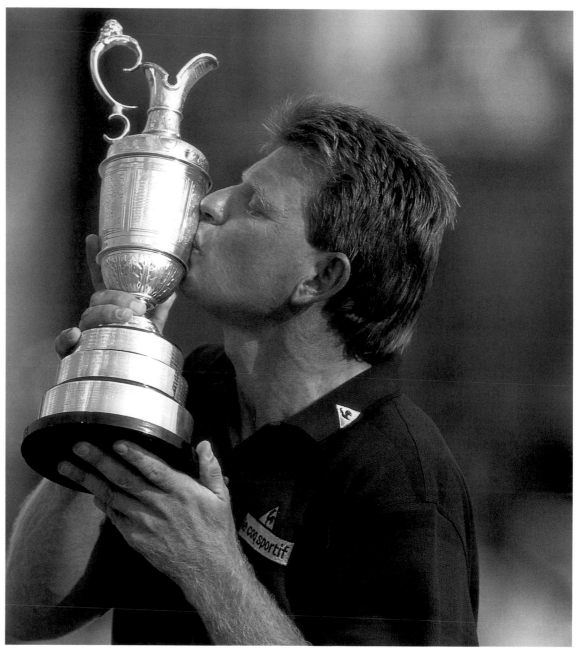

G olf is a game of refinement played by courteous players whose behavior shows respect for the history of the game, the playing field and their fellow golfers. It is no wonder then that etiquette is the first section in *The Rules of Golf*, a priority driving home the point that certain

Being awarded the Claret Jug is one of golf's greatest honors and Nick Price receives it graciously and, in good form, gives it a kiss after his 1994 British Open victory.

standards of behavior are an integral part of the game.

Some guidelines

Teeing off

On the teeing ground stand a safe distance to the side of (never directly behind or ahead of) the player who is about to hit. You should stand still so as not to distract their eye. Be complimentary of good performance when they are through making their shot. Poor performance merits either silence or sympathy.

Players in front of you

Hitting into the group in front of you is not only dangerous but very discourteous. A fail-safe way to avoid this is don't hit until all the members of the group ahead have left the area you're hitting to. When it's your turn to play from any position (the tee, the rough, the trees), take a head count to be sure that all the players in front of you have hit their shots and are well on their way to their next shots.

If you hit a ball that looks as if it might strike or land close by to someone, holler "FORE" so that they can take cover.

Distractions and noise

Golf is played on a "quiet" stage so it is very poor form to be the source of distractions of any kind. Jingling change, loud whispering and banging about in the cart while another golfer is trying to play should be avoided.

Avoiding slow play

In the interest of all, play without delay. You don't need to "run" around the course but there's no cause to dawdle either. You can avoid slow play by mentally preparing for your next shot as you're approaching your ball. And you'll be a sought-after playing companion if you limit your practice swings to one.

Lost balls

Golf balls are expensive and a lost ball costs you a penalty stroke, but searching for lost balls is a time-consuming task that can plug up the entire golf course. Under the rules you have five minutes to look but unless you're in a tournament, you'll be a very unpopular golfer if you take more than a minute or two. To cut down on the number of lost balls, everyone in your group should watch each other's shot and mark the landing area.

Golf carts

In riding carts, there's a tendency to cluster around the person who is hitting. Unless your ball is ahead of everyone else's, make sure that you go directly to your ball so you'll be ready to play when it's your turn. If you're dropped off or must leave your cart on the path and walk to your ball, take an array of clubs so that you'll have the right one. Once you've hit your shot get into your cart with your club, waiting to replace it in your bag until the next stop. If you are

To understand the different scoring systems involved in golf you'll first need to understand the basics of Par and the Handicap System.

Par

Par is a numerical standard based on the layout of the course. The average course is a total of 18 different holes, each being either a par three, four or five. Par for each hole is based on the amount of strokes required by an expert to negotiate its distance plus two putts on the green. For example, on a par three, the shortest hole, an expert is allotted one shot to get to the green, plus two for putting, for a total of par three. Note, however, that par is a standard based on an expert's performance and therefore the standard is often not reached by the average golfer on a regular basis.

Individual scores are often expressed in relationship to the par for the course. For example, if you were to take 80 strokes on a par 72 course, you would have a score eight strokes over par. If your score is 70 on a par 72, your score could also be expressed as two under par. If, on a par three, you hit your ball short of the green, pitch it onto the green and then two putt, your score would be four or one over par for that hole. This terminology is necessary in understanding the handicap system.

Handicap

Handicap systems were devised to allow players of varying skill levels to compete against one another. Your handicap is related to the number of strokes over par that you average. Although the USGA uses a much more complicated formula to compute handicaps, an easy way to understand the basic idea of handicaps is as follows: if you play 20 rounds of golf and you average a score of 82, i.e. 10 over par, your handicap would be about a 10. If you don't have access to the formal calculating system, you can get an idea of where you stand by using this very general guideline: subtract par from your score to arrive at your handicap.

Forms of play

Stroke play and match play are the two basic scoring systems that apply to both tournament and recreational golf. In the world of amateur golf, a handicap system is often used in conjunction with these forms of play.

Stroke play

You'll win at stroke play when you complete your round in fewer strokes than all your fellow competitors. In a handicapped stroke play competition, your actual score is known as your gross score and from this your handicap is deducted to arrive at your net score. The player with the lowest net score is the winner of a handicapped competition.

The lowest net score is determined as follows. Say the two lowest net scores for this tournament are a 70 and a 73. The player with a net score of 73 was a 10 handicap who had a gross (actual) score of 83 (83 minus 10 = 73). The player with a net score of 70 was a 20 handicap with a gross score of 90. In handicap competition, the player with the lowest net score is the winner; in this example, the 20 handicap would be the winner based on the net score although the actual gross score was higher

Match play

This is a hole-by-hole competition between two individuals or two teams. Each hole is either won, lost or halved (tied). To win at match play you or your team has to win the most holes.

Handicapping match play events is different from the method used in stroke play where you simply deduct the handicap from the actual score. Each hole of a golf course is rated for its difficulty and this rating correlates to handicap. The most difficult hole on the course is known as the number one handicap hole and the system continues for all the holes. Score cards are arranged so that the stroke holes alternate from the front nine to the back nine causing the strokes to be evenly distributed over the course of 18 holes. For example: the # 1 stroke hole is on the front nine and the # 2 stroke hole is on the back nine; the # 3 stroke hole is on the front nine and the # 4 stroke hole is on the back nine.

Before a match play competition, the players compare handicaps. The lower handicap player "gives strokes" to the higher handicap player on the more difficult holes. For example, a 10 playing a 20 handicap would give 10 strokes to the 20 handicap, which is the difference between their handicaps and their skill level. This way they can compete as equals. The strokes are given in this instance on the ten most difficult holes on the course, the five most difficult on the front (handicap numbers 1, 3, 5, 7, 9) and the five most difficult holes on the back (2, 4, 6, 8, 10). Note that these are not hole numbers but the handicap rating that applies to the specific hole. So the 20 handicap could score one stroke higher on these holes and still tie the hole.

Note: stroke play and match play are the official forms of play and the handicap system is a unique and attractive feature of the game of golf which allows golfers of all abilities to play together in a competitive atmosphere.

Learning the game

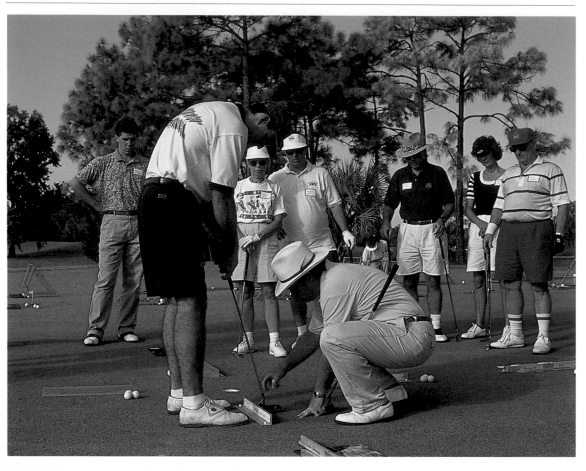

There are a number of ways to learn to play better golf. The first step is to choose a model. This involves not only copying the mannerisms and swing motion of an expert player with whom you match up well but also breaking the golf swing down into manageable parts, finding the perfect model for each and then copying that model perfectly until it becomes ingrained as a habit.

One way to do this is to take lessons where the models for every part of the swing are presented to you. Then you take your models and practice them, piece by piece, until you have built a functional swing. Once you've done this, it's time

At the Academy of Golf at PGA National, you will find Director Mike Adams involved in every single school.

to play the game on the course and that involves knowing how to manage the course and, just as importantly, how to manage yourself.

Please remember, however, that the swing, no matter how well memorized, is still a creative act born out of the conditions of the moment, no two of which are ever the same. Whereas you can reduce the swing to its individual pieces, you cannot reduce the game to a science. It is an art and you are the artist.

Modeling

Human beings are experts at modeling. A young child watches closely how its mother reacts in a certain situation and copies that behavior. If the situation occurs often enough, the behavior becomes a habit. Learning is a combination of nature, the potentials we are born with, and nurture, the experiences that shape our lives. We all have the potential to play better golf; that's the nature part. The question is how well do we organize our experiences so that our learning is efficient and rapid. That's the nurture part, the part that's under your control.

Chuck Hogan in his excellent book, *Learning Golf,* outlines the modeling process as follows: first you pick a model for the piece of the swing you want to learn—it might be the grip, stance or the position of your club at the top of your swing. Then you match that model in every detail. Once you're able to match it perfectly, then you repeat your perfect match until it becomes so ingrained that you can do it automatically every time. At this point it's in your long-term memory and you can now go on to the next "piece."

Learning the game by using a series of precise models as templates is nicely augmented when you choose a golfer as a model. Linda Vollstedt, one of the most successful college coaches in the history of women's golf, encourages her players to use models to enhance what she feels is the common trait among champions: self confidence. Linda says: "You have to practice self confidence, so I have my players think about the qualities associated with being self confident and then practice them." Her first step is to have her players pick "a role model" because, as she points out, "they are going to have to model that behavior." Similarly she advises beginners to pick a model for their swing, but she stresses that when doing so you should realize that everyone is built differently and

has a different swing, so pick out a role model who you feel you can be like, i.e. someone with the same body type and a similar level of fitness.

When learning the fundamentals of your set up, even down to the grip, pick a model to try and emulate.

Linda Vollstedt, Head Coach of Arizona State University Women's Golf Team, says, "As the skills and mechanics get to the point where you have a better understanding of the movement of the golf swing (the importance of rhythm, balance and timing), then you can get on the course and learn how to play.

"Learning golf is not just about standing on the driving range hitting balls; you need to get out on the course and learn to play. Many teachers don't teach how to play golf; they teach how to 'swing golf.' But my teaching philosophy is the opposite of most. I feel most teaching should be done on the course, even with beginners. Especially when someone has learned to swing the club and hit the ball. I can teach more in 30 minutes on the course than I can in three days on the driving range."

Choosing an instructor *continued*

Group lessons

Many resorts, clubs and driving ranges offer clinics on different aspects of the game. One session may be dedicated to putting and another to bunker play. Usually the sessions last for an hour or two. Clinics start with a presentation from the teacher on the chosen topic, after which you'll work on these skills. Depending on the size of the group, you'll have varying amounts of individual attention. This is a good way for beginners to get a taste for instruction without a big investment of time or money. It's also a good idea for intermediate golfers who need to brush up on their fundamentals. Group lessons are probably a

Arranging a group lesson for yourself and some friends can be a comfortable way to get started with golf instruction.

waste of time for the good player.

If you don't know of a clinic held in your area, it's easy to arrange one for your own group of friends or business associates. First, find out how many participants you'll have and what part of the game your group would like to learn. Then contact your golf professional and arrange the time, date and price structure. Many people find this is an excellent way to get started with instruction, because they are among friends and the program is tailored specifically to their requests.

Short game lessons

Be sure to dedicate at least an equal amount of your lesson to your short game, especially putting, since putting alone accounts for more than 40 percent of your game. If distance isn't your strong suit, a good short game can be a great equalizer. Remember that a two-foot putt counts for just as much on your score card as a 250-yard drive. So either schedule separate short game lessons or divide your lesson time between the full swing and the short game.

Playing lessons

You can have your pro take you on the course for what's known as a playing lesson. The objective here is not to work on your mechanics but your course management skills, and such things as shot selection and how to handle adversity. To do this efficiently, you won't play each shot in succession as you do with your friends, but you'll go to different "situations" and learn to manage your way around the course based on your current golf skills. It is impossible to learn to play golf on a driving range so, once you have some basics, be sure your golf pro takes you on the course and teaches you the essence of the game.

1 ⟩ If you're serious about lowering your handicap, be sure to dedicate at least an equal portion of your lesson time and practice to your short game skills.

2 ⟩ When you take playing lessons, you will learn strategy and course management techniques.

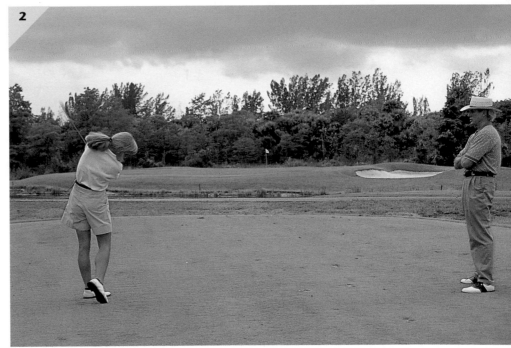

Golf schools

When choosing a golf school be sure to check not only the package price but also make a careful inquiry as to the following:

■ Find out who actually does the teaching. Is there a "big name" associated with the school? Determine to what extent that person participates in the school you plan to attend.

■ Find out the teacher-student ratio; it should be at least four to one if you are going to get enough individual attention.

■ Ask about the format of the school: how much time is dedicated to the short game, on-course instruction, etc?

■ Ask if your progress is video-taped and if they give you the tape to take home to work from.

The teacher-student ratio is important. Ideally, there should be no more than four pupils in a group.

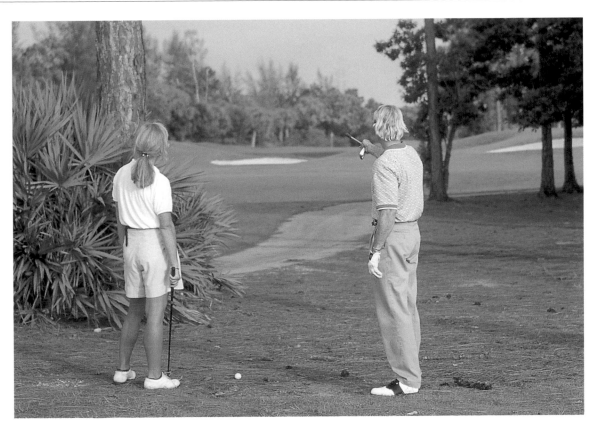

The Players School at PGA National features course management and mental strategy instruction from Dr. T.J. Tomasi.

Course management and strategy schools

If you are satisfied with your ball striking but need help with your playing ability you can go to a school specifically designed to enhance these skills. Like an in-depth and extended playing lesson, you'll learn how to handle the inner game of golf. Golf is a thinking person's game and schools like this can teach you how to manage your game, your shot selections and your emotions once you get to the course.

Summary

Regardless of what format you choose for instruction, make sure you don't mix yourself up with too many theories. Carefully select your teacher and then stick with that person. Expect to learn golf at a similar rate to which you learned other sports. If this is your first attempt at a sport, relate the learning process to other skills you've acquired: playing the piano, trigonometry, chess, gardening. Regardless of the skill and unless you're a prodigy, learning something new is a process that requires instruction, a dedication to practice and the exercise of your new skills on the course. Golf is no different and you'll get out of it what you put into it.

Course design and strategy

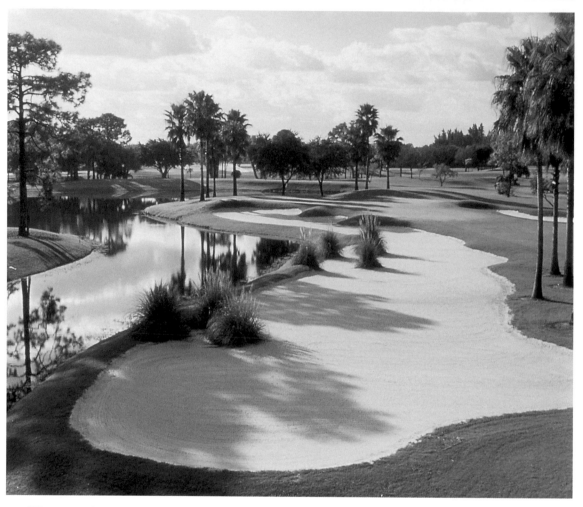

One of golf's most compelling features is its playing area. Unlike the uniform boundaries of a soccer field or the rigid dimensions of a tennis court, golf courses come in an endless array of shapes and sizes. At their finest, they are truly a work of art, sculpted by the architect and the whims of nature, to offer golfers a field of play unrivaled in any other sport.

A course can be short in distance and tightly bounded by trees and water, or long and open with heavy rough and treacherous greens. Depending on the location, be it seaside, moun-

The Champion Course at PGA National is the annual host of the Senior PGA Championship. To beat the "champ," you'll need to conquer its many challenges, such as sand, water, trees, rough and wind.

tainous or desert, each course offers special situations that challenge you to adapt your skills and strategies to the design features built in by the architect. To conquer the inevitable variations you'll face, you need to understand the features that all golf courses have in common.

The concept of par

A championship course features 18 different holes consisting of a mixture of par threes, par fours and par fives, so named for the number of times it takes an expert to hit the ball from the teeing ground into the hole.

Regulation par

Although there are many ways to "make par" the standard is as follows.

■ **On par threes**, the shortest distance holes, you'll hit your ball from the tee to the green in one shot.

■ **On par fours**, the intermediate distance holes, you'll hit your tee shot to the ideal landing area in the fairway and from there hit your "approach shot" on to the green.

■ **On par fives**, the longest holes on the course, you'll hit your tee shot and your second shot to the ideal landing areas in the fairway, then hit

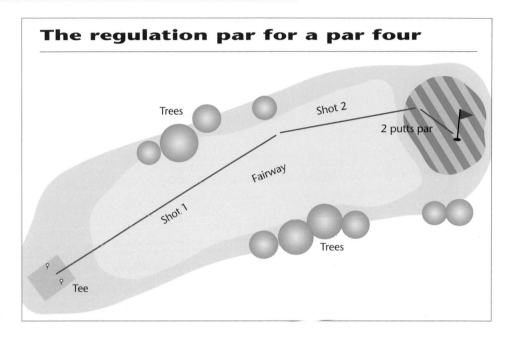

The regulation par for a par four

Trees

Shot 2

2 putts par

Fairway

Shot 1

Tee

Trees

On a par four, you will make a par in "regulation" when you hit your tee shot on to the fairway, your approach shot on to the green, and take two putts to get the ball in the hole.

Design without women in mind

In the past, golf courses were often an intimidating place for women because they were typically designed with two considerations: the professional male golfer and the amateur male golfer. The "ladies" tees were generally an afterthought to course design, if they existed at all. Often these tees were just a few yards ahead of the men's tees, a totally insignificant distance adjustment. When ladies' tees were finally added to courses, they did provide distance adjustments, but often these tees were placed "off to the side" of a hole, forcing women to play from odd angles. Modern-day course architect Rees Jones says: "In the past, forward tees weren't given any thought or as much as they are today so that even if the distance was adjusted, the angle would create an obstacle."

Fortunately, the world of golf course design has changed dramatically and today architects give special attention to the strategic location of each tee box. Even the terminology has changed. Jan Beljan of Fazio Golf Course Designers echoes the modern sentiments of her fellow golf course designers: "We don't call them 'ladies' tees' any more because we have our tees assigned as gender neutral and age neutral." Today's golf courses feature the forward, middle and back tees and golfers are encouraged to choose the tee most appropriate to the distance they hit the ball and their current playing ability. Most newer courses are built with four and five sets of tees so golfers of all levels have an appropriate challenge.

The concept of par *continued*

your approach shot on to the green. Once you reach each green, you are allotted two putts to make your score equal to par.

These examples are what's know as a "regulation par," but since golf is a game where mis-hits are common, even the world's best players sometimes struggle to make par in "regulation," if at all.

The "non-regulation par"

You can still make par even though your tee shot misses the fairway or your approach shot

misses the green. For example, on a par four, you might hit your ball into the trees and make an excellent "recovery shot" out of the woods but land just short of the green. From there, you could make what's known as an "up and down" by hitting a difficult pitch shot from heavy rough to within six feet of the hole and sinking the putt. Although not a "regulation" par, you've still made par and on the score card what counts is not "how" but "how many."

At other times, your score will be more than par or "over par" and sometimes when you're firing on all cylinders, you'll get the ball in the hole in fewer strokes than par or "under par."

When you take one stroke more than par, you've made what's known as a bogey; two strokes more than par is a double bogey. Triple and quadruple bogeys follow, and after that nobody's much interested in talking about their score, to say nothing about writing it down. If you take one stroke fewer than par, you've made a birdie, two strokes fewer is an eagle, three fewer is a double eagle. If your tee shot goes in the hole that's known as a hole-in-one. There's nothing normal about a hole-in-one but, when it happens, it's almost always on a par three. In this case you've actually made an eagle (two shots under the par).

There's an endless variety of ways to make a non-regulation par. In this example, your tee shots finds the trees, your recovery shot is short of the green, your third shot lands close to the hole and you one putt for par.

The non-regulation par

Guidelines for course management

Rees Jones says: "Definition is important in golf course design today. If an architect designs a hole to help the golfer determine what to do, then the golfer has a better chance of hitting the proper shot and achieving their goal." So when you arrive at the tee box take a few moments to identify the shape of the hole and what the architect had in mind. Each hole has a route from the tee to the green, which is indicated by the fairway, but rarely is it a straight line. Like chess, golf is a game of strategy and you'll need to think a move or two ahead to make a successful plan of attack.

If you're at a new course and the layout of the hole isn't clear from the tee, be sure to look at the map of the hole on your score card or on a placard that's often by the tee box as you drive up to the hole. Or ask one of your playing partners, who knows the course, to give you an idea what's out there.

Know thyself

A successful strategy for playing golf involves knowing your strengths and weaknesses and matching them to the demands of the course. Keep an honest and up-to-date inventory of your current skills and play to your strengths when you get to the course. The more you know about your capabilities the better you can adapt to the demands.

For example, if you're a great fairway wood player but not so great with the driver, use your three or five wood off the tee when you absolutely have to hit the fairway. If you're a good pitcher of the ball but not a good bunker player, you might play short of a deep green side bunker, then pitch your ball safely onto the green. We're not advocating that you be content with your weakness but that you play to your current strengths. Make a note of your weaknesses and then give them special attention on the practice tee. Your strategy is simple: to improve your game, keep your strengths up to date and focus on eliminating your weaknesses.

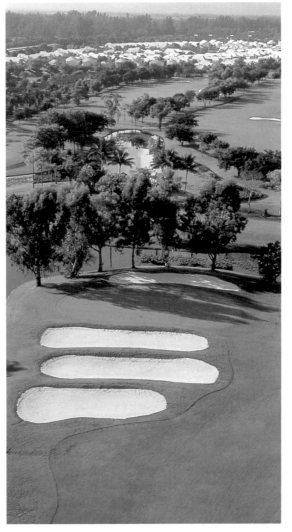

As you approach the teeing ground, you should check the map of the hole, which is usually located by the back tees.

When faced with difficult bunkers surrounding a green, you should evaluate your current skill level and plan your strategy accordingly.

Guidelines for course management *continued*

Tee shot strategy

Once you've evaluated the layout of the hole, be sure to look at your options from both sides of the tee. Sometimes, a short walk to the other side of the tee gives you a better angle to your target. A good rule of thumb is to tee up on the side of trouble but aim away from it. If you're a slicer of the ball, tee the ball on the right side and aim down the left side of the fairway. If you hit it straight, you're in good shape; if you slice it, the worst result may be that you land in the right rough. The opposite is true for a hooker of the ball.

However, remember that "trouble" is relative to the way you hit the ball. If you tend to mis-hit to the right, you'll be more concerned about the fairway bunker on the right than the large pond on the left. But even if you rarely hit the ball straight, never aim your ball at the trouble and expect it to curve back to safety.

In general, the idea is to always play away from the trouble. What do you do when there's big trouble on both sides of the fairway? Choose a club you know is going to get you on the fairway even if it's a long hole and you have to hit a five iron. You may not be able to reach the green in regulation but you'll avoid penalty strokes, and if you follow your tee shot with a couple of solid shots, you'll be close enough to the green to rely on your short game to keep your score down.

Although the same teeing ground is shown in both pictures, each side of the tee offers a different perspective of the hole. A golfer whose ball flight usually curves from right to left has a better angle from the left side of the tee (1), but from the right side of the tee (2) the margin for error is much smaller due to the proximity of the trees on the right.

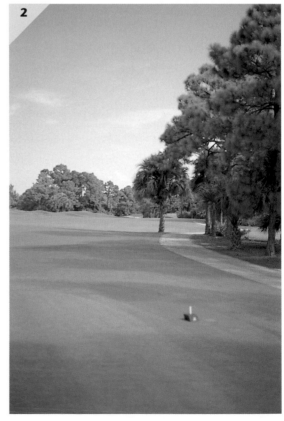

Approach shots

On par fours and fives your attempt at hitting your ball on to the green is called your "approach" shot. The first piece of information you need to make a good approach is the yardage to the pin. Most courses have markers or colored disks in the center of the fairway, indicating 100 (red), 150 (white) and 200 (blue) yards to the center of the green. You may also find yardage markings on the cart paths, sprinkler heads or posts on the sides of the fairway that indicate 150 yards. Check to find out how the course is marked and if the yardage is measured to the front or center of the green (it's usually to the center).

Once you have your yardage to the center of the green, locate the pin in relation to that figure. Most greens are at least 30 yards deep so if the pin is in the back of the green, you need to add about 10 yards to your distance; if it's in the front, you need to subtract about 10 yards. Once you know the yardage, take into consideration how conditions, such as wind and elevation, will affect your ball flight.

Most courses feature markers or colored disks in the fairway which indicate your yardage to the green.

Wind

If you're playing in windy conditions, you need to determine exactly how much distance it will effectively add to or subtract from your shot. You can ignore anything less than five miles per hour but if it's blowing more than that, you'll need to adjust your club selection. You won't have a scientific way to measure the strength of the wind, but as a golfer you'll learn to use the measuring devices available to you.

■ For example, if your shirt sleeves are fluttering in the breeze and your hair is blowing about, you probably have more than a five-mile-per-hour wind.

■ Look at the clouds to see how quickly they're moving, as well as the flagstick to see if it's waving and in what direction.

■ If the shot you're planning will get above the tree-tops, pay close attention to the amount and direction in which they are moving.

Once you've made your analysis, adjust your club selection as follows: for every five to ten miles per hour of wind, add one club if you're hitting into the wind, and subtract one if it's behind you.

A side wind is not a helping wind because for most of its journey, your ball is fighting the wind. It's only at its apex when it blows your ball sideways that the wind can be considered helpful. You adjust for a side wind, using about two-thirds of what you would adjust for a head wind of the same speed—for example, a side wind of nine miles per hour is treated as a head wind of six miles per hour.

Lie and elevation

First, you must take your lie into consideration.

■ From the rough, if the grass is moving in the same direction as you intend to hit your ball, it causes the ball to jump off the club face so you can figure your ball will travel a greater distance.

The key to playing in the wind is to hit the ball solidly. So the old saw, "When it's breezy, swing easy," is a good guide. Since you've already compensated for the wind by adding a club, avoid the temptation to swing "hard" in a head wind. If you do, the chances are that you'll mis-hit your ball and the wind will have an even greater effect. Be confident that you have the right club and make "solid contact" your objective.

In a side wind, most players over-estimate its force and aim off the green expecting the wind to blow it back on. As you learned in Tee Strategy, never aim where a straight shot will get you into trouble, or, in golf lingo, don't "give the green away." You should favor one side or another, but never aim off the green as a compensation for a side wind.

In windy conditions, tee your ball as you normally would and keep your ball position the same. Unless you're an expert player, making variations to your set up often contributes to mis-hits.

Approach shots *continued*

■ If the grass is against you, it slows down the club, robbing you of distance, so take one club more.

You should also adjust your club selection depending on how much the green is below or above you. The guideline is that for every 30 feet of elevation, add (uphill) or subtract (downhill) 10 yards.

Pin placement

The location of the pin has a major influence on the type of shot you should play and there are many times during each round where you should not be aiming directly at the flag. Knowing when to attack and when to play safe is the hallmark of a good player.

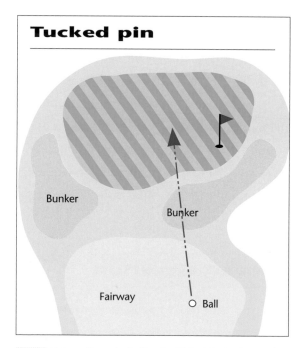

Tucked pin

When the pin is "tucked" behind a hazard as shown here, you should always be sure to play to the safe part of the green.

Tucked pins

In golf lingo, a flagstick that is set behind a bunker or a water hazard just a short distance from the edge of the green is said to be "tucked." In this situation, it's difficult to get your ball close to the hole on your approach shot unless you know how to fade and draw the ball on command. Even expert golfers allow some margin for error for these difficult shots. If the pin is tucked left, and you can reliably draw the ball, aim at the center of the green and let the ball curve to the left, close to the pin. This way, if you happen to hit it straight, you're still in the middle of the green.

The cardinal sin in this situation is aiming straight at the flagstick. Unless your shot is perfect,

Front, middle and back pins

When using the red, yellow and green lights method, remember not to confuse this mental strategy with the actual colors of the flags. Many courses feature different flag colors to indicate whether the pin is in the front, middle or back of the green. Each course is different, but often you'll see red flags for front pins, white flags for middle pins and blue flags for back pins. These colors are often chosen because they have a loose correlation to the yardage disks in the fairway and the traditional colors of the tee markers. Thus red indicates short distance, white—medium, and blue—long distance. Before you play, be sure to ask about the color coding and don't confuse it with your red, yellow and green lights strategy.

your margin for error is too small—which is why it's called a "sucker pin." A mis-hit aimed directly at a tucked pin usually winds up in the bunker or rough with very little green between your ball and the hole. This is called "short siding" yourself because you have a short amount of green on which to stop your ball. So when the pin is tucked, the smart player, depending on strengths and weaknesses, aims to the middle or safe side of the green.

Red, yellow and green lights

A good way to identify the type of pin you're dealing with is to label it in your mind by colors.

- Red light = don't go for it.
- Yellow light = proceed with caution.
- Green light = go for it.

Here's how it works. Evaluate the location of the pin based on the conditions. If a pin is protected by two conditions, such as a bunker, with a strong side wind that will blow your ball toward the bunker, then that's definitely a red light pin. If so stop aiming at the flag and select a

different part of the green as your target.

If the pin is protected by only one condition, such as a bunker, then you can aim closer to it, but proceed with caution by giving yourself about a 10- to 15-foot margin of error on the safe side of the pin (the side the bunker is not on). When there is no trouble surrounding the pin, or the pin's in the middle, go right at this green light situation.

Obviously, pin accessibility depends on your talent level so once again you need to compile a realistic catalogue of your strengths and weaknesses.

When the flagstick is protected by one condition, such as a bunker in this instance, use the "yellow light" strategy.

1 Red light pin — Water, Bunker, Fairway

2 Yellow light pin — Fairway, Bunker

3 Green light pin — Fairway, Bunker

Your first year as a golfer

From the outside, golf seems like a simple game but your first few rounds can prove an arduous task. The golf course offers a variety of situations, each requiring a different club, and sometimes a modified swing and set up. There are rules to learn, customs to follow, and a pace of play to be maintained. All combine to create a good bit of confusion for the beginner. And though this book will clarify some of your confusion, you'll need time to master your skills, learn golf's nuances, and make yourself at home on the course.

For this reason, we offer modifications you can make during your first year as a golfer. Keep in mind, our suggestions are not in accordance with the official Rules of Golf, and are by no means suggested for play when your swing matures. But when you're just learning golf, it's almost impossible to know all the rules, let alone follow them and still complete 18 holes in four hours. Golf is a complex game and, just like anything else you learn, you need to start simple and work toward the more difficult. If you begin your golf career trying to play in strict accordance to the rules it's akin to learning algebra before you learn addition.

Once you're more comfortable on the golf course, begin to familiarize yourself with the Rules of Golf. They are the essence of the game and a true round of golf can be played only when you follow the rules to the letter.

Your first few rounds

If possible, arrange to play your first few rounds with an experienced player. Don't worry that you won't play as well as they do—you're a beginner and therefore you have a perfect excuse. Another choice is to schedule a playing lesson with your golf professional. In both cases, you'll have someone to answer your questions and show you around the course.

A group of beginners

If you decide to play your first round with other new golfers be sure each of you makes some advance preparations. First, make a tee time (an appointment to play) when the course is less crowded so you can take a little longer than more experienced players need. Next, be sure to watch a few rounds of golf on TV. Though your shots probably won't look like those of the pros, observe how they move around the course and the conditions of play subject to commentary. Most importantly, be sure you have taken a lesson or spent some productive time on the practice range before you venture on to the course.

The first tee

This can be a nerve-wracking place even for more experienced players. It's often in view of the clubhouse so you'll feel like a lot of eyes are on you. The common reaction is to rush, but slow down, evaluate your target, and go through your pre-shot routine. This way you'll increase your odds of getting off to a good start. If you badly mis-hit your first shot, a common practice is to take one "mulligan" (another try). Since "mulligans" are not in accordance with the rules, you'd only do so in a casual round if time allows.

Improving your lie

Especially during your first few rounds move your ball from difficult lies (heavy rough, bare ground, difficult stances) to good ones. If someone tells you you're breaking the rules, explain that you're

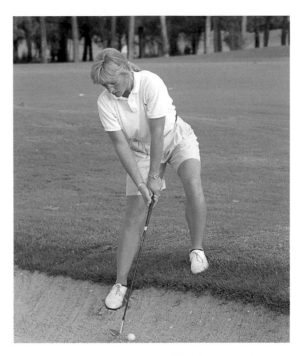

Especially during your first few rounds, move your ball off difficult lies like this one and play from a good lie.

trying to learn the easier shots before you tackle the more difficult ones and you're not playing for an official score. There is little sense in trying to hit a ball from heavy rough when you're still challenged by a shot from a good lie in the fairway.

Moving along

If you hit a ball that travels only a few yards from the tee, pick it up, bring it out to the fairway where the other members of your group have hit their shots, and play from there. During your first few rounds you may find that several shots in a row go badly. Instead of worrying about holding up the others, just pick up your ball, collect your thoughts, and take another turn after the other members of your group have hit.

Do-over's

Taking a "mulligan" is a common practice on the first tee, but you should avoid this unofficial custom after that for several reasons. First, do-over's are time consuming and, as a beginner, it's likely you'll struggle to keep with the pace of play even without trying the same shot twice. Second, since golf is a social game, it's important to remember the other members of your group are eager for their own turn to play, and hitting a second ball from the same place means your playing companions must wait for you. Third, the superintendent won't appreciate the extra divot you might take. Most courses frown on players who turn the golf course into a practice range. Finally, though we advocate bending the rules to make the game easier during your first year, one of golf's defining features is the fact that you're forced to play your mistakes. Do-over's are contrary to the nature of the game and not a good habit to start.

General rules and safety

- Never position yourself ahead of a player whose turn it is to hit.
- Engage the parking brake on your cart before you leave it unattended. If you're not sure how to do this ask the cart attendant when you collect your key.
- When playing out of the woods, remember a misdirected shot could hit a tree and ricochet back at you. Weigh the risks according to your skill level and choose the safest play. Alert your playing partners so they too can be prepared for the possible ricochet effect.
- If you're looking for your ball along the edge of water, woods, or the desert be careful of snakes. In this situation, it's good to carry a "snake iron" (any iron will do) in case you encounter one of golf's unofficial hazards. Many tropical locations also feature alligators—steer well clear of them.

On the putting green

Beginners can sometimes be too diligent about the rules they know, especially putting until the ball goes in the hole. But if you've already taken four or five putts, do yourself and your companions a favor and pick up the ball. Before you putt on the next hole, evaluate what went wrong on the last green. If you kept coming up short or long, adjust the force of your stroke accordingly. Limit putts to three and fairway strokes to eight—then carry your ball to the green and putt.

Beginners' par

Par is the standard for an expert golfer. As a beginner you should set appropriate goals for yourself during your first year. One method would be to take the par for a particular hole, say four, and make it your goal to get on the green in that many strokes. Then add the normal two strokes for putting, to arrive at a beginner's par of six for that hole. As you begin to meet your goals, refine them by trying to reach the green in one fewer stroke.

Golf carts

Exercise caution when driving your golf cart, even more so than you would in your car. Sharp turns at full speed can cause a cart to tip over, in which case your open-framed vehicle provides you little or no protection. Be especially careful on steep or wet slopes and avoid injury by keeping your arms and feet safely inside the cart.

Be sure to engage the parking brake on your cart, otherwise it might end up in a hazard.

Novice rules

It's vital to eventually learn and play by the Rules of Golf, so here's a simple description of some you'll deal with most frequently. The official rules are far more complex and the following is only a generalized description.

- One of golf's most basic rules is to play the ball "as it lies," meaning the rules preclude you from moving your ball except under certain conditions. Once you're on the putting green, the rules allow you to lift and clean your ball after you've marked its location with a coin or similar object.

- When your ball lands in a bunker, you're not allowed to let your club touch the sand until you actually make your downswing, so hover your club above the sand when you take your address position. If your ball trickles just inside the boundary of a water hazard you're allowed to play it if you can but, as in the bunker, you can't "ground" your club at address.

■ Usually, when your ball enters a water hazard, you won't have a play. The procedure is to add a stroke penalty to your score and drop your ball according to the rules. To do so, first identify what type of water hazard you've entered. A lateral water hazard is marked by red stakes and is mostly to the side of a hole. Though the rules allow several options, the most common is to drop your ball within two club lengths of where the ball last crossed the margin of the hazard. A regular water hazard is defined by yellow stakes and mostly bisects a hole. You can drop your ball any distance behind this hazard on a line formed by these two points: where your ball last crossed the hazard, and the hole.

■ When your ball comes to rest "out of bounds,"

an area literally outside the boundary of the course indicated by white stakes, you're not permitted to play from this location under any circumstances. Under the rules you'd re-play from the place where you originally hit the ball that went out of bounds and add a one stroke penalty to your score. For example, if you hit your tee shot out of bounds, you'd then hit another tee shot and compute your score as follows: one stroke for your first shot, plus a one stroke penalty for going out of bounds and one stroke for your second shot, a total of three strokes to that point. You'd follow the same procedure for a lost ball.

■ The complete Rules of Golf are available at most golf shops. If not, ask your golf professional how you can acquire a copy. Like golf itself, you'll learn the rules most easily if you first understand the basics and then take time to study the details.

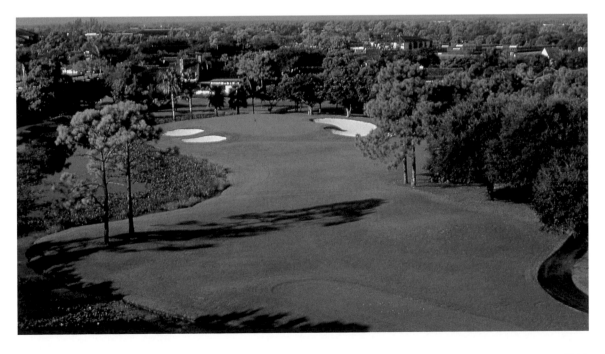

The Rules of Golf govern play on all areas of the golf course.

Glossary

Address (outside a hazard)

Taking your stance and setting the club behind the ball in preparation to swing your golf club.

Albatross

Three strokes under par for a particular hole. Exceedingly rare.

Approach

A shot that you intend to hit on to the putting surface.

Ball position

At address your ball rests on an imaginary line extending toward the target, and its position is referred to in relation to your stance. A ball back in your stance means that the ball is further away from the target, more toward your right foot. A ball forward in your stance means the ball is closer to the target, more toward your left foot.

Birdie

This is holing out your ball in one swing less than par.

Bogey

Holing out your ball in one swing more than par.

◾ Double bogey: this is two strokes over par.

Carry

This is the distance your ball must fly in the air not counting the roll after it lands.

Choke down

This is the action of placing your hands further down the grip of your club so that there is an inch or two between the butt end of your club and the top of your hand.

Closed

With regard to the club face, closed means that the face aims to the left of your target. With regard to your body, closed means your shoulders, hips and/or feet are aligned to the right of the target.

Dogleg

Golf hole that is curved or angled from right to left or left to right. (Resembling the shape of a dog's hind leg.)

Draw

When struck, the ball curves slightly from right to left.

Eagle

Two strokes under par for a particular hole. This is most commonly achieved on a par five where a long hitter may be able to reach the green in two shots, rather than the allotted three, and one putt for a score of three.

Fade

When struck, the golf ball curves slightly from left to right.

Fairway

Closely mown grass down the central line of play between the tee and the green.

Fat (heavy)

This term is used to describe a mis-hit shot where the club comes into contact with the ground before striking the ball itself.

Flag stick (pin)

A pole with a flag on top of it that sits in the hole on the putting green to indicate the location of the hole. The USGA recommends that it should be at least seven feet high and three-quarters of an inch wide, but in other areas of the world the dimensions vary.

Fore

A warning signal called out by golfers to warn others that they may be in danger of being hit by an errant shot.

Fringe (or apron or collar)

The area immediately surrounding the putting surface, which is often cut at fairway height.

Green

This is the putting surface.

Handicap

A scoring adjustment based on ability (see scoring systems, page 170).

Heel

The portion of the club face that is located toward the hosel or neck of the club.

Honor

The right to tee off first, due to having the lowest score on the previous hole, or awarded on the first tee on the basis by lot.

Hook

When struck, the golf ball curves severely from right to left.

Hosel

A tubular extension of the club head where the shaft is inserted, located at the heel end of the club.

Iron

This is a club with a thin, flat head, which is usually made of steel, and designed to hit the ball higher, straighter and a shorter distance than woods.

Lag putt

This is a putt that assures that the next putt is easy A long putt that would be difficult to hole out should be lagged close to the hole for an easy two putt.

Leading edge

The bottom edge of the club face, where the face and the sole meet.

Less club

As in "use less club": choosing a more lofted club that produces less distance, for example, an eight iron instead of a seven iron

Lie

This has two possible meanings:

■ The condition of the ground on which your ball comes to rest.

■ The way in which the sole of your golf club rests on the ground. It can lie toe up and therefore be too upright; it can lie with the heel up and therefore be too flat; or it can lie with the sole flush to the ground and the toe slightly up which is the standard.

Lob wedge

This is more lofted than the average sand wedge with about 60 degrees of loft. It is used to hit high shots that produce minimal roll.

Loft

The angle of the club face as measured from the leading edge to the top line of the club when the club is soled flush to the ground.

Mark

Used as a verb, "mark your ball," for example, means to place an object such as a small coin behind your ball to identify its original position once the ball is removed. As a noun it refers to the object used for marking.

Marker

This may refer to the following:

■ Tee markers—objects defining the forward boundary of the teeing ground.

■ Yardage markers—monuments or markings on the course which indicate yardage from that distance usually to the center of the green.

■ In a tournament, a marker is a person who keeps your official score, most often a fellow competitor.

Metal wood

An oxymoron used to describe the materials (metal) that have for the most part replaced the wood in your driving and fairway club heads.

More club

As in "I need more club to reach the green": using a less lofted club that produces greater distance (a five rather than a six iron).

Open

■ With regard to the club face, open means the face aims to the right of your target.

■ With regard to the golfer's body, open means your shoulders, hips and/or feet are aligned to the left of the target.

Par

The score an expert is expected to make (see scoring systems, page 170).

Pull

The ball travels on a straight line but to the left of the target.

Push

The ball travels on a straight line, but to the right of the target.

Reverse C

The follow-through position where the spine is bent backward in a comma-like shape with the head and back foot in alignment.

Rough

The areas on the golf course, usually adjacent to the fairways and surrounding the green, which are comprised of thicker, longer grass than found in the fairway. Should be avoided.

Skull (thin)

The term used to describe a mis-hit where the ball is struck more toward the sole of the golf club, producing a low, out-of-control running shot.

Shank (lateral)

A mis-hit shot where the ball is struck on the heel of the golf club near the neck. It flies severely to the right of the golfer and is also known as the "lateral" or the "pitch out."

Sky

A mis-hit ball that is hit very high with drastically reduced distance. It is similar to a pop-up in baseball. It may sometimes leave scratches on the top edge of the driver called "idiot marks."

Slice

The ball curves severely from left to right.

Stroke

Any forward motion of the golf club made with the intention of hitting your ball. You do not have to make contact for a stroke to count. Each stroke counts toward your total score.

Tee

A peg, usually made of wood, on which to place your ball from the teeing ground. The teeing ground itself is also referred to as the tee.

Toe

This is the end of the club face opposite the heel.